GREAT BRITAIN

AN EMPIRE IN TRANSITION

GREAT BRITAIN

AN EMPIRE IN TRANSITION

BY

ALBERT VITON

THE JOHN DAY COMPANY
NEW YORK

Manufactured in the United States of America

VAN REES PRESS • NEW YORK

TO

E. P. ADLER

IN GRATITUDE

AND ADMIRATION

PREFACE

I THINK that readers have the right to know that this is in no way a war book. Not only was it planned, outlined, and largely written before the storm burst over Europe; all arrangements for publication were completed by June, 1939. The war has of course made necessary certain revisions and additions; but there have been more of the latter than of the former.

A few words in a preface is a poor way to express the extent of my debt to Mr. Richard J. Walsh, editor of *Asia* magazine, but for whose suggestion this book might not have been written. His penetrating, sometimes devastating, criticism has been the more helpful for his anxiety not to wound; his generous encouragement lingered long. At Northwestern University I am especially indebted to Professor A. R. Hatton, who has been a great friend and teacher; Professor K. W. Colegrove, from whose valuable advice on many points I benefited; and Professor Paul Haensel, who kindly read the chapter on the Financial Empire. My thanks are due, too, to the officials of the British Library of Information, in New York City, who placed their complete collection of British Documents at my disposal. Also, I am grateful to The Macmillan Co. for permission to quote from *India and the Simon Report* by C. F. Andrews and from *The Dominions as Sovereign States* by A. B. Keith; to Charles Scribner's Sons, publishers of *Australia* by W. K. Hancock and *South Africa* by Jan H. Hofmeyr; to Robert M. McBride, publishers of *Turkey, Greece and the Great Powers* by J. F.

Abbott; to Alfred A. Knopf, publishers of *India and the Future* by William Archer.

As to my debt to my wife, Susan Yuval, the less said the better. The pages of this book, on which she labored with me, may not reflect her fine appreciation of style, but there is hardly a paragraph which has not benefited from her criticism and suggestions.

Northwestern University

Evanston, Ill.
January, 1940

CONTENTS

THE STRUCTURE OF THE EMPIRE

THE EMPIRE AT THE CROSSROADS

MAPS AND CHARTS

THE STRUCTURE OF THE
EMPIRE

I

THE EMPIRE AND
THE WORLD

WHAT IS THE BRITISH EMPIRE? What position does it occupy in world affairs? How is it constructed? Wherein lies its strength? What are its weaknesses? Since the beginning of this century, cataclysms of world-wide magnitude have shaken the foundations of Western civilization and swept away political structures which had appeared as solid as granite. How have those forces affected the British Empire? How has it been able to survive them? Are we to conclude, as Anglophiles are proud to tell us, that its history proves it to be the "finger of God moving through the centuries"; or, as the no-less-outspoken Anglophobes proclaim, that it is a Satanic Frankenstein bringing wars and misery to humanity? Finally and most important, whither is it moving—to destruction or to new life? Can Great Britain repeat the amazing political and economic revivals of the past, or will the new problems which are bound to arise in the future prove too perplexing even to this phoenix-like political entity?

No questions in the whole range of bewildering contemporary social and political phenomena are more pregnant with implications to humanity. Even the United States, although thousands of miles away from the heart of the Empire and from the center of its problems, cannot conceivably isolate itself from the effects of major movements within the Empire. It is not only that the presence of Canada in the north and numerous British possessions in the south bring the affairs of the British Empire close to its gates; even if there were no Canada, no Jamaica, no Bermuda, no Guiana, the sheer immensity of the Empire in other parts of the

3

world, its vast population, its immense markets and resources would be bound to affect our fundamental interests more vitally than the affairs of any other political structure. More than 40 per cent of our foreign trade is transacted with the British Empire. England—our best customer—took in 1937 close to 17 per cent of our total exports, while Canada was a close second.

For the British Empire holds the world's largest grouping of peoples; its wealth is enormous; its potential wealth defies computation; its naval power has been the terror of the seas. The British Empire has affected since the beginning of the eighteenth century the lives of more human beings than any other political structure ever erected; its influence has spread over territories more vast than that of any previous human organization; for good or for evil, its tremendous power enabled it, during the past two or three centuries, to direct the course of world history with more authority than that exerted by any other state.

One can hint at, not outline, in the space of a few pages the greatness and immense power of the group of small islands in the North Sea which, although territorially only about a third of the area of the state of Texas, have sent out their tentacles to every part of the globe. During the nineteenth century British traders and missionaries, explorers and political administrators penetrated almost every section of the world, leaving behind them a trail of British interests. How can one tell the story of Dark Africa without mentioning the British in every paragraph? How is one to trace the development of China, Tibet, Afghanistan, obscure Arab tribes on the Trucial Coast and in the fiery deserts of Arabia Deserta, of cannibal peoples in the islands of the South Sea, without writing at the same time a story of British daring, influence, and overwhelming power?

That this gigantic Empire has not been able to assure world peace by its own power is due only to the hopeless mental astigmatism and muddle-headedness of its rulers. Until the last few years, certainly, Great Britain had the resources and influence to crush potential disturbers of world peace by diplomatic and economic weapons long before resort had to be had to arms. Russia in the last century, Germany, Japan, and Italy since the beginning of this century, could have been prevented with no great efforts from becoming menaces to the security of the Empire and the peace of the world. If the *Pax Britannica* has been no more real than the *Pax Romana* in ancient times, the explanation does not lie in lack of potential power.

Yet even if unable or unwilling to assure permanent world peace, the British Empire has been powerful enough to prevent dozens of wars during the past century and a half. There is hardly a European or Asiatic state which has not been prevented by British disapproval or threats from grasping the sword. Russia, Greece, Japan, almost every Balkan country, Portugal and Spain—even France and Italy—have been prevented at one time or another from disturbing the precarious peace of the world; and the *Pax Britannica* has been real in the Near East, in the robber-infested regions around the Persian Gulf and around the Red Sea. It is not impossible that Kaiser Wilhelm II would not have loosed the first World War had he known for certain that the British would fight. Until the end of 1938, not an important diplomatic conference was held without Britain's playing a leading and often a decisive role. Great empires have had to forego the fruits of military victory because London so ordered; in boundary disputes, as at Fashoda, the British needed only to threaten to gain acceptance of their views. Nor did British diplomats have to pound tables and clatter swords to obtain a hearing for their opinions. Every swaggering potentate knew that behind their quiet, measured words lay the might of the greatest imperial structure ever erected by man.

IF IT CAME TO PASS

To realize Britain's position in the contemporary world one need only consider what would happen if as a result of military defeat the British Empire ceased to exist tomorrow. A few minutes' reflection will show that the very foundations of Western civilization would be shaken by such a cataclysm more profoundly than by any other event since the collapse of Rome. Not because the British Empire has been so invaluable a civilizing force; rather, civilization would tremble because all the aggressive powers—as well as many states at present without aggressive foreign policies—would immediately rush to occupy the vacuum created by the disappearance of Britain. Armies, navies, and air forces would be set in motion from one end of the world to the other; forces of destruction far greater than those which swept across Europe in the fifth century and created the Dark Ages would be unleashed now. And not only Europe would be affected; the impact would be felt by every human being from the lonely shepherd in the mountains of Tibet and the fisherman off the coast of Newfoundland to the highly civilized and gregarious dweller on Park Avenue, New York City.

The solemn fact is that collapse of the British Empire would serve as a signal for all the hungry powers of the world to launch new and greater wars of aggression. It is a grave mistake to think that nothing more tragic would happen than the replacement of Britain by, say, Germany as the dominant power in the world; that instead of a British Empire there would be a German Empire. The situation is not nearly so simple. Aside from the all-important fact that a German Empire would mean a fundamental cultural change, the repercussions of which would affect every section of the world, the tragic reality is that a victorious Germany would be unable to establish even a temporary settlement. A German victory would be followed not by peace, but by wars which might extend over a century or more. Such a victory would release a new imperialist cycle over the world, and all the suffering which that would entail. Britain, however, is a satiated empire, having long since reached the limits of her possible expansion; and a British victory would be followed not by new imperialist expansion, but by the beginning of the disintegration of the Empire.

Britain's defeat would be the signal for a general scramble between Germany, Russia, Japan, and Italy for parts of the Empire. For not only does each have designs on certain territories; the hungry states are not in agreement among themselves as to the division of the spoils. Their conflicting claims are too fundamental to be resolved in any other way than by force of arms. Further: aggrandizement by these states would compel Turkey, Holland, Belgium—if only to main-

tain their relative position in the delicate European balance
of power—to enter the race. To make confusion worse confounded, many of the small states not directly in the race
would exploit the resultant chaos to pay off debts of their
own, and civil wars would break out in a dozen places.

Nor could the three score and six states forming the British Empire defend their independence. During the century
of its world preponderance Britain became the policeman
for more than a quarter of the globe, and the members of the
Empire came to depend on her for protection against foreign aggression. Some handed over their safety into British
hands voluntarily as a measure of economy; others were
compelled by the British to do so for their selfish imperialistic
reasons. The protection the mother country has been able to
give them until now has been, no doubt, effective; but, as a
result, those states have come very close to complete disarmament. Not one of the colonies could resist a foreign attack; even among the wealthy Dominions not one has had
a military machine comparable to that maintained by fourth-
rate European states. In addition, fear of Britain kept the
wolves away from more than a score of states not colored
red on maps.

Take the Near East as an example of what would happen
over the whole world in the event of a sudden collapse of
the British Empire. Germany, Italy, and France among European powers have their eyes on this part of the world; of the
native states, Egypt, Saudi-Arabia, Turkey, Iran, and even
Iraq have ambitions to attain hegemony by conquering the
others. Only the ubiquitous British agents, policemen, and
soldiers have until now been able to keep in check these
potential aggressors and to maintain a semblance of order;
their disappearance would leave the gates wide open to all
the forces of chaos. The European powers would certainly
not wait long before landing troops; the native aspirants to
hegemony would ally themselves with one or the other of
the European aggressors. Russia, too, would certainly not
remain a passive spectator while the potentially hostile
major powers established themselves in this strategic part
of the world. Since the beginning of the last century Russia
has dreamed of outlets to the warm waters of the Mediter-

ranean and the Persian Gulf. What better opportunity for fulfilling the ancient unrealized ambition could there be than such a crisis?

In addition a dozen civil wars would inevitably flare up throughout the length and breadth of the Near East. In Iraq, Kurds and Assyrians would be on the march against their Arab Moslem compatriots; the Wahabis, whose lust for loot is sharpened by a fanatical hatred for all the less puritanical of the Faithful, would renew their periodic raids into Iraq and Trans-Jordan if there were no Royal Air Force to bomb them back into their dreary deserts; the Bedouin everywhere would no longer have to stifle their sincere contempt for the townsmen and no less sincere craving for their wealth; ancient scores between the Moslems and the Copts of Egypt would not have to wait long for settlement. And what a massacre there would be in Palestine! Zionist and Arab, who fought from ambush even when thousands of British troops filled the country, would now fly at each other's throat in the open. The blood of tens of thousands of men, women, and children would saturate the earth before peace could be restored.

No better certainly would be the situation in Africa, India, and Central Asia. The Italian dictator, already established in Africa, makes no secret of his ambition to expand at the expense of the British and French empires; Nazi Germany dreams of recovering its pre-1914 colonies and is hungry for the raw materials of others; imperialists in the Union of South Africa, though they are unable to protect their own frontiers and would sooner or later fall prey to the major European powers, dream of a "protectorate" over all the native territories south of the equator. In the Far East, Russia and Japan eye each other distrustfully and would not wait long before coming to blows. Immense prizes would be in the balance: there are Hong Kong and Singapore; there are Malaya, Burma, and India; there are Tibet and Afghanistan —all states which would be completely unable to defend themselves. The rival European states would not remain passive while frontiers were being re-drawn. France, Holland, and even Portugal, with immense vested interests in these continents, would be driven to join the scramble. In addition, a hundred civil wars would sweep over the continents like prairie fires. Africans have been waiting for just such an opportunity. Ancient feuds among them, kept down at present by the British, would flare up. The Indian Moslems, better armed and more militant than the Hindus, would certainly attempt to re-establish their ancient hegemony, in which they would be aided by the fierce tribesmen of the North West Frontier. Japan has been waiting for the day when world chaos will deliver into its hands Australia and New Zealand with their immense areas for colonization, their wool crops, valued in 1936 at three hundred million dollars, and their vast food resources. Neither could for long protect its independence. In the end, two or three powers would divide among themselves more than half of the world; but the end would be far removed, and tens, perhaps hundreds, of millions of human beings would not live to see it. Rivers of blood would sweep away every trace of civilization in all these areas; cities and whole states would be ruined and destroyed.

It is inconceivable that such world-shaking convulsions would not leave their imprint on every person in the Americas. International trade would disappear; new cultural problems would confront us; even more pressing would be the new political currents. Certainly we would not have to fight for Canada; it would come on its knees begging for protection or incorporation in the Union. The British possessions in the southern part of the continent would also fall under our wings, while self-protection would doubtlessly force the United States to establish effective domination over the whole Western Hemisphere and adjacent islands. But can anyone imagine that we would tolerate the extension of Japan's domination over Singapore, India, Australia, and New Zealand, which would give it complete control over the Pacific? Even if sacrifice of our vital interests on other continents kept us out during the first stages of the gigantic scramble, the day when one or the other of the new mighty world empires would cross hot steel with us could not be far postponed. For the new Napoleons would dream, as did all those of the past, of world domination.

A few simple figures are sufficient to indicate the magni-

THE BRITISH EMPIRE

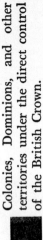 Colonies, Dominions, and other territories under the direct control of the British Crown.

Areas where the influence of the British government is paramount.

States strongly influenced by Britain's financial power.

Note

Because the British Empire contains so many diverse political forms and includes such a vast number of states, it is impossible to divide it into hard-and-fast classifications. The method of classification can always be disputed; and there can always be dispute whether a particular territory should be included under one category or under another. The method of classification employed in preparing this map, which follows that of the book, is intended by the author to give as clear and accurate a picture of the Empire as possible.

For the sake of clarity, names of all areas (except continents) which are not closely associated with the British Empire are omitted from this map.

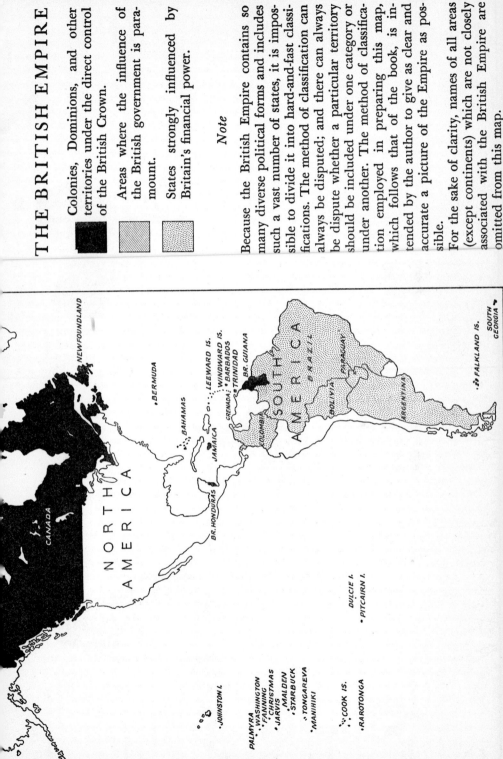

NEWFOUNDLAND

BERMUDA

BAHAMAS

LEEWARD IS.

WINDWARD IS.

GRENADA • BARBADOS

TRINIDAD

BR. GUIANA

JAMAICA

COLOMBIA

SOUTH AMERICA

BRAZIL

BOLIVIA

PARAGUAY

ARGENTINA

FALKLAND IS.

SOUTH GEORGIA

BR. HONDURAS

NORTH AMERICA

CANADA

JOHNSTON I.

PALMYRA

WASHINGTON

FANNING

CHRISTMAS

JARVIS

MALDEN

STARBUCK

TONGAREVA

MANIHIKI

COOK IS.

RAROTONGA

DULCIE I.

PITCAIRN I.

tude of the Empire. Excluding spheres of influence and states with which Britain is on special treaty relationship—taking, in other words, the "British Empire" in its narrowest meaning—we find that it spreads over twelve million three hundred thousand square miles, or a quarter of the earth's land surface, and possesses a population of five hundred million, or a quarter of the world's total. Every type of climate, from the frozen coldness of the Antarctic to the blazing heat of the tropics; every type of scenery, from the unscalable heights of the Himalayas to the Dead Sea thirteen hundred feet below sea level, is to be found in it. There is hardly a human race, a religion, a civilization which is not represented. Though the King of England is the Defender of the Christian Faith, his Empire is the world's greatest Moslem and Buddhist power. Peoples of every race from blond Nordic to black Bushman live in the areas colored red on world maps, which are to be found on every single continent.

Staggering are the figures of the Empire's wealth. Its total imports in 1937 reached the sum of nine and a half billion dollars; its exports of domestic products mounted close to eight billion dollars. Britain alone accounted for more than 11 per cent of international trade; the empire as a whole, for more than a quarter. It is by far the world's largest producer of agricultural products, industrial goods, and all types of minerals. More than a third of the world's industrial goods is produced in the areas ruled by King George VI, more than a third of the world's supply of tin and manganese, more than half of its cocoa, 70 per cent of its nickel, more than nine-tenths of its jute, asbestos, and other products. A large part of the world's wool and cotton comes from the areas colored red on the map, which contain also more than 40 per cent of all cotton spindles. Britain alone owns more than a third of the world's ocean steamers, and almost half of the world's shipping tonnage enters and clears in Empire ports.

Indeed, were an Empire trade policy adopted, self-sufficiency in most essentials and nearly all non-essentials would be possible. Only in petroleum is the Empire seriously deficient; but Britain controls almost 20 per cent at the source of production and the total output could easily be increased.

But the British Empire is far greater than the maps show. At least a score of states not colored red on British maps fall under its shadow and their policies are strongly influenced, if not controlled, by the views of London. Like small stars they revolve around the central planet, whose powerful gravitational pull holds them tightly in their orbits. Some are bound to Great Britain by political ties; others are kept in their allotted places by Britain's immense economic power, by golden threads composed of hundreds of millions of dollars worth of investments. So persuasive is Britain's economic influence that a change in the value of its currency immediately affects the currencies, and therefore the economic structures, of almost half the world.

POPULAR MISCONCEPTIONS

Today, when the lives of millions of men are in the balance and a false step may spell the doom of nations, informed clear thinking on international affairs is no longer a virtue and luxury for the few; it has become of vital interest to the multitude. For the first time in history, public opinion now determines internal and foreign policies of governments; the mistakes of officialdom and the consequent disasters can no longer be blamed on a closed caste separated from the "masses." And, as I have attempted to indicate, events in no political structure hold greater interest to humanity than those in the British Empire—a league of nations by itself and the only league which so far has been able to give effective security to its members. Its immensity, and the position the Empire has occupied in the world make its affairs of universal importance.

Yet experience has abundantly demonstrated to me that there are more misconceptions of the nature, structure, policies, and aims of the British Empire than of any other important political organization. There is less solid knowledge about the problems of the Empire than, say, about those of the Third Reich. Not only among the "masses." During lectures before audiences composed of university graduates and in conversations with people to whom foreign affairs is not a closed book, I have been amazed and shocked at the primeval ignorance shown when problems of Britain and the Empire came under discussion. And that in spite of the fact that newspapers and periodicals devote more space to the Empire than to any other political structure—or perhaps just because of that. Newspapers invariably write of the Empire as if it were a unit which Britain owns, administers, and exploits as one owns a house, an automobile, or a farm.

Even serious writers have contrasted the tremendous natural resources that Britain "owns" in its empire with the poverty of Japan, Italy, or Germany. A learned publication, established to enlighten the American public on world affairs, recently contrasted the vast spaces available in the Empire for every British national with the overcrowded conditions in the so-called "have-not" states. Few have heard of the Statute of Westminster; fewer still of the recent efforts to overhaul the structure and to establish it on more solid foundations. Collapse of the Empire has been an article of faith to too many for too many years. In America especially, prejudices dating back to the eighteenth century have prevented a realistic understanding of the forces at work. Many apparently intelligent men and women have told me with utmost seriousness that Canada, Australia, New Zealand, to mention only the most prominent territories, are impatiently waiting for the collapse of Britain to fulfill their ancient ambition to apply for membership in the American federation.

The ignorance betrayed by such views is perhaps inevitable. It is to be expected that the British Empire should be beyond the comprehension of all except the few who make its affairs their special study. The diversity in physical conditions is paralleled by an even greater variety in political and social forms. The Empire follows no blueprint of any political theorist; history offers no parallel. A comparison with other imperial structures would only emphasize differences. The variety of political forms in the Empire is bewildering. Dictatorial autocracy is found not far from the most progressive democracy; experimental socialism and feudalism, semi-slavery, advanced capitalism, and pre-capitalistic aristocracy exist side by side. Political and economic realities are in a state of constant flux; and the time of one man is hardly sufficient to keep up with the changes in the imperial kaleidoscope.

Unfortunately, words remain in use long after their real meaning has changed beyond recognition. The word "empire" brings to mind pictures of the exploiting Romans who annually carried away from their colonies immense quantities of wheat and other products; of the freebooting Spanish grandees who robbed their colonies of precious accumulations; or, for that matter, of eighteenth-century British officials in India, who followed in the footsteps of their imperial predecessors. But conditions in the overwhelming part of the British "Empire" are entirely different. Strange as it may seem, England has no more control over the governments of Canada, Australia, New Zealand, or the Union of South Africa than it has over the government of the United States. England cannot impose an immigration policy on any of the Dominions; the same is true in matters of commerce, industry, agriculture, and everything else. The writ of the United Kingdom's Government does not run at all over seven and a half million square miles of the British "Empire." These huge areas, which contain most of the empty spaces, are in every respect self-governing. An Englishman can no more emigrate as of right to Canada or to the Union of South Africa than he can to the United States or Bulgaria; indeed, an unemployed English worker can emigrate more easily to the United States than to the Union of South Africa.

Only a small fraction, then, of the area painted red on maps is controlled by the Government of the United Kingdom; and there in varying degrees. Britain has today less authority in India than in Ceylon, less in Ceylon than in Fiji, less in Fiji than in Palestine. The type of control which the majority of people have in mind when speaking of the British Empire is rapidly becoming an anachronism even in the colonies. Everywhere the trend is in the direction of greater and greater local autonomy; everywhere Britain has been driven to relinquish some of its former unlimited power and to give back territory to those to whom it belongs —the native inhabitants. What is it if not giving away when Britain permits India to levy protective duties which diminish importation of British goods to the tune of some two hundred fifty million dollars annually? What if not giving away is it when the Palestine Government, under pressure of local industrialists, imposes a duty on raincoats to diminish imports from England? Is Britain not giving away Ceylon when a Legislative Assembly is set up to control a native ministry?

Insufficient awareness of this distinction has resulted not only in muddled thinking, but inevitably in actions costing an enormous amount of human misery. The fascist and militarist powers, which justify their aggressions by pointing to the immense territories colored red on maps, prefer to overlook that Britain has been steadily relinquishing the kind of imperial power they are attempting to re-establish now, and that the overwhelming part of the new type of influence which Britain has evolved—and it is all-pervasive —far from being due to military power, is actually hampered by it, since maintenance of a military machine entails great financial expenditure. The truth is that Britain owes its position as much to its financial power as to its navy. Germany too could have built up great financial power had it chosen to concentrate on productive economic enterprise instead of wasting its resources on armaments. To equate the British Empire with, say, those of Japan or Italy is simply meaningless and shows either prejudice or ignorance.

STRUCTURE OF THE EMPIRE

A series of circles revolving around a common center, Great Britain, can illustrate best the variety of structural forms included in the general expression, "the British Empire." Dependence on England lessens the further we go from the center, until, in the last circle, we find states which are completely independent politically, and whose special relationship with the Empire springs from financial and economic reasons.

Dependence upon London is greatest in the sixty-odd territories of the first circle, which includes the crown colonies, areas under condominium, and mandated territories. Here the writ of the British Government is supreme on all important matters; special constitutional provisions, even in the most autonomous of the crown colonies, enable Britain to enforce policies unpalatable to the native population; and control of all administrative forces is vested in British officials in the overwhelming number of territories. But the tendency even in this imperial category is in the direction of greater local autonomy. If we start this circle with dependencies like Palestine, where the native population does not elect even an advisory body and all power is concentrated in a British high commissioner or governor, we come in a series of gradual transitions to countries like Ceylon, Jamaica, Bermuda, and others, where native officials have assumed increasing authority and London's erstwhile absolute control has weakened.

India and Burma occupy the second circle. Here the power of London has been reduced *de jure* as well as *de facto* since the beginning of the century. Britain still has absolute control of India's military establishment and its foreign relations; it has a great deal to say about such matters as finance, relations between the communities, industrial and agricultural policies; but since 1935 at least, India has had far more home rule than the most advanced territory of the first circle and it has been able to carry through measures directly counter to British interests. Its entrance to the third circle, now occupied by the six Dominions, is only a matter of time.

Political dependence on London has been reduced to zero among the Dominions. They are in every way self-governing independent states, equal in status to Great Britain itself, and members of the League of Nations in their own right. The King's representative in each, known as governor general, exercises no power and does not represent the British Government: he is completely subservient to the will of the local government, which is responsible to a democratically elected parliament. It is no doubt difficult to realize that the "British Empire," even in its narrowest interpretation, contains governments ranging from the autocracies found in some of the colonies to the highly democratic, completely independent government found in a Dominion like New Zealand; yet the Dominions remain a very real part of the British Empire, to the strength of which they greatly contribute.

With the fourth circle, however, which I label the Outer

Empire, we leave the boundaries of the Empire proper.
Members of this and the succeeding category are not colored red on any map; in only a few territories could Britain claim direct power by virtue of treaty arrangements;
all the members of this category have been fully independent

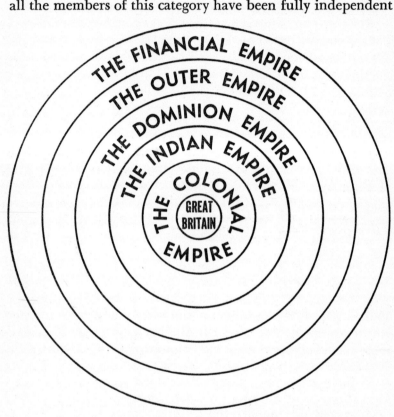

    The British Empire can be conveniently represented
by a series of concentric circles, the power and influence
of Great Britain being greatest at the center and diminishing gradually towards the outer circumference.
    In the Appendix at the back of the book is a list com-
prising every component territory of the British Empire,
divided according to the classifications in the above chart.

states. Nevertheless during periods when Britain was strong,
influence and common interest have been sufficient to make
Turkey, Greece, Portugal, and the other members of this

circle as much part of the British political structure as Canada and perhaps more so. And this prediction may be ventured with safety: when and if the British Empire begins to disintegrate, it will be in the areas of the Outer Empire —the so-called spheres of influence—that the process will set in. The real outposts of the Empire lie outside the red areas.

Completely different is the relationship represented by the fifth and final circle, the Financial Empire. Aside from reinforcing the bonds connecting all the states of the preceding circles with Great Britain, financial links carefully forged during the past hundred years have connected about a dozen countries with Britain which otherwise would have had no more special relations with her than has had the United States or Italy. That the financial connection did not spell loss of political independence of the members of this imperial category is obvious; Britain's influence here has been weaker than in any other of the circles. Nevertheless, the effects of the special financial connection have gone far beyond the spheres of economics, and have given Britain a certain amount of political influence as well.

Such have been the fundamental divisions in the British imperial structure. Of course, an intricate inter-relationship has existed between the various parts. The greatness and might of the Empire cannot be attributed to any one of the groups. It has been due, rather, to Britain's extremely adroit balancing of forces and counterforces. Strength drawn from the existence of one part of the structure has been used for keeping the others in their appointed places, while the power resulting from preponderance in the other spheres has reacted on the first part. In a sense, the Empire has been a house of cards, each card supported by the other, and Great Britain has been the master builder. A political structure as great and as complex as Britain's could not exist on any other principle. Even military force, decisive in holding together normal political systems, would have been totally useless had all the component parts decided at one time to break away. True, the colonial empire has been the foundation of the whole structure; on the other hand, it is extremely doubtful whether even the foundation could have been preserved without the superstructures.

II
THE COLONIAL EMPIRE

EVERY TYPE OF CLIMATE, topography, and scenery is to be found in Britain's colonial empire, which spreads over close to three million square miles of territory and is made up of sixty-one separate administrations. Lowlands baked by the tropical sun of Africa; highlands fit for white habitation; the beautiful Mediterranean lands; the fertile islands of Malaya; islands in the steaming Indian Ocean, and in the frozen Antarctic—everywhere British officials and policemen, traders and missionaries are to be found. Peoples of all colors and in all stages of cultural development—from tribes just emerging from cannibalism to proud holders of Oxford diplomas—are to be found among the seventy million inhabitants of the colonies; and there is no major religion which is not represented.

The colonial empire falls into seven clear geographic groups. First there are the Mediterranean dependencies—Gibraltar, Malta, Cyprus, Palestine, and Trans-Jordan. Then come a group of six colonies in West Africa; three in South Africa; and seven more in East Africa. The most important galaxy is situated in the Far East, and includes the various Malay States, Ceylon, Hong Kong, Borneo, and others. A somewhat larger, though less important, galaxy is to be found in the West Indies and America, while a large number of islands, many practically uninhabited, are strewn throughout the Western Pacific.

Colored peoples constitute the overwhelming majority. There are fewer than three hundred thousand whites in the whole of Africa exclusive of the Union of South Africa; only one white in twenty-six square miles. Needless to say, all the productive physical work is done by colored peoples. Natives have been conscripted for building roads, bridges, and railways and for working on plantations and in mines; millions of Indians, Chinese, and other peoples have been imported to do the hard physical labor. The whites manage and govern.

Scarcity of population undoubtedly militates against progressive development in the colonial empire. The average density is twenty-seven per square mile, while in some African territories it is less than fourteen persons to the square mile. India with an area less than a third larger, supports a population twenty-six times as large. The birth rate is high, having averaged in 1936 about thirty births per thousand of population, compared with twenty for Great Britain and the Dominions. On the other hand, the death rate is also abnormally high, averaging nineteen per thousand against ten in the United Kingdom and the Dominions.

Potentially Africa could support a population five to eight times the present one if science and capital were put to work on a rational basis. Palestine is a good example of what capital, science, and human energy can do to semideserted land. Jewish resources more than doubled the country's population in less than a score of years, and the limit is not yet in sight.

Under existing conditions, however, the colonies cannot absorb large scale immigration; probably they are already overcrowded. There is a real land hunger in all the colonies; millions of people engaged in agriculture live perpetually on the border of starvation. Their present holdings, though large, do not yield enough for a decent standard of living. During the recent refugee conferences not one colony offered to accept immigrants, Jewish or otherwise.

How is one to explain so glaring a paradox? The full answer to this question will emerge when we come to consider Britain's industrial and agricultural policies in the colonies; suffice it to say at this point that the present low absorptive capacity is due to no more inherent cause than unmitigated neglect, intentional or otherwise, by the British administration. Nearly all the land cultivated at present— and vast areas of good land remain fallow—is worked in the most inefficient manner possible. Native methods of cultivation, which the British administrators have left practically unchanged, are extremely wasteful; but the vast estates owned by European settlers are farmed in a manner hardly more productive. Nor have serious attempts been made to implement the wealth of the colonies by exploiting their natural resources. Although the greater part of the colonial empire has been under British rule for more than a century, no survey of the underground wealth has yet been prepared. No one knows what riches are buried in the wilds of Africa, in the Pacific and Indian possessions. New natural resources are being discovered by chance and accident every year; under scientific management production could be increased a hundredfold.

Immigration constitutes a serious problem; for while it can be a great benefit to the backward natives, it is also open to serious abuse. In the past, European administration and settlers everywhere created frightful problems which will take decades to solve. First, European settlers have not been colonists. They came to grab huge estates which they worked with colored labor. Lord Olivier has shown that white "settlements produce...first, slavery, predial or domestic; second, compulsory or indentured labour; third, the expropriation of natives from the land in order to compel them to work for wages on the estates; fourth, pressure on the natives to labour for wages through direct or indirect taxation—each of which has in turn given rise to reactions of the humanitarian conscience."

Second, Indian and Chinese indentured labor was imported into many colonies where the native inhabitants were too slow to recognize the benefits of working for a pittance on plantations and in mines. Extremely serious minority problems have thus been created in many dependencies. In Fiji there are almost as many Indians as natives. In Sarawak, where there are four hundred fifty thousand natives, the one hundred thousand Chinese monopolize most of the trade, and are responsible for the production of copper, gold, rubber, and oil. In the Straits Settlements the number of Chinese and Indians in 1936 was close to eight hundred eighty thousand, compared with a quarter of a million Malays.

Until recent years the British authorities were content to leave bad enough alone. They neither troubled to regulate the flow of immigrants, nor took any steps to eliminate the inevitable antagonisms between the indigenous and the foreign populations. Probably they saw the possibilities of using the foreign groups to counterweigh native nationalism —in other words, *divide et impere*. But severe criticism in England and outside has at last forced Britain to recognize the evils of unregulated immigration, and laws prohibiting further alienation of native lands have been enacted in many dependencies. In Fiji and other colonies an attempt has been made to protect the natives against the sharp practices of foreign traders. An official Statement of Policy has declared that whenever the interests of natives conflict with those of the foreign population, including whites, the interests of the former must predominate. His Britannic Majesty's Government has rejected the view of many imperialists that Africa be treated as an adjunct to Europe, to alleviate the latter's population pressure. The new policy, aiming to safeguard the interests of the natives, represents a revolutionary change, and deserves the acclaim of every humanitarian.

Unfortunately this policy has been used as a cloak for inactivity. Instead of evolving a positive policy which will protect the interests of the natives, facilitate their orderly progress and at the same time provide room for European and Asiatic settlers, Britain has oscillated between extremes, the common denominator of which has been inactivity. Instead of initiating large schemes of development and irrigation; instead of adopting long-range measures to improve productivity and substitute intensive for extensive cultivation, which would raise the native standard of living and at the same time create vast fields for immigration, the authorities have limited themselves to negative measures which are ultimately against the best interests of the natives themselves.

The problem of immigration has not yet been attacked in a serious manner. Immigration pressure is great; and as one member of Parliament has said, "We are not entitled to take up a dog-in-the-manger attitude. If we do we shall lose our moral right to control this vast territory." But minority problems causing inestimable harm to everyone concerned except the imperial power must be avoided at all costs. It is not right that a few thousand white settlers should control the destinies of the indigenous inhabitants and deny them their natural rights, as is the case under existing conditions. On the other hand, a complete ban on immigration is as unfair to the natives as to Europeans. A scheme of large-scale development will have to be evolved to meet the interests of both. Such a plan might involve resettlement of natives to compact areas where colored states will ultimately arise, while opening no less clearly defined compact areas to European colonization.

REMOTE CONTROL

How is Britain's vast colonial empire governed? One could reasonably expect that a modern organization would be at work to develop the tremendous potential wealth of the colonies, that an efficient and highly experienced government system would have been evolved during the past few centuries. The fate of millions of helpless peoples depend upon the few thousand British officials in the colonies and their supervisors in London; great responsibilities rest on the shoulders of the few hand-picked administrators and there are almost unlimited opportunities for benefiting the millions of natives. Have they risen to those opportunities, have the responsibilities been honestly executed?

One examining the system of colonial administration in London, whence issues all policy, is amazed at how lightly the task has sat upon British shoulders. The feeling is unavoidable that Britain has somehow stumbled into imperial responsibilities and has never stopped to decide how to deal with them. No adequate machinery for directing and coordinating colonial affairs has ever been set up. The methods and structure of the Colonial Office are as antiquated as the Downing Street building which houses it. Muddling has been carried to an absurd degree; and unfortunately there has been more muddling along than muddling through.

The supreme head of the whole colonial empire is the King, in whose name are made all appointments and decisions; but the King delegates his authority to a secretary, who is a member of the Cabinet. Although since the end of the eighteenth century Britain's colonial empire has been almost as large in area as it is at present, the office of Colonial Secretary is of comparatively recent origin, dating only from 1854. Until then the colonies were managed in turn by a Committee of the Privy Council, a Council of Trade and Plantations, and, appropriately, by the Secretary for War. However, even after the creation of a cabinet post for the colonies, nearly all attention was devoted to the areas settled by Englishmen, which now constitute the Dominions. The territories inhabited by colored peoples continued to receive very scant care indeed. Not until 1930 was a special Secretary for the Dominions appointed. Can one cite a better example of perfunctory administration?

Theoretically the Colonial Secretary determines policy. His signature goes on all documents; governors in the colonies can scarcely take a step without his endorsement; and he is responsible to Parliament for all developments. In reality, however, the colonies have traditionally been managed by a very small number of families, which have made imperial administration their specialty and have monopolized all the important positions. The Colonial Office is, next to the Foreign Office, the most exclusive club in England. An extraordinarily vigorous minister—as was Mr. Winston Churchill—succeeds sometimes in asserting his authority over the civil service officials; usually it is the other way around. And the permanent staff always wins in the end.

Learned, shrewd, and highly experienced in the art of governing, the permanent officials have been bitterly reactionary, fearful of innovations which might lead to diminution of the power of England and of the privileges of their class. Every reform in the colonial empire or the services has had to be pushed through against their opposition. As Colonel Wedgwood recently said in the Commons: "The permanent officials, the bureaucracy, have for nineteen years struggled against the House of Commons, and they have beaten us. The Secretary of State tells us," Colonel Wedgwood continued, "that we are admirably conducting in this House the democratic control of the British Empire. Was there ever such humbug? On every question that has been taken up in this House recently we have been defeated by the permanent officials, and we have no possible means of bringing them to book."

Hence the stagnation which has characterized colonial administration. During the colonial debate in Parliament on June 14, 1938, Colonel Ponsonby suggested that it was high time to appoint a "Royal Commission to investigate the whole question of the methods of colonial administration." The speaker found that three policies characterized British administration in various colonies during the past thirty or forty years. "In some places there is a policy of stagnation ...that [a] particular colony may dribble along with nothing done for it and nothing happens at all until a crisis occurs. There is another type...where there is a policy of inaction. Then there is a third form of policy, which one might call a policy of jerks and spasms, and which is suddenly evolved as a result of a crisis." But the changes introduced as a result of uprisings and riots are usually short-lived. A return to the policy of inaction and stagnation is effected at the first possible opportunity.

The very air of the Colonial Office smells of a museum, and the administration is ideally suited for dealing with collections of fossils. Although the problems of all the colonies are strikingly similar, the Colonial Office never set up a machinery to deal with such matters as education, health, agriculture in the colonial empire as a whole. Instead, administration has been along geographical lines. The section in charge of Mediterranean territories, for example, has had little or no contact with other territorial sections; each unit within a geographical group has been administered autonomously. Hence one need not be surprised to find colony after colony repeating the policies which had proved disastrous in others, while social experiments which should have been of great benefit to the whole Empire have remained unknown outside the frontiers of the experimenting colony.

Widespread criticism has forced the permanent staff to

introduce a few reforms. An Economic Section has been set up to deal with the economic problems of the colonies, and advisers have been appointed to specialize in others. But, as Colonel Ponsonby has said, the Colonial Office is "like a boy who has outgrown his suit. At first it can be lengthened, or a bit can be let in, but after a time it is necessary to have a new suit altogether." The Colonial Office has remained stationary in a fast-moving world for too long for slight adjustments and changes to be sufficient.

There is not a colony which does not suffer from the rigidly bureaucratic system at the headquarters of the Empire. Important matters are held up there for inordinate lengths of time, and important laws have been known to fly back and forth between London and colonial capitals for two years or more. Life may not move very rapidly in the Federated Malay States or in Fiji, but even there questions come up which require immediate action. In more dynamic colonies this system has produced disastrous results. The number of communications entering and leaving the Colonial Office has increased by no less than 30 per cent between 1934 and 1938. Much of the antagonism to colonial rule in the more highly developed colonies is due to the feeling that, while private commercial and industrial life has to adjust itself to modern conditions, government still proceeds at the leisurely eighteenth-century pace.

The attitude of the British Parliament, which is the final authority on all questions of policy, is characteristic of the utter negligence prevailing in the management of colonial affairs. The House of Commons devotes no more than a few hours each year to a debate on colonial problems, and that one annual debate usually takes place in an empty House. The colonial debate of June 7, 1939, was attended by fewer than one hundred members; no more than a dozen rose to speak. The opening speech of the Colonial Secretary was described by the *Manchester Guardian* as a fine example of what "an after-dinner speech to the Junior Imperialist League" ought to be. "Indeed, Mr. MacDonald was so complacent that Mr. R. V. Grimston, Vice-Chamberlain of the Household, who was sitting beside him, fell asleep during the speech."

It is true that Parliamentary intervention is usually "to some effect." Many an official misdeed in the colonies has been checked in Parliament and many an injustice has been righted. As one member recently said, "If we look at the history of the Colonial Empire and the history of India we see that the history of progressive measures comes from the House of Commons." But to this day colonial matters are taken up only sporadically, as after an uprising. Parliament has never awakened to the realization of its tremendous responsibility; there is complete lassitude towards the Empire. Special committees have been set up to study foreign affairs and other matters; but no committee for the systematic examination of colonial questions has been formed, and no organized machinery for hearing colonial complaints has yet been evolved.

The only way open to M.P.'s for obtaining information and for exercising some control over the permanent officials in the Colonial Office is to table questions which the minister answers each Wednesday afternoon. "But that is not really a satisfactory manner of dealing with the matter," Sir E. Grigg said during the 1939 debate. Information obtained by this method is scanty; ministers have found it fairly easy to evade persistent critics; and the permanent officials as a result have usually been at liberty to pursue their reactionary policies. Another member, Major Sir Ralph Glyn, confessed feeling "ashamed sometimes when in Westminster Hall we meet at the Empire Parliamentary Association people from some of the British Colonies who say, 'I have been looking up Hansard since I have been here, and our affairs have not been considered during the last six years.'" Colonies have found that to obtain any hearing at all in Parliament, they have to maintain expensive offices in London for soliciting the interest of selected members in their particular problems.

The supervisory machinery in London awaits a thorough overhauling. Assured that one makes no blunders when doing nothing, the Colonial Office has done its best to show as little animation as humanly possible. But organizational reforms will no longer suffice. The root of all evils is that the Office has not yet really reconciled itself to the idea that colonies are a trust which must be managed for interests other than selfish. The permanent staff needs a new goal at which to aim; at present, unable to pursue any more the old goals, it wanders aimlessly and marks time.

GOVERNMENT ON THE SPOT

Autocratic, aimless, and desultory supervision in London might have been at least tolerable if efficient liberal administrative machines had existed in the colonies. Such, however, is very far from being the case. Colonial administrations are neither efficient nor liberal. Democracy is unknown in the colonial empire. Even where elected bodies have been set up to co-operate with the executive, the franchise is open to only an insignificant fraction of the native population. The situation is even worse in those colonies which have had the misfortune to attract considerable numbers of European settlers.

At the head of each colonial government stands a governor or a high commissioner, who holds office for five years and may be reappointed. He is always chief executive; frequently he is the legislative body as well; in certain cases he partakes of the powers of the judiciary. He is commander-in-chief of the armed forces; he can declare martial law and set aside civil courts; he can order the imprisonment of persons and the confiscation of property. He draws up budgets, decides on financial policy, and can remove and appoint officials.

Each governor is an autocrat free from control by the local population. Whether he really exercises all powers entrusted to him by regulation depends on his own character and on the character of the man who at the moment happens to be Colonial Secretary. A vigorous governor can leave a lasting imprint upon a territory. His advice is always sought by London and his recommendations are usually accepted. Men like Lord Lugard, Viscount General Allenby, Lord Lloyd, Sir Percy Cox, knew how to force their decisions upon the authorities at home. More and more, however, during recent years the importance of "the man on the spot" has decreased; instead of initiating policy he has tended to become a local agent for executing decisions

reached in London. The amount of paper shipped back and
forth between London and the colonies has more than kept
pace with improvements in transportation.

The governor is always flanked on one side by a chief, or
colonial, secretary and, on the other, by a number of senior
officials. Heads of departments in nearly all colonial administrations are British. Next in importance are the district commissioners—again nearly always British—who are
responsible for general administration within certain areas.
Co-operation between these district authorities and the de-
partmental services is usually not well organized; frequently
one branch does not know what the other is doing and
there is a great deal of bickering over jurisdiction. The
heads of five or six departments form an executive council
which the governor is supposed to consult on all major
matters. The importance of this council is not great.

All power, therefore, is concentrated in the hands of
British officials. "No Barotse or Nyasa native," the High
Commissioner for Southern Rhodesia wrote in *The Times*
of London on August 8, 1939, "would be accepted by the
Colonial Office for the higher ranks of its service although
he could show university qualification for the post. The
higher ranks of the Colonial Service are reserved for Europeans not by the Act of any Parliament, but by a color bar
of custom, which is equally effective." In the dependencies
which do admit natives to senior posts, the native official
does not have the influence which should go with his rank,
and in practice he has to take orders from British junior
officials. This irregularity stands high on the list of native
complaints.

No one can say that colonial governments have been very
democratic; yet efficiency has certainly not been one of their
characteristics. The best that can be said of the British is
that they have maintained order, have abolished internecine
warfare and slavery, and have placed justice within the
reach of everybody except labor leaders and strikers. But
that is about all they have done. As to what they have *not*
done, subsequent pages will show. To call them missionaries
of civilization would require redefinition of the key words.
Left to themselves, British officials could rule for centuries

without introducing perceptible changes. Nothing irks them
so much as new activity: their one ambition is to enjoy
the sweet fruits of their well-paid offices and to do as little as
possible that might disturb the existing social framework.
Colonial governments are invariably bureaucratic to the extreme. The amount of paper work done is tremendous, and
frequently years pass before action is taken on matters however slight.

Invariably the officials take credit for all the progress
which has taken place in the colonies; but anyone with personal knowledge of conditions will have to agree that missionaries and even traders have been far more efficient in
bringing western civilization to backward areas. British
traders have not been philanthropists, obviously. They went
to the colonies not to bring civilization but to exploit riches
of the earth and native labor. In so doing, however, they
set up industrial enterprises which showed the natives modern machinery, and they set an example of foreign ideas
and ways of living.

Normally every attempt is made to hide the mailed fist
beneath a velvet glove. Administrators try to win at least the
passive consent of the natives, and even make concessions
to avoid bloodshed. Showing the flag and teaching the
natives a lesson "to remember us by" has been exceedingly
unpopular in Britain; every colonial administrator must
consider the reaction in Parliament, where Labor and liberal
members might ask unpleasant questions. Yet the inescap-
able reality is that the system rests on force; both colonial
administrations and natives realize that there are always His
Majesty's Navy and the Royal Air Force to do a bit of dem-
onstrating whenever necessary.

Such is the essential framework of colonial government.
However, since the beginning of this century and especially
since the World War, Britain has evolved two methods of
satisfying native demands for self-government and of teaching the colonials, in the words of the present Colonial Secretary, "to manage their own affairs." First, many colonies have
been endowed with a legislative council or assembly, which
debates laws, the budget, and other administrative matters.
However, these bodies are usually little more than law-de-

bating societies: if they refuse approval of a government-sponsored measure, a governor is still free to enact it on his own authority. Second, there is the method known as indirect rule, which leaves local affairs to the management of native chiefs. Choice of method has not been left to accident. Legislative councils have been introduced in dependencies containing permanent European settlers on whom government can always rely; in purely native areas, necessity dictated the adoption of the second method.

No doubt, some legislative councils exercise more real authority than others; yet a number of basic features are characteristic of all. First, there is no question of responsible government. Second, every council contains a body of officially appointed members who vote as instructed, and who in most dependencies constitute the majority. Third, even the number of white voters is reduced by high property qualifications, which everywhere makes the legislative councils the organs of the white plantation and mine owners. In Northern Rhodesia, for example, only 3,580 of the 10,588 Europeans in 1936 had the vote. Fourth, natives simply have no voice at all: in Kenya, to cite one fairly typical case, eighteen hundred whites elect eleven members to the council (and fifty-five thousand Indians and Arabs are represented by five); but the three million natives do not elect anybody. They are represented by an appointed white missionary.

Evolution towards a wider franchise is so slow as to be almost imperceptible. In Jamaica only sixty thousand of a population of one million two hundred thousand are on the franchise rolls; and the rolls are not increasing. In Mauritius ten thousand out of four hundred thousand, and in Barbados, five thousand out of one hundred ninety thousand may exercise the "rights of man." In British Honduras 3.5 per cent of the population may vote; in British Guiana, 2.8 per cent; in the West Indies, about 5 per cent.

Ceylon is the most notable exception to this type of self-government. Having had until 1931 a legislative council of the usual colonial pattern, Ceylon was then granted, in celebration of the centenary of British rule, a new constitution which introduced far-reaching changes. Representative, and to a certain extent even responsible, government was established. Legislative power is now vested in the Council of State which consists of three official members, not more than eight nominated members to give the European and other minority communities adequate representation, and fifty members elected on a territorial basis. The franchise is very wide. The Council elects seven executive committees from among its own members which deal with the various branches of administration; and the chairman elected by each committee is appointed a minister by the Governor.

But even Ceylon is still very far from responsible government. The new Constitution has not abolished British control. First, the legal and financial departments and the office of chief secretary are reserved to British ministers. The executive committee cannot refer a decision on financial matters directly to the Council without first obtaining the approval of the Board of Ministers, where sits the British financial adviser. Very much power is left in the hands of the Governor. He may decline to appoint as minister a member elected chairman of an executive committee; it remains within his power to declare a state of emergency and thereupon to assume control of any government department. The Governor is also the final authority on all matters pertaining to the civil service.

Indirect rule, invented by Lord Lugard while governor of Nigeria during the early years of the century, has been hailed as a great missionary effort to educate the natives in the art of self-government. The idea was to leave native chiefs in control of purely black areas, where native administrations with courts, police, educational and medical services would remain under native management subject to the advice of white advisers and the remote control of the Governor. The native administrations would levy and collect their own taxes, and spend the money in ways deemed best by them.

Indirect rule is no longer confined to Nigeria; today it is practiced, in various forms, in large sections of the colonial empire. Unfortunately the system which raised many bright expectations, has turned out to be no more than a method for running the Empire cheaply. Resort has been had to it when vast areas with poor communications could not find the funds necessary for paying the high salaries of numerous European officials. All sorts of abuses have grown up; tyranny is rife under the rule of chiefs bolstered up by white armed force; progress has been retarded. "What fascism means to the white workers," George Padmore writes, "Indirect Rule means to the Natives in Africa, for under this system of Government the Blacks have absolutely no voice in affairs of state." Even Lord Hailey, one of the originators of indirect rule, has recently acknowledged that its "rapid development ...can take a course which may hamper...introduction... of parliamentary institutions." What is worse, the system enables the white overlords to escape responsibility for the deeds of their native pawns. When asked about floggings in Nigeria for failure to pay taxes on time, a colonial secretary replied: "The flogging was administered by the Alkali or Native judge, without the authority of the Administration Officer."

PUBLIC FINANCE—NOT FOR THE PUBLIC

It is wholly in keeping with the nature of British colonial administration that public finance should present many features no longer found in civilized states. A government of British aristocrats rapidly becoming government by plantation and mine owners, has to exist for the benefit of plantation and mine owners; and public finance offers one of the best ways of maintaining the present social inequalities. Consequently colonial governments have not yet accepted the idea of progressive taxation. The rich are not called upon to pay for social services to the poor: indeed, in many colonies the practice seems to be to make the poor—and often the very poorest—finance services for the rich.

The feature that strikes the observer is that an extraordinarily large part of the revenue of the colonial empire, which amounted in 1936 to 270 million dollars, comes from taxes on those least able to pay. First, 16 to 43 per cent of the revenue of the African colonies is raised by a head or hut tax of $2.50 to $5 on every native above eighteen years of age, and this tax takes a tenth or even a fifth of the native's miserably low yearly cash income. Second, high duty is levied on cotton prints, cheap shoes, and other articles imported

primarily for natives. Colonial tariffs are not high enough
to stimulate industry; but they are sufficiently high to constitute a burden on the native consumer. That such a system
of taxation is not the fairest in the world is acknowledged
even by British authorities. "A system of native taxation
which has no regard for ability to pay is unsatisfactory," a
royal commission on Rhodesia-Nyasaland wrote about the
head tax. Nor are the natives blind to the obvious unfair-
ness of these taxes. They have been the cause of much ill
feeling and have led to numerous riots; but changes have
been very slow in coming.

On the other hand, the prosperous sections of the population contribute very lightly to public revenue. The few
colonies which now levy tax on income have kept the rates
considerably below the nuisance line. In Jamaica in 1935 incomes exceeding one hundred thousand dollars were taxed
less than ten thousand dollars; in England those incomes
would have been taxed fifty-two thousand dollars. In Northern Rhodesia, natives who rarely have a total annual income
exceeding fifty dollars have to pay a head tax; for Europeans,
income tax begins at the thirty-six-hundred-dollar level and
a generous exemption of five hundred dollars is allowed for
each child. But many colonies have no income tax of any
kind, which should make them a haven for all who find
taxation in Western countries unbearably heavy.

What wonder if colonial administrations never have sufficient funds for public services? They have large sources of
untapped revenue; but they are not inclined to tax whites
for social services to the indigent natives who produce all
the wealth. Public finance is like that in every colony—not
in the interests of the public.

Assistance provided since 1930 from the Colonial Development Fund of the British Treasury compensates for these
evils only to a very slight extent. The 1939 report of the
Colonial Development Advisory Committee shows that a
total of $18,800,000 had been granted until 1937 to the
whole colonial empire—not a tremendous sum, obviously.
In addition, loans totaling $32,500,000 were made during
this period. But only a small fraction of these negligible
sums went for social services. Public health received 12 per

cent; education apparently was not considered a cause deserving any assistance at all. Most of the money has gone to help colonies construct major works which are frequently of military importance. The lion's share of the "assistance," 43 per cent to be exact, went to improve communications; 11 per cent went to aid the development of mineral resources.

How funds raised by taxation are spent will become evident when we come to examine colonial social policies. Suffice it to say at this point that very few colonies spend on all social services more than 30 per cent of their budgets. In Nigeria, for example, 21 per cent was absorbed by debt charges in 1936-37; 29 per cent went for administration; 12 per cent for economic development; defense and pensions ate up 18 per cent; but social services received no more than 18 per cent. Everywhere a large and increasing portion of the expenditure goes for payment of salaries, allowances, and pensions of British officials, who receive up to fifteen times the wages of native employees.

INDUSTRIAL PROGRESS

Colonial governments have never considered it their duty to improve the native standard of living through industrialization. On the contrary, development of local finishing industries, which alone could pull the colonies out of their present poverty, has been definitely discouraged. Consequently, the colonial empire remains industrially at the stage where England stood at the beginning of the last century.

Probably the strongest weapon in preventing colonial industrialization is the tariff, which has been kept everywhere too low to give protection against foreign dumping. More than that: in some colonies manufacturers who relied on the low cost of native labor and started factories without tariff protection found that before long, tariffs as high as those on the finished products, or even higher, were imposed on the raw materials which they had to import. In Palestine, to cite one example, chocolate manufacturers were bankrupted because the administration imposed for years a higher tariff on sugar than on foreign chocolates. Not until one or two factories went to the wall were changes secured.

The absence of trained workers has militated strongly against industrial development. Imperialism has taken good care not to provide colonial youth with technical training, and the few technical schools started during the past decade aimed at supplying government needs exclusively. Lack of skilled labor is becoming an increasingly serious factor in retarding industrialization; more than one colonial manufacturer has publicly attributed the failure of his establishment to this deplorable situation. Some manufacturers have gone so far as to import skilled labor from Europe.

III

LIFE IN THE COLONIES

THE PICTURE WHICH the colonial empire presents is not a happy one. There is no escaping the conclusion that Britain has in the past neglected it to an extent bordering on the criminal. All the government has had to do was to provide for law and order, which came to constitute the chief burden of all administrations; to set up police forces which absorbed anywhere from 15 per cent to 35 per cent of total revenue; to provide a general administration which proved its usefulness by doing as little as possible; and, above all, to provide a system of justice.

This last, British adminstrations have done with conspicuous success. Legal systems vary; everywhere, however, a fair amount of objective legal justice has been provided. Peoples who never knew that justice can be honest and that judges may decide without regard to personal interest have benefited immensely from the example set by British courts. Labor has not fared exceedingly well; nor have cruelties, nor cases of undue severity, been lacking. The West African Court of Appeal not long ago set an example of civilized justice by sentencing a prisoner charged with the offense of stealing yams valued at two shillings (fifty cents) to ten years' imprisonment. The fact remains, however, that legal justice has constituted the most valuable commodity exported by the British to their colonial possessions.

As a result of the extremely narrow interpretation of duties of government, private enterprise in the guise of white settlers and speculators has had the whole field open to itself. Since it has not been part of the duty of government to see that labor is protected, entrepreneurs have been free to pay starvation wages. Social services have been neglected; wherever possible, education of natives—though not of Europeans—has been left to missionaries. In the field of agriculture this policy has produced disastrous results.

THE GOOD EARTH

Agriculture has been, and will remain for a long time to come, the cornerstone of colonial economy. About 90 per cent of the population depends on it for livelihood; it shapes the whole course of native life. Yet colonial administrators have not considered it their duty to safeguard the interests of those tens of millions of natives. A landless peasantry has been created in countries with abundant land for all, and from every colony goes up a cry from tens of thousands of peasants asking that the land stolen from them in one way or another be given back. Chiefs unable to read and write have been required to sign away vast stretches of land, which in any case did not belong to them but to their tribes; not till the results of the chiefs' marks on the contracts were brought home to the natives by means of forced evacuation did they realize what had happened. Then they either revolted and suffered the consequences; or they submitted to overwhelming force.

Vast areas have been alienated to plantations in every colony. In Kenya, 2,107 whites own 5,200,000 acres or close to twenty-five hundred acres per settler; in Nyasaland, Cecil Rhodes' South African Company acquired ownership over 2,700,000 acres, and in Northern Rhodesia its subsidiary still owns more than two million acres. Twenty per cent of the cultivated area of Fiji belongs to a British sugar company. Plantations of between two thousand and six thousand acres are considered small. "I would like to ask," exclaimed a speaker in the House of Commons, "how much of the poverty and the unemployment that exist in St. Helena today is due to the fact that most of the cultivable land on the highlands is in the ownership of three people who are members of the executive council nominated by the Governor?"

The plantation system has given birth to social and economic evils which are everywhere causing tremendous hardships. Not only are colonial plantations primitive and of very low productivity; their great size makes mixed farming unprofitable. To pay, estates must concentrate on cultivation of simple plants, which can be sold in bulk. Colonial agriculture has thus become extremely specialized and overdependent on world markets; and there is hardly a colony whose economy does not depend on a single crop for export, while much of the food requirements has to be imported. A fall in the price of sugar brought ineffable suffering to thousands and thousands of families in Jamaica, Trinidad, and other dependencies whose economy was tied up with that article. In the Gold Coast, for example, production of cocoa was increased from four hundred dollars in 1881 to fifty-five million in 1928; and it is easy to imagine the social consequences when the value of the exported cocoa declined to less than twenty million dollars five years later, although there was an increase in quantity. Even worse were the social results following the fall in the price of rubber, of which the colonial empire is by far the world's largest producer.

"The West Indian Colonies," a speaker in the Commons exclaimed after a description of the results of agricultural overspecialization, "today are what Britain has made them, in their people, their trade and their social life. Great Britain has drawn men from many parts of the world, from Africa, China, and India to populate those islands and to work in order to supply our needs." Nobody but the British authorities is to blame for this lopsided development; it could have been checked at any time had they so desired. Laws protecting native landownership would have made impossible the unwieldy plantations; and hundreds of measures could have been taken to increase production of food for local needs.

Very little has been done to modernize agriculture and to create a healthy native peasantry. Natives are planting and reaping by the same methods used one hundred or five hundred years ago. Much and valuable research has been carried out in a number of dependencies, but very little has been done until now to bring the new knowledge to the attention of native farmers. Soviet Russia, Turkey, and other countries have found out how much can be accomplished,

and in an incredibly short time, if modern methods of propaganda—films, posters, illustrated books, lectures by trained
natives in villages and over the radio—are intelligently and
intensively used. Unfortunately, their example has not been
imitated by the rulers of the British Empire. Some colonists,
certainly, publish agricultural bulletins; unfortunately again,
the vast majority of natives cannot read.

Other measures are long overdue. At present the whole
Empire is almost entirely barren of irrigation and water-
control schemes. The amount of land under intensive cultivation is insignificant. The system of landownership has to
be modernized. The present system works decisively against
agricultural progress. In some parts of the Empire land is
held in communal ownership which makes individual effort
useless. Land registration and parcellation are proceeding
at a snail's pace: at the present rate, it will take no less than
125 years to execute in Palestine a land settlement scheme
begun a decade ago. Cyprus languishes today under old
Turkish land laws abolished in Turkey long since. And
everywhere, agriculture stagnates under a terrific burden of
debt, on which an interest rate of 50 per cent is usual, and
100 per cent is not unknown. Indebtedness is increasing, and
the usurers eventually get hold of the best land. Cyprus,
with a mortgage debt representing 13.1 per cent of the total
value of immovable property, had more than thirteen thousand forced land sales during the years 1935-1938. But though
this problem recurs everywhere with monotonous regularity,
administrations have done practically nothing to cope with
it. No serious and concentrated efforts have been made to
develop peasant co-operatives, which alone can solve the
problem; to establish government banks to lend money at
reasonable rates; to educate the peasantry how to handle
money. Laws prohibiting forced sales of small holdings have
been negative and ineffective.

How these policies have affected the daily lives of the
sixty million human beings in the colonies is graphically
brought out by the report of a Committee on Nutrition in
the Colonial Empire. It constitutes one of the severest in-
dictments of the British management—or lack of it—ever
written. "There are few of the constituents considered nec-

essary in Europe for a nutritionally adequate diet which are generally available in sufficient quantities in the Colonial Empire," the Committee concludes. "After studying all the reports submitted by Colonial Governments and all the other available material, we have no doubt at all that there are few parts of the Colonial Empire (or indeed of any tropical country) where the diet of the majority of the population is at present anything like sufficient for optimum nutrition. Diets are frequently insufficient in quality. If they are bulky, the bulk is too often made up of foods that do not supply all the needs of a balanced diet. Judged by European standards they lack variety and they lack protective value."

The results of this widespread malnutrition are evident everywhere. The large numbers of deformed and disease-ridden natives cannot fail to impress every visitor to a colony. "Amongst definite deficiency diseases those caused by lack of vitamin A are perhaps the most common in the Colonial Empire, and there are reports from a wide selection of territories of affections of the eye, changes in the skin, and other symptoms which may be attributed to a deficiency of this vitamin. Beri-beri, known to be caused by a deficiency of vitamin B_1, occurs with frequency in rice-eating countries and is found in various parts of the Colonial Empire. Cases of some degree of deficiency of this vitamin are probably widely prevalent where the full disease has not been recognized. Pellagra, due to the absence of another member of the B group of vitamins, is reported fairly frequently.... Apart from these well-recognized disorders there are reports of a number of diseases which are possibly of dietetic origin, but which have not yet been positively identified. These include *chalchaleh* in Somaliland, *chiufa* and *onyalai* in Northern Rhodesia, *decoque* in Seychelles, *kwashiokor* in the Gold Coast and burning feet and butterfly wings in British Honduras."

Even more important perhaps are the general effects resulting from constant food deficiency—general ill-health, lowered resistance, impaired efficiency, mental sluggishness. "There is now a general consensus of belief that there exist with great frequency, especially in the tropics, deficiency states which while not resulting in manifest disease prevent the full enjoyment of health. These states, although less obvious, are more insidious than the clearly-defined deficiency diseases and are a much more important factor in the lives of the people. Moreover, the prevalence of malnutrition aggravates many other diseases. This is particularly the case with ulcers and a number of skin affections, leprosy, tuberculosis and malaria."

"We should go so far as to say," the Committee on Nutrition has written, "that for every recorded case of a specific deficiency disease there are hundreds of cases of absence of full health due in part at least to malnutrition. This conclusion is supported by the observations of competent observers in every part of the world and by the evidence of the startling improvement of physique, well-being and efficiency which have been discovered to result from additions to the normal diet in areas so different as Malaya, Ceylon, East Africa, West Africa and the Indies."

Painfully little has so far been done to remedy these conditions. Reports from individual colonies on their "practical measures for improvement of nutrition" show that committees have been established, "recommendations" have been made; and that has been about all. The most effective solution is to divide the large estates for settling peasants on small-holdings to grow food for local consumption. This solution was recommended by commissions appointed half a century ago; but very little has been done. "As far back as forty or fifty years ago, members in this House were pleading for land settlement schemes in the West Indies," an M. P. said in 1938, but "today we find that the same sort of demand has to be made."

AN EMPIRE OF SLUMS

The British Empire is a disease-ridden, pest-infected, slum empire, in which very little attention has been devoted to improving human life. Every year millions of human beings die who under different circumstances would be alive; for the Empire's maternity and infant mortality rate is among the highest in the world. I do not know of a single colony in which the infant mortality rate has fallen to less than one hundred per thousand births, and a mortality of three hundred has been all too frequent. Social services in the richest colony are much below the standards prevailing in the poorest and most backward European country.

A visit to any colony will disclose housing and living conditions infinitely worse than anything found in the West. One commission after another has reported on the horrible slum areas around every industrial compound and every city. "It is hardly too much to say that on some of the sugar estates the accommodations provided are in a state of extreme disrepair, and thoroughly unhygienic.... We visited 'barrack' dwellings in Port-of-Spain which are indescribable in their lack of elementary needs of decency and for which ...monthly rents varying from 12s. to 15s. [$3.00 to $3.75] a room are paid." A medical witness has described the native workers' quarter in Port-of-Spain as "an entangled conglomeration of unsightly ruinous huts and privy cesspits placed helter-skelter on a sloping, steep, and slippery hillside—a danger to health, life and limb for the local residents and a menace to the surrounding city population." Usually the hovels are completely devoid of furniture except for some sacks filled with straw for beds. Round holes in the walls serve for windows. But these conditions have not disturbed the Olympian equanimity of colonial administrators.

Nor has more than a meager beginning been made to provide medical services. Only an insignificant fraction of natives suffering from trachoma, syphilis, tuberculosis, and a hundred other diseases receive any medical attention. Hundreds of miles of thickly settled territory are without medical facilities of any kind. Sleeping sickness and other tropical scourges have not been eradicated to this day. Observers agree that everywhere the natives' capacity to work is impaired by diseases which weaken his body and brain.

Rather than fill pages with dreary statistics let us look at one fairly representative colony with a history not strikingly different from many another. Northern Rhodesia was occupied during the last decade of the nineteenth century by Cecil Rhodes' South Africa Chartered Company, which extracted concessions from the chief of the Barotse tribe. The company employed a number of medical officers for its European staff; no attempt was made, however, to study health conditions of the natives. "Not before 1915-16 did the annual report of the Secretary of the Administration contain a reference to health matters in general," says one official British publication. In 1922 the company's medical staff of fifteen gave treatment to a grand total of five thousand native patients. Transfer of government to the Colonial Office in 1924 brought no improvements. "No change worthy of note appears to have taken place," an investigating commission reported. The health department was a "garrison service" which was "doing little more than tick over until 1937."

"Increases of staff and activity became possible" in 1937, and the following year saw nineteen medical officers at work in the whole colony. As to the increase in activity, I can do no better than quote the following official sentences: "Taking the Territory as a whole the present medical provision for a native population of 1,366,000 spread over a country a quarter as large again as France is entirely inadequate. Including every Government medical post and every missionary medical post aided by Government, no matter how small, how primitive, and how few and ill-trained its staff, a total is reached of some seventy posts where Government makes provision for medical aid to natives. On the generous assumption that each of these covers an area of twenty-five miles radius or about two thousand square miles, more than half the Territory remains unprovided" for entirely.

Unfortunately the situation is infinitely worse than the passage indicates. Not all of the seventy posts are intended for natives. On the contrary, only the worst equipped serve them; the best are intended exclusively or primarily for Europeans. "The sites of 10 of the 12 medical stations were chosen primarily in the interests of groups of European officials or settlers.... Further out of 29 posts occupied by matrons and nursing sisters 20 are solely concerned with the care of Europeans and four with both Europeans and Natives. The European hospitals at the main centers are very good and those at the smaller centers generally adequate, that at Fort Jameson being about twice as large as is now necessary.... For Africans the position is very different. The

Medical Officers at nine of the 12 stations find themselves
so tied by the claims of the European population that they
rarely get out among the natives of the districts.... Some
of the doctors are overworked and the demands on them
are continually increasing. The same circumstances make
adequate supervision of outlying dispensaries impossible.
... There are large concentrations of natives outside the
reach of any doctor.... In the whole vast area west of the
railway line there are two Government doctors and one
medical missionary.... Moreover of the 12 Government hospitals for Natives, only two... are good, while three... are
primitive . . . five are very bad."

I doubt if there is in the whole range of imperialist depravity anything which is as scandalous as the color bar in
health work. Northern Rhodesia far from being an exception is only too typical in this respect. Everywhere the distribution of medical facilities for European and native is
shamefully unfair. While tens of thousands of natives are
rotting away with disease, a hospital reserved for Europeans
is "twice as large as necessary"! In Kenya, the three best-
equipped hospitals are reserved exclusively for Europeans,
while three hospitals containing one thousand beds have to
suffice for an African population of more than three million. In Nigeria, to cite another example, twelve excellent
hospitals are maintained for four thousand Europeans; fifty-
two of various grades for twenty million natives. In the city
of Ibadon, the largest native city in Africa, thirty-four beds
are provided for three hundred ninety thousand natives;
eleven beds for half a hundred whites.

Better medical facilities are admittedly provided in more
wealthy dependencies; nowhere, however, is there anything
approaching adequacy. Ceylon, which ranks highest in the
whole colonial empire, boasts 108 government hospitals for
a population of 5.8 millions and about seven hundred dispensaries and visiting stations. Conditions are also fair in
Palestine, where the Zionist funds enable the government to
do health work among the Arabs. Even there, however, the
Zionists spend on their own health organization serving a
third of the population more than the government spends
for the whole country.

Characteristic of the speed with which colonial administrations attack social problems is that Nyasaland was without a public health service until 1931. Until this day the government does not even know whether sleeping sickness exists in certain localities. Those colonies which have sanitation departments limit their work to the cities and more particularly to the European sections. Hygiene propaganda, which has worked miracles in a number of backward European countries, was totally unknown in the colonies until the last few years. Maternity and child welfare centers are completely unknown in the larger part of the Empire. What wonder that colonies are allocating as little as 5 per cent of their revenues on public health! In 1909 total expenditure for this purpose in the whole African empire amounted to $745,000: even today less than a dollar per head is spent per annum on the colonial population.

Colonial governments are always short of funds when it comes to social services. There is enough money, from revenue or borrowed funds, for meeting debt charges, paying the large salaries of white administrative officials, constructing public works which are usually more helpful to the Europeans than to the natives; but treasuries become dry when called upon to pay for social services. Nor can anyone say honestly that the best use is made of the available funds. Instead of training native personnel, who work for one-fifth, or even one-tenth, of the salaries paid to foreign officials, colonial governments have until recently been bent on employing only European medical men. The number of native doctors in Africa can almost be counted on one's fingers. The native medical orderlies now used in some dependencies lack the most elementary training and no real progress is to be expected from them.

The truth is that even Italy and Holland have done more to improve the health of their colored subjects. Never did the British Government consider it its duty to institute upon occupation of a new territory a searching general investigation of local diseases and their causes, and to execute thereafter a fundamental health campaign, with funds provided, either as a partial loan or as a grant-in-aid, by the imperial government. It has been suggested more than once

that a corps of medical and sanitation experts be formed
which should go from colony to colony to tackle local health
problems. Instead, matters have been left to chance; the
small improvements which have taken place have come in
driblets and have nowhere effected fundamental changes.
In many areas the number of new diseases that have taken
root since the British occupation is greater than the number of old ones that have been eradicated; and the white
men with their cities and industrial compounds have everywhere created problems of sanitation which did not exist
before and with which governments have failed to cope.

THUS COLONIALS ARE TAUGHT

Until very recently the British did not consider education part of "good government." If Christian missions established schools, well and good; if not—perhaps so much the
better. Uganda became a British protectorate in 1894; but
until 1924 education "was left entirely in the hands of the
Missions." Fiji came under British control in 1874; but it
had no educational department till the beginning of this
century. "There," says Mr. Arthur Mayhew, Joint Secretary
of the Advisory Committee on Education in the Colonies,
"as in several African dependencies, a fully developed and
effective department came into existence only after the
war."

Everywhere education has been neglected and treated as
a stepchild of the administration. Though control of the
Gold Coast forts was assumed in 1821, a census in 1931 revealed that only 35,418 out of 3.2 million natives had completed an elementary course. Only in such European colonies
as Malta and Cyprus has a beginning been made to provide
elementary schooling for the masses. "In Tanganyika there
are 1,250,000 children of school age, and more than 1,000,-
000 of them attend no institution of any description." In
Uganda fewer than a third of all children attend any kind
of school; in Trinidad fewer than half; the Protectorate of
Sierra Leone, boasted in 1934 a total of eight government
primary schools, with an attendance of 4,500 out of a school
population of 426,000. In rich Ceylon no more than 20 per
cent of the children are accommodated in government

schools, while fewer than 50 per cent receive any kind of education.

The British Empire is an empire of illiterates. Probably not more than 2 per cent of the natives are literate; and, as the Commons was recently told, "In some parts of West Africa, the rate of progress in education is such that it would take seven hundred years before the whole of the population would be able even to read and write." The situation would be worse but for the presence of missionary schools. Tanganyika has three missionary schools to every one maintained by government; Kenya, Nyasaland—all rely entirely on missions to provide elementary schooling for natives.

Girls' education was neglected almost entirely until recent years. "One cannot help feeling that the establishment of a girls' school (in Nigeria) ought not to have been deferred till after the end of thirty years of British rule," writes Mr. Mayhew. Even today, women's education is left almost entirely to missions. Probably fewer than 10 per cent of all girls of school age receive any kind of instruction. In the British Cameroons 1,142 girls out of about one hundred forty thousand attended any type of school in 1937. The apology of colonial officials, that "natives do not want their girls educated," can be thrown out of court. Natives are demanding increased educational opportunities for their girls, and more than one native witness before investigating commissions has put forward the neglect of female education as a serious grievance.

Everywhere in the colonial empire education is being starved in order to provide for expensive general administrations; and a good part of the sums allocated to departments of education goes to pay the high salaries of the British supervisors. Rarely indeed does education receive more than 5 per cent of the total budget; in some colonies—Nyasaland, for example—its portion is less than 3 per cent. Northern Rhodesia devoted in 1937 to education the sum of $355,000 out of a budget totaling close to seven million dollars.

Yet in some colonies even those niggardly sums are monopolized by the European settlers, while the indigenous population gets a crumb. In Southern Rhodesia $1,805,000 was spent in 1938 for the education of the children of sixty thousand non-natives; the magnificent sum of four hundred fifty thousand dollars went for those of a million and a quarter natives. In addition, $1,150,000 was spent on Europeans from the Beit Trust; 1 per cent of this sum was given for natives. While thirty dollars was spent on education per head of the European population, thirty-five cents sufficed for each native head. Southern Rhodesia devoted two hundred eighty thousand dollars in 1938 to educate the children of eleven thousand non-natives, and two hundred twenty thousand dollars for those of 1,366,000 natives (in 1923 not a cent was given to the latter): or twenty-five dollars per European and fifteen cents for each native taxpayer. In Tanganyika—$4.53 per European; six cents per native.

Nor is any progress to be expected from the existing schools. The standard of vernacular schools for the masses, which make up 90 per cent of the system, is so low that children learn next to nothing, and the teachers themselves could profit from a few years in a high school, which the vast majority never attended. Although the schools are not scholastic in purpose, they dispense far too much useless book knowledge not integrated with local life and environment; instead of using the schools as a vehicle for reforming native life, the administrations devote little or no attention to such matters as hygiene, agriculture, sanitation, arts and crafts; and the three "R's," mechanically and imperfectly learned, are forgotten before long. Most of the elementary schooling in the colonies is a complete waste.

But divorce from reality can hardly be carried further than has been done by the so-called "English schools," intended for the select few able to afford secondary education. Chained to the requirements of the Oxford or Cambridge entrance examinations, all, whether in the West Indies, tropical Africa, in the dependencies of the Mediterranean or the Western Pacific, require that students memorize masses of data about the British climate, British geography, British animal and plant life, and study the history and government of a society totally alien to them. I once happened upon a literature class in such a school where Chaucer, not the works of native writers, was considered appropriate for study. These schools, from elementary classes up, have little relation to local life and the problems of the immediate neighborhood. Education there is not an organic part of life, but an unpleasant exercise in a foreign gymnastic, which, after a series of trials and tribulations, will lead to a certificate and ultimately to a clerkship in a government office.

If this education has not done much damage, that is because there has been so terribly little of it. Secondary education was neglected until after the World War, and neither Nyasaland, the Rhodesias nor Kenya possesses as yet a single secondary school for Africans. In Zanzibar the first secondary school for boys was established only in 1935. Non-African dependencies are somewhat better provided, but even there only an insignificant fraction—much less than 1 per cent—of the youth has an opportunity to attend high schools.

No less serious is it that technical and agricultural training has been neglected almost completely. A commission appointed in 1937 to study "higher education in East Africa" found that on a "conservative basis...a large expansion and improvement will be required" before it would be possible to meet the demands of the government alone for trained medical assistants, sanitary inspectors, and agricultural teachers. It is a sad fact that the oldest government agricultural school in the whole colonial empire dates only from 1910. Today there are twenty-seven such schools, most of which have been opened within the last decade. Three colleges in Africa, though of a standard not much above secondary schools in western countries, are doing excellent work; obviously, however, the number of graduates is far too small to influence effectively native life.

The unfortunate truth is that, aside from a manifold increase in the number of elementary and primary schools and a complete change in their programs, there will have to be a hundred-fold increase in the number of secondary, technical, and agricultural schools before there can possibly be any appreciable improvement in the standard of colonial life and before those sixty million subjects of His Britannic Majesty can become citizens of the modern world.

WHAT PRICE LABOR?

No optimist—not even a colonial secretary addressing the Junior Imperialist League on Empire Day—can assert unblushingly that the life of a colonial laborer is an attractive one. Compared with the life of colored workers in the colonies, that of the most oppressed sections of the working class in the most backward areas in the West is princely. The following is a composite picture of a typical colonial worker.

Though he was born to the leisurely life of a primitive countryside, where very little work is done, a number of forces beyond his control have driven him to migrate, perhaps over a thousand miles of roadless jungle, to seek employment in mine or plantation. The first of these circumstances is that the relentless encroachment of white-owned plantations has reduced the tribal area and the plot to which he is entitled by custom will not suffice to feed a family. Second, tax collectors have come to demand that he pay a head or hut tax of two to five dollars, a sum not to be earned in the village. Third, if he stays at home, government officers will force him to work a certain number of days on roads and other public works. Fourth, new cultural influences have given him a taste for cheap manufactured articles to be had only with coin of the realm. Finally, perhaps, he may desire medical treatment, or adventure or education in modern civilization.

Employment is not difficult to find in most colonies. The European establishments are crying for hands. But our black Odysseus must settle down quickly. Laws providing severe punishment for blacks wandering about without cards of employment have been enacted in most African dependencies. A place of employment having been found, he will live in a corrugated iron barrack together with dozens of other natives. If his wife and children are with him, they too will have to crowd into the small room. Guards will wake him before sunrise, sometimes at three or four o'clock in the morning, and he will work till sunset. There is no eight-hour day for colonial labor; nor need employers go to the expense of providing healthy working conditions and safety devices. Life is cheap in the colonies. The monthly rations of the black laborer will consist of ten to fifteen pounds of meal; two pounds of meat; less than a pound of nuts; two pounds of beans; two to three pounds of vegetables, some salt and fat; if he is accompanied by his wife and children, about ten pounds of maize will be added. As to wages, thirty days of work—that is, five full weeks—will entitle him to three to eight dollars, out of which will be taken his hut or head tax and perhaps the tax of some members of his family left in the village. And so, after a year or two, the black treks again to his native area with a few trinkets and a couple of yards of Manchester print on his back; enriched now by experience of modern civilization; and with his head tax paid. However, the forces which first drove him to leave the native area will still be in operation; and more likely than not, he will repeat the journey before long.

That this picture is in no sense an exaggeration is borne out by more official data than I can possibly marshal here. A member of Parliament who visited ginneries in Tanganyika found that "the dust inside was almost incredible, and people should not have to work eleven hours in such conditions." An average labor day of eleven hours is the rule in all colonies, and wages are terribly low. Cotton ginneries in Uganda pay an average wage of less than $2.50 for thirty days of work. In Northern Rhodesia agricultural workers earned in good years $1.75 to $2.50 per month, while those engaged in industry received from $1.75 to $5. In Southern Rhodesia firms pay an average of $3.10 monthly with food. According to the present Colonial Secretary, "in the four great African Colonies, wage rates from $1.25 to $3.75 a month are the regular rule for the vast majority of people, and...most families...have cash incomes of probably less than $15, and certainly less than $25 per year"—which is just about sufficient to pay all the taxes.

True, native labor is not as productive as white. But whose fault is that? A man cannot give out more than he takes in; and natives receive very little in the way of food. A vicious circle exists: undernourished, weak, and disease-ridden, the native cannot produce very much; unable to produce, he is paid very little and given the cheapest rations possible. The low cost of food does not compensate for the meager wage. "It has been calculated that the minimum sum required to obtain a reasonably good diet (not an optimum diet) in Freetown [Sierra Leone] is between 6d. and 7d. per head per day, or say 15s. a month. That is just about the average wage received by the urban laborer, so that according to this computation if he is to feed himself decently there is nothing left at all for the food of his wife and family let alone for his housing, clothing, etc., unless he has other sources of income." But experiments have shown that the circle can be broken. When the 200 workers at the Kampala railway station, Uganda, "drawn from a tribe which was notorious for its poor physique and inefficient work," were given a full diet including meat, "it was soon found that they turned into as good workpeople as exist anywhere in East Africa."

As was to be expected, child labor is prevalent, and recent years have witnessed a definite upswing in the employment of children especially on tea, cotton, and sugar plantations, where they can be driven to do the work of adults at less pay. A recent law in Kenya permits employment of children ten years of age. In Uganda children of nine can be contracted and "forced away from their homes and subjected to penal sanctions." The existing labor law in Northern Rhodesia permits "contracts" with children; a commissioner sent in 1938 to study conditions advised that "the section should be deleted as contracts with penal sanctions for children under sixteen are undesirable."

No wonder natives do not like to work for Europeans and resort has to be had to all sorts of methods to supply laborers. World opinion having forced colonial officials to outlaw the indenture system, more refined methods have been evolved, the most effective of which is taxation. I know that many now try to minimize the importance of this method in driving natives to seek paid employment; but anybody who has any first-hand knowledge of colonial conditions knows how naïve are those attempts at whitewashing. The native may be able to resist all kinds of pressure and inducements; he cannot, however, resist the tax gatherer. The Governor of Kenya has frankly admitted "that taxation is the only possible method of compelling the Native to leave his Reserve for the purpose of seeking work."

Once in employment, the worker is kept at his job in many colonies by laws providing extremely severe penalties for breach of contract. Master and servants ordinances provide for fines, amounting sometimes to fifty dollars, or two years' imprisonment, or both, if an employee runs away from his job. An "Ordinance to Regulate the Employment of Servants," which includes skilled and unskilled laborers, enacted in Kenya in 1939, provides that a worker "may be fined a sum not exceeding one-half of his monthly wages, and in default may be imprisoned for a period not exceeding one month," if (a) he fails "to commence his services at the stipulated times"; if (b) "he absents himself" from work; or if (c) "he neglects to perform any work which it was his duty to have performed or if he carelessly or improperly performs any work which, from its nature, it was his duty under his contract to have performed carefully and properly," and so on.

One must not forget that forced labor for public works —but for public works only—still exists throughout the colonial empire in practice, though not in theory. A missionary in Rhodesia wrote in the *Manchester Guardian*: "I was shown an astounding extension of roadmaking work which had been achieved in the last few months by the Native Departments' authority. The amount of work accomplished must have been a stupendous burden upon those who were called out from their employment to do it with their own tools, without any food being given them or any pay.... *No wage has been given, no rations supplied, no remission of the poll tax promised.*" The Native Authority Ordinance of 1929 gives chiefs the right to impose forced labor for public works. "The District Officer is told that such and such buildings or roads ought to be made or put in order. He in turn sends for the chiefs and tells them what he wishes to be done. The chiefs in turn summon the headmen and sub-headmen, telling each how many men he must produce, and they in turn go to the village and choose the men to be called." At least half of the roads in the colonies have been built by forced labor.

This description of life in British colonies might lead the reader to conclude that British imperialism is more exploiting than all others, more tyrannical, and socially more reactionary. Such, however, is not the case. It is true that native labor is exploited almost as badly in British colonies as in those ruled by other European imperialist nations, that the land problem is almost as serious, that poverty is almost as great. Indeed, in the matter of public works, sanitation, hygiene, agricultural improvement the Italians, Dutch, and perhaps even the French have better records than the British can show; and there are more literates per thousand of the population in Dutch Java than in most British colonies. Yet after all these facts have been considered, any true yardstick will show that British imperialism has been the lesser evil. Compared with all the others, Britain has indeed been "the great schoolteacher of colored peoples"—even if unintentionally so.

There has been a difference in the degree of cruelty and in the method of exploitation. Imperialism is imperialism and it retains its inherent characteristics regardless which nation practices it. The important word is "inherent": imperialism is inherently authoritarian; inherently antidemocratic; inherently exploiting. To survive it must be static. But British imperialism degenerated only in exceptional circumstances to the bestial cruelties that have been all too characteristic of the other regimes.

British officials brought with them the English conceptions of individual liberty, freedom from government regimentation, and common justice. While liberating the natives from the tyranny of their chiefs and of civil wars, they usually refrained from setting up a new administrative tyranny, the more oppressive because so much more efficient. British colonies have traditionally been devoid of the spirit of regimentation and militarization found in the pre-1914 German colonies and the contemporary French possessions. That fascist laws and denial of civil liberties have not been unknown in British colonies goes without saying. In Cyprus, for example, Hansard was not so long ago declared to be seditious literature; one recalls the Rowlatt Acts in India, the Denishwai incident in Egypt, the illegal methods used in breaking strikes in Barbados, Mauritius, India, and elsewhere; yet there is no denying that such high-handed actions have been sufficiently exceptional not to disturb the reign of law. Only in British colonies does one find a bench which dares to make "it perfectly clear that there had been a complete outrage in the administration of justice and that the men [who instigated a strike in Mauritius] ought never to have been sentenced."

Of course, compared with American standards the freedom found in British colonies has not amounted to much. There is no escaping the fact that ultimately all imperialisms rest on force and no amount of sugar-coating can remove the bitterness of the pill. But the fact is also that the extra bit of freedom has stood British colonials in very good stead and has made possible educational, cultural, and even political progress not found in any other system.

Second, if British officials have not done much to advance native education, neither have they interfered, as have other imperialist officials, when the natives began doing something for themselves; or when non-official bodies such as missionaries appeared on the scene to open schools which produced a native intelligentsia imbued with ideals that official government schools would have been less anxious to encourage. Hence the vast influence of missionary organizations in British colonies; hence the importance which private charitable institutions have occupied in all fields of social work; hence also the greater industrial and economic progress of British colonies than those of any other nation. In the heyday of British rule, that is, before 1914, capitalists, merchants, prospectors, promoters were free to do anything that seemed profitable in their eyes; and it is notorious that, during its vigor, private capitalism accomplishes more in months than bureaucratic government can in decades. Obviously, besides being virtuous and in its day socially progressive, this practice was also very profitable to British capital.

Probably British colonial officials would have been no better than those of all other imperialist nations and would

just as soon have resorted to brute force in coping with natives; but in Great Britain more than anywhere else there
has been a fairly vigilant press, a House of Commons with
liberal and Labor members who have always been ready to
make trouble for colonial secretaries, and, as Lord Hailey
has correctly pointed out, "a large public with a very genu-
ine interest in colonial questions, much better informed on
the realities of colonial conditions than the public of most
other European nations." The difference in degree of cruelty
has had greater influences than one who has not lived in
colonial countries can realize, and has been sufficient to
place British imperialism in a category by itself.

As to method of exploitation, the fundamental fact is
that all imperialist nations except the British have either
not grasped at all the implications of capitalist dynamics,
or, as has been the case with the French, have grasped them
only to so limited an extent that capitalism in the colonies
lost its progressive qualities. All these states have ruled according to the ancient Roman principles of tribute. That
is what Lenin meant when he wrote in his study on *Imperialism* that "unlike British colonial imperialism, French
imperialism might be termed usury imperialism"—while the
others might be called feudal imperialism. Their exploitation has traditionally assumed two forms. First, they despoiled their colonies of all movable wealth accumulated
during previous centuries. After all wealth was drained interest declined and the colonies settled down to a stagnant
existence. Second, in line with their pre-capitalist conceptions, they have grabbed lands for vast estates, relegating
the natives to the position of slaves. Both of these forms of
exploitation are essentially static even economically, and
therefore much more so politically and culturally.

The British, too, have practiced these forms of exploitation. But as a nation of traders—as the creators of modern
industrial and financial capitalism—the British have sought
the greater opportunities for profit which capitalism makes
possible, and thereby have opened the door to political and
cultural influences. Possessing large financial resources
awaiting profitable investment, the British built roads and
railways, developed mines, constructed telephones and tele-

graphs. Colonial administrations, as was shown above, have not encouraged development of finishing industries; private entrepreneurs, however, have not always toed the official line. British banking and credit institutions, British exporting and importing houses, industrialists in search of raw materials—all these, while enabling Britain to draw greater profits from her colonies than has any other imperialist nation, have introduced a progressive dynamics and have recreated, if on a limited scale, all the social forces that have revolutionized the West since 1775.

And supremely confident of their own infinite superiority, the British have not had to degrade the natives at every turn, as other imperialist nations have done. They have had no objection if the natives retain their self-respect—an attitude which is greatly appreciated by all colored peoples and which, probably more than any other single factor, accounts for the scarcity of revolts in British colonies until after 1920. Not worried lest every grumbler start a revolution, they have not set up complicated spy systems, and the hand of the police has not been made to fall nearly as heavily as in other administrations.

Is respect for civil rights—and on a very limited scale at that—sufficient to compensate for administrative inefficiency which has resulted in neglect of social services? History, I believe, answers these questions; and the reply is in the affirmative, except in the cases of peoples still in the "barbarian" stage of development and therefore unable to make use of the greater freedom. If a people has the right to criticize, if it is permitted to demand and to protest, it will forge ahead, in the long run, much faster and certainly in a more healthy manner than one which is spoon-fed by a paternal administration and gets knocked over the head every time it dares to criticize.

Let this be clear: the greatest evil of foreign domination is not that it robs poor countries of their little wealth, that it exploits colonial labor, that it does not provide good government and those nation-building social services we deem essential in a progressive administration. The greatest evil, to quote the words used in 1882 by John Seeley, one of the profoundest students of imperialism, to describe the *Ex-*

pansion of England into India, is that "subjection for a long time to a foreign yoke is one of the most potent causes of national deterioration" since it diminishes "what little power" a colony may have had for "evolving out of itself a stable Government." Fortunately British imperialism has been less destructive of the moral fiber of colonial peoples than all other imperial systems. This factor in conjunction with the economic progressiveness of the British has made possible considerable political progress and has gradually prepared colonies for self-determination.

And the fact is that the British have always insisted that self-determination must be the ultimate result of their rule. To be sure, as was shown above, they have thought of this end more as an abstract possibility in some remote future, and day-by-day administration has not been conducted so as to realize that end in the shortest time possible. Lord Hailey has had to admit "that our governments have shown themselves unduly slow to realize the necessity of educating the Africans not merely to take the routine of administration off the shoulders of the European officers, but to take part, in a more real sense, in the actual work of administration." But the fact is also that Egypt and other colonial territories have already attained full self-government, while many more are slowly or rapidly reaching that goal. No other imperial system has provided for a similar development; in no other scheme has the direction been so clearly defined.

It is significant that the British have never conceived of any political system as something fixed, frozen, and final. On the contrary they have incorporated change into the very essence of their structure, and they have constantly made adjustments to fit unprecedented conditions. Unwillingness to give up power and privileges is not characteristic of British administration: in so far as the British have resisted colonial demands, they have been as all other imperial nations; but unlike all others, they have given up both power and privileges whenever sufficient popular pressure was brought to bear. They have crushed revolts with blood and iron as have all other empires; but unlike all others, they have invariably made concessions afterwards, which have given the colonial peoples greater liberty and self-rule than they had before.

One needs only to compare a British with a French or Italian or Dutch possession to see what these differences, slight as they appear when contrasted with the fundamental evils of imperialism, have meant in reality. Compare, for example, contemporary French-ruled Syria with Egypt. In 1914 Syria was far more advanced than Egypt economically, politically, and culturally. Syrian townspeople were more energetic than all other peoples of the Near East; their economic consciousness was far more highly developed; in trade they held first place; Syrian craftsmen and workers were not only the most energetic but much the best. Socially Syria was modernizing itself very rapidly. Decay of feudalism had gone further there than anywhere else; movements for the emancipation of women had started. Even greater was Syria's cultural superiority. Education had developed there more than in any other Near Eastern country; Syria's newspapers and periodicals were the best in the Near East; its literature the most vigorous. Indeed, the whole Arab world drew on Syria's intelligentsia for teachers, writers, doctors, businessmen, and officials. If any Arab territory was prepared for self-government, it was certainly Syria and the Lebanon.

But since 1920 the French have run the country—and have run it down. Who can doubt now which is the more advanced? In 1920 Syria's political life was far more vigorous than that of Egypt; today, however, Egypt is an independent country with complete self-government, while Syria is further from independence than ever. Intentionally or otherwise, the French have introduced bacilli which have eaten at Syria's vitals, and have made the country sick indeed. Culturally, economically, socially there has been not progress, but distinct retrogression. No longer is Syria the teacher of the Near East: Egypt passed it long since, and so even did Iraq, which in 1920 was very far behind. The literatures of both the latter are today more vigorous than that of Syria; their economic structures are much healthier; modernization has gone further; both now lead fairly orderly national lives, progressing in every way. But it will take

Syria at least a generation or two to overcome the disruptive forces the French have released during the short period of their administration and to recover its erstwhile vigor.

Or compare India with Java. Which of the two has had the smoother and the more efficient administration cannot be doubted; Java's social services have been much better than those provided by the British for India. Yet the former is almost as far from self-determination as it has ever been, while India has not only had a very vigorous political movement, but has demonstrated its ability to lead an almost completely independent life. Even British imperialists admit that India needs nothing more than supervision, since normal daily administration can now be safely entrusted to Indian hands. While Java's moral fiber has strengthened hardly at all during the past centuries, or to a degree that is almost negligible, that of India has grown in a manner that is nothing short of amazing. In 1882 Seeley feared that "the few facts we know about the ancient Hindus confirm what we should conjecture about the moral effects produced on them" by foreign rule. We know now that British rule has not only not had disastrous results, but has perhaps done "more than ever was done by former Governments to make... possible" for India to "begin to breathe as a single national whole."

That the differences between British and other imperial rules should add up to such imposing totals may be surprising. However, history shows that they do. The results are seen throughout the colonial world, regardless which colonies one will compare. Even the British possessions in Africa, more neglected than all others, compare favorably with those of France, Portugal, or Italy; and the differences will become even greater during subsequent years, when the British colonies will be better prepared to make use of their greater freedom. The slowest development in British territories takes place while the foundation is being laid— while the first few thousands of natives are being educated, while the simplest attempt is being made to cope with the most widespread diseases, while the first few agricultural reforms are being introduced and the first few factories built. Once that part is finished, advance becomes rapid and develops with accelerating tempo. The other imperialist administrations, the Dutch and the French, lay the foundations comparatively quickly; afterwards, however, native attempts to build on those foundations are crushed mercilessly and a dead silence ensues.

SUMMING UP

These peculiarities of British administration—miserable social conditions on the one side, and a considerable amount of civil and political freedom on the other—have given Britain's colonial empire a history unlike that of any other empire and have produced problems which all others have been spared until now. It was inevitable that these conditions should sooner or later produce nationalist movements aiming to obtain the political self-determination which the British promised but were slow to realize.

Broadly, British colonial history has fallen into two distinct periods. During the first period the British had very little trouble with their colonies. Rebellions were rare; both the people and their chiefs accepted the foreign rulers with little protest. The duration of this stage varied. In India, the British encountered very little opposition for more than one hundred and fifty years after Clive's victory; in Jamaica and other old colonies the period was even longer; in Egypt nationalism blossomed much more rapidly, appearing as a force only thirty years after the Occupation; the African and Asiatic dependencies made no trouble till after the first World War.

Paradoxically enough, the long absence of rebellions in the African and Asiatic colonial possessions was due to the social conditions, which were even worse than those described above. To rule peoples in the lowest stages of development is much easier than English imperialists would have the world believe. Knowing nothing about the Western world and Western conceptions of human life, primitive peoples made no demands on the British administrators and the absence of social services was no cause for dissatisfaction. Such peoples are too poor, too ignorant, too weak physically and mentally to protest and to revolt.

The very fact that British colonial administrators were too easy-going or too reactionary to bother with complicated schemes of social reform did much to prevent the outbreak of rebellions such as constantly marred Germany's colonial record. Throughout I have followed—rightly, I believe—Western standards of judgment; but natives knew nothing of these standards, and were not dissatisfied when the British failed to live up to them. In the early days of an imperialist rule, far from complaining that nation-building social services are inadequate, natives resent their existence. The less they are bothered with schools, sanitation, road-building, vaccination, and so forth, the better they like it. That is why the British have traditionally got along so well with primitive peoples.

Another factor which made for peace was the absence of forced labor for private purposes. In colonies as a whole, more rebellions have been caused by the practice of imperialist officials of using military might to drive natives to work on European-owned estates and in mines than by any other single factor; the British, however, outlawed this evil practice comparatively early. Having learned the wisdom of moderation, British administrators turned a deaf ear to the constant demands of white plantation owners that armed force be used whenever they could not obtain sufficient native labor by any other means. The natives were not slow to appreciate this bit of humanitarianism. Refugees from neighboring territories ruled by other imperialist states gave wide publicity to the terroristic methods used to compel them to work.

What happened was simply that the British transplanted to the colonies the *laissez-faire* conception of government which had worked so well in their own country. That the best government is the one which governs least had been a British dogma at least since the middle of the eighteenth century; why should it not prove as useful in the colonies as it had proven in England? That conditions in the colonies were totally different from those prevailing in their own country, they did not stop to see. However, if this system did not make for rapid social progress, neither did it produce those practices which brought about innumerable revolts in other empires.

Whatever its shortcomings when judged by Western standards, then, British rule until 1914 was a well-integrated system, logical and not out of harmony with the social reality in the colonies. Civilization filtered in, but slowly and without dislocating the social system. Under normal circumstances, this system could have survived centuries, and the Empire would not have been menaced. But it was destined not to continue peacefully. Outbreak of the first World War introduced revolutionary changes which shook colonial society. It was not long before the British discovered to their great chagrin that their somnambulant dependencies were awakening, and not slowly either.

Thus began the second period of Britain's colonial history. Western doctrines of liberty, self-determination, social progress, and the duties of government suddenly made their appearance, and the native inhabitants applied those ideas to themselves. Everywhere movements of protest and of revolt sprang up; there is hardly a colony where British rule has not been challenged. Industrial workers began to stage strikes and demonstrations. No longer were backward peoples grateful for being left undisturbed by schools, hospitals, public works; they now began to demand those as of right, and revolted when their demands were not satisfied. The characteristics which constituted a source of strength before 1914 in all British administrations now became their greatest weakness. The social conditions described above, as will become obvious in subsequent pages, contributed a great deal to the weakening of the Empire during the twenties and the first part of the last decade.

Impetus was added to the protest movement by the greater political freedom prevailing in these colonies. The colonials of the French Empire, too, became increasingly dissatisfied with their foreign masters; unfortunately for them, they were not given the slightest opportunity to express their dissatisfaction, which was nipped while still in the bud. And unlike the French or other imperialist nations, which had never held out self-determination as the ultimate result of their rule, the British had frequently proclaimed that autonomy was the inevitable end of their system. Now the hour of reckoning began to approach constantly nearer. The far-flung colonies, so submissive and quiescent until 1920, emerged as one of the menaces to the continued existence of the Empire.

IV

INDIA: BRIGHTEST JEWEL
OF THE CROWN

INDIA OCCUPIES A UNIQUE position in the Empire: it is less
dependent on London than a crown colony yet lacks the
full independence of a Dominion. The manner of its occupation, its early company government, the peculiar relationship
between the East India Company and the British Government, which came gradually to control yet did not rule till
the middle of the last century, the type of administration
set up—all these, as well as innumerable factors inherent in
the nature of the country itself, its people, its civilization
and socio-economic life, have co-operated to make India
alone and incomparable in the whole vast imperial structure.

No wonder India has been called "the brightest jewel of
the British Crown." Every consideration entitles it to that
dubious honor. Placed over the map of Europe, it would
cover the whole except Russia. Though smaller than Canada
or Australia, its area of 1,575,000 square miles contains more
cultivated land. Its immense population makes it an empire
in its own right. The last census, that of 1931, showed a total
population of more than 338,000,000; by now, the 370,-
000,000 mark has been passed. British India alone registers
every year about nine million births—a number which is
thrice as large as the total existing population of Lithuania
or many another European state.

India has also been unique in her social organization.
Hindu society has lacked real cohesion. A galaxy of religions
and cults bewildering in variety and complexity has added
to the confusion. There is, first, the large Moslem minority,
constituting 23 per cent of the population, and the majority

in some provinces. Obviously, the presence of this large minority has provided a fertile ground for conflict, especially as the Mohammedans had once conquered India and ruled it. Add to the religious groups Buddhists, Sikhs, and numerous smaller communities such as Jains, Parsees, Christians, and others; add also differences in language and administrative traditions. The two major tongues have been Urdu and Hindi; but the census enumerates a total of 222 languages and dialects.

More than any other colony, India provided endless opportunities for beneficent administration. The British could have revolutionized Indian life and brought the country into the vortex of modern movements. The people were backward, no doubt; but their past culture showed high ability, great artistic prowess, and no mean administrative capacities. Hundreds of millions of human beings would have benefited, and the influence of a reformed India on Asia would have been immense. On the other hand, the variety of social divisions and religious antagonisms offered no fewer opportunities for the unscrupulous imperialist interested only in the enhancement of his power and aggrandizement. With no great difficulty they could be turned to selfish ends.

Which of these two policies have the British followed? One regrets to say that they have followed the second. Few if any of the fundamental Indian problems have been solved since Clive's victory at Plassey in 1757, when the British became the effective rulers of the vast peninsula. On the contrary, the British have aggravated all the old problems and created many new ones.

Not that the Indian Civil Service—that silent, autocratical governing body—has given bad rule. Its rule has been good as far as it has gone; but as we have seen in the colonial empire, the civil service either has not gone fast enough or went nowhere at all. Paid high salaries to keep them beyond the temptation of bribery, British officials have been neither cruel nor corrupt; but their conception of the duties and functions of government has been extremely narrow. Government to them has had no meaning beyond the collection of taxes, administration of justice, and, above all, maintenance of law and order. They have given no thought to social reform; there has been no trace of purposeful economic development; even education and public health remained beyond their range.

The India Act of 1858, which transferred rule from the East India Company to the British Crown, did not lead to the slightest reform in administration. As the years went by, authority became more than ever centralized in British hands. The authority of the governor general grew; the central government stretched its tentacles further. As a purely administrative machine, no doubt the government became fairly efficient; but it was a machine without life and without a soul. Taxation was its fuel; law and order its only product. The provincial legislative councils set up not only were farces; they served to divide Indians and to miseducate them in the art of responsible democratic government. Projects for instituting some simulacrum of popular government in the smallest political units faded into smoke. The famous Resolution on Local Self-Government of 1882 was as far from real democracy as anything could possibly be. Subsequent "reforms" went all in the same direction. The Morley-Minto reforms in the early years of this century aimed to create "a constitutional autocracy," and did not succeed even in this. The autocracy remained no different from what it had always been.

The representative councils set up under the reforms not only lacked all real power and responsibility, but were not even representative. They were packed with officials and other nominated members; Moslems and other minority communities were granted representation far above their numerical strength. The people were not given the slightest share in government. High property and other qualifications required for the right to vote made even the elected members representative not of the nation but of the privileged classes which would be most ready to co-operate with the administration. A total of 5,818 persons out of a population of three hundred millions were given the right to elect representatives for the Indian Legislative Council. In Bombay, eight Moslem electors were represented by a member;

the representative for Burma—possessing a population of about eleven million—was chosen by nine men.

There was a tolerable amount of freedom of speech and of press until the rebellion of 1858, primarily because there was no danger of either's being used to menace British rule. A radical change then brought forth ordinances to control the press and other measures restricting personal liberty. The continuance of agitation led to further repressive measures against the press in 1908 and 1910. Publishers were required to deposit security which might be forfeited in case of publication of seditious matter; on repetition of the offense, the printing press was liable to confiscation. These laws failing to restrain expression of the growing discontent, a whole series of new ones were enacted which culminated with the fascist Defense of India Act and the Rowlatt Act at the end of the war. Under these and numerous other enactments all traces of personal liberty disappeared from the official ken; and in practice the Indian person or his property has had not many more constitutional guarantees than a German under the Nazis.

Discriminations against Indians both in government employment and in law courts, far from diminishing with the passage of years, actually increased until the World War. An Act of 1833, declaring that "no native...shall by reason only of his religion, place of birth, descent, color, or any of them, be disabled from holding any place, office or employment under the Company," remained a dead letter. Not even lip service was paid to it by the local administration. Artificial difficulties were created to prevent an Indian from entering the sacred ranks of the Senior Civil Service; a measure introduced in the eighties to place Europeans and Indians on an equal basis in the administration of criminal law led to a furore and was finally emasculated. Only the judiciary offered respectable careers for natives. A royal commission in 1930 found that natives could not, apparently, advance beyond a certain rank even in the railway administration.

LIFE, WORK AND UNHAPPINESS

Before proceeding with political matters it might be well to glance at the socio-economic realities of this imperial jewel. For the key to all India's political problems is its backward social state: its all-pervasive poverty; its vast illiteracy and cultural backwardness; its minority conflicts which play into the hands of the British rulers; its feudal classes which rely on the British to protect their exploitation. Britain did not conquer India with arms nor has it held that continent by the sword. Far truer is it to say that, like a trained elephant, India bent her knees to the British masters and submitted to the goad; and it was only necessary to play on India's internal divisions to keep it obedient.

First we must turn to the five hundred thousand villages. Here live almost nine-tenths of the Indian population, which depends on the soil for livelihood. This fact alone reveals how medieval India still is. How is one to portray to Western eyes the tragedy of those hundreds of millions? In a poverty such as is never seen and is almost unimaginable in the West they are born; in poverty and squalor and with disease they live; in poverty and in debt they die.

In all discussions on India the most fundamental fact to bear in mind is that at least a third of the population is perpetually hungry, while the overwhelming majority does not know the meaning of a satisfactory meal. Professor D. Dubey has demonstrated that "64.6 per cent of the population lives always on insufficient food, getting only about 73 per cent of the minimum requirements for maintaining efficiency. In other words, two-thirds of the population always get only three-quarters of the amount of food-grains they should have." The production of grains and pulses, after allowing for exports, provides only 1.2 pounds per head per day—which is about the standard allowed by government for famine relief and less than the diet given to prisoners. The ryot, or peasant, neither drinks nor smokes; his clothing consists of a cotton loin cloth which he uses till it disintegrates. The village in which he lives has nothing in common with the idyllic picture of peace drawn by some Western romanticists. It is an ugly place, not a beautiful one. It is an unusual hovel that has more than one room; windows are rare; the roof of sticks and palm leaves is a poor protection against the periodic heavy rains. Inside, the monotony of the gray mud walls is hardly relieved by a single piece of furniture. There are neither tables nor chairs nor books nor pictures. The bed, if there is one, is made of twisted twigs which raise the straw mattress a few inches from the ground.

That the population of one of the greatest agricultural countries in the world lives in perpetual semi-starvation is due to a variety of factors. First, there is not enough land to satisfy the whole national land hunger. An Indian economist has shown that under "Indian conditions" twenty acres of dry or five to seven acres of "wet" land suffice for a subsistence existence; yet if holdings were divided on the basis of even this low calculation, "more than half of the existing population would be displaced." The average holding in Bengal is 3.1 acres; in the United Provinces it is 2.5; in the Deccan, three-fifths of all holdings are less than five acres. And even these small holdings have been scattered by divisions and sub-divisions into minute fragments all over the village area.

Second, production per acre is extremely low. The yield of India's staple products—wheat, sugar, cotton—is between half and one-quarter of that obtained in Western countries. This low productivity is not due to laziness. On the contrary, every study shows that the ryot works very hard, toiling in season with all the members of his family from sunrise to sunset; and he works thoroughly. He may plow as many as a dozen times, and weeds carefully. Unfortunately, factors outside his control impede progress. Schools have not been provided for him to learn modern agricultural methods; he tills and reaps exactly as did his ancestors a thousand years ago; and he is far too poor to afford the modern machines or such a luxury as manure even if he knew about them. The wooden blade he uses no more than scratches the ground a few inches deep during a dozen plowings; centuries of intensive cultivation with little or no manuring have extracted from mother earth all her life juices. Consequently the Indian farmer has to devote no less than forty days to cultivating a single acre against the one day devoted by his American counterpart, who obtains a yield two to four times as large. There can be no better indication of the frightful human wastage!

However, this is not the end of the tale. Not only does the ryot have too little land for cultivation; the plot he cultivates does not belong to him. Half of the land in India is owned by rich landlords; the other half is mortgaged to usurers. The land hunger has driven up rents till half or even two-thirds of the income goes to idle *zamindars,* or landlords. Cultivating four acres, the ryot might earn as much as thirty-five dollars a year, from which a rental of ten to twenty-five dollars has to be paid. To meet extraordinary expenses or to survive years of famine, he has to resort to money lenders, or *banias,* and once in their clutches the chances of release are very small. Reliable estimates place the debts of peasants at two to three billion dollars, the average interest rate on which is about 30 per cent. The ryot's income being too low to pay such usurious rates, the debt grows until the *bania* seizes title of the land. Thus the number of landless peasants grows continuously; those who still own petty plots are life-long slaves to the usurers.

What a year of famine means to such a population can be easily imagined. Constant exploitation has exhausted the soil, which yields less and less notwithstanding the peasant's hard work. The road to improvement is barred by both *zamindar* and *bania.* To avoid the possible necessity of paying compensation when they evict the peasant from his land, they do not permit plantation of fruit trees, construction of wells, or any other improvements. The government, also, has helped to keep the peasants in perpetual debt by collecting taxes before, not after, the crop is reaped.

The people, too, have become exhausted. Constant undernourishment, unsanitary surroundings, and lack of adequate medical provisions have diminished the people's vitality and their ability to work. Irrigation works built by the British have considerably increased the fertility of a large part of the cultivated area; but very little has been done to provide good drinking water and village latrines, and even less in the way of rural hospitalization. Periodic plagues ravage the country, taking millions of lives and disabling even more; few of the fifty million cases of malaria every year receive medical treatment. Hence, this bacillus takes every year about a million lives which could be saved and disables another two million, while the vitality of other millions is considerably sapped. Hookworm takes its annual toll in lives and in national energy; there is ancholostimia, and there are many other tropical diseases.

These frightful conditions give India a mortality rate of twenty-three to twenty-eight per thousand, a rate which is double that of England and three times that of Australia or New Zealand. Climate cannot be blamed for this human wastage; statistics show that among the European communities in India mortality is not higher than in England or the United States. Rarely does the infant mortality rate fall below two hundred per thousand live births; usually it is closer to three hundred—which means that almost one of every three children does not survive to see its first birthday. One might expect that the sturdy ones who survive the perils of childhood would live to ripe old age. Such, however, is not the case. The average Indian can expect to live only 23.5 years—less than half of the average life expectancy in the United States.

As in the colonies, insufficient production of food spells undernourishment for three-quarters of the population and a low standard of national energy; this in turn leads to poor work and low production. The social evils aggravate the situation by making for an unfair distribution of the wealth produced. But even if every ryot owned the land he cultivates and retained his whole production, the improvement would not be very great. The basic fact is that the total amount of wealth produced is insufficient for India's immense population. The per capita income in India is less than twenty-five dollars a year, as compared with about seven hundred fifty dollars in the United States.

Only industrialization could have broken this vicious circle. The experience of all Western countries has shown that industry alone can produce a significant increase in the quantity of goods available for distribution. At present, more than half of India's male population is in reality permanently unemployed. Peasants are occupied on their land less than a third of the year; millions of men are entirely without work.

Unfortunately, industry has been slow in developing. Although the second most populated country in the world, India is only eighth or ninth on the industrial ladder. France, England, Italy, Germany, and other countries with a tenth of its population outrank it as industrial producers. The total number of factories is around nine thousand, which, although it represents a significant increase over the fifteen hundred in 1900, is still extremely low for so large a land. Fewer than two million workers are employed in modern industry; no more than a quarter of a million in the two thousand mines. Even if small handicraft shops are included, the total number of wage earners will be well below fifteen million.

How do these millions live? Is their lot in the city better than it was in the village, whence the vast majority have been pushed out by hunger and debt? The answer to these questions is provided by a royal commission appointed a dozen years ago to study labor conditions. The report, with its eighteen volumes of evidence, lays bare the morphology of India's industrial misery; and the conditions revealed go far towards explaining the disturbances which periodically are reported on the front pages of Western newspapers. Indian labor would not have been as solidly devoted to the ideal of national independence had the British authorities shown greater zeal in protecting its interests.

To India belongs the honor of having some of the worst working conditions in the world. The vast majority of factories are in filthy, dilapidated buildings lacking all sanitary arrangements. Only a small fraction of the larger factories are equipped with latrines, wash stands, and similar luxuries. In the cotton factories high humidity is maintained in spite of the oppressive heat; the prevalence of dust frequently results in pulmonary disease. "The atmosphere is so very hot that people often faint and have to be carried to the hospital," weavers reported. An almost complete absence of safety devices results in an abnormally high rate of accidents. Ginning factories are perpetually filled with a thick layer of dust which enters the lungs and causes serious diseases. "Dust asthma, bronchitis, consumption and other diseases of the respiratory system prevail in the industrial centers of the cotton country," the government of the Central Provinces reported. Even worse are conditions in small shops employing fewer than twenty workers. Exempt from all legal control, they are invariably located in unhygienic cramped premises, lacking provisions for ventilation or adequate lighting.

Hours are frightfully long. The Factories Act of 1922, limiting work to ten hours a day and sixty a week, has never been adequately enforced. A working day of twelve hours or more has therefore been no rarity, especially in the small shops, where work starts at sunrise and—thanks to electricity—continues till after sunset. Women, too, have to work these long hours, a fact which shows that in industry, at least, Western ideas about the equality of the sexes are penetrating. "We get up at four o'clock in the morning to do our household work so that we may be ready to go to the mill at seven o'clock. We work in the mill from seven in the morning till five-thirty in the evening. Then we go home and work till seven o'clock in our houses," said a woman who works "in one of the best mills"; in many factories work lasts from five-thirty to seven in the evening. But though equal with men in working hours, women receive considerably lower wages; and many have no choice but to supplement them with income from prostitution.

What do Indian workers get for their semislavery? On the average their wages are well below thirty cents a day; unskilled workers rarely earn more than five or ten cents. A representative of the Indian Railways, who estimated that the barest minimum necessary for sustaining life is four cents a day per person, had to acknowledge that even on the government railways—and conditions in private industry are far worse—thousands of workers do not receive enough apiece to support a wife and two children on that starvation level. "Of 759,000 employees on . . . railways . . . , 408,000, or 54 per cent, were in receipt of less than" six dollars a month.

"Yet he lives," was the triumphant reply of the representative of the railroads. Yes, he lives, for a time anyway; but how? Every investigation shows that most workers are perpetually semihungry, spend next to nothing on clothing, and are too poor to marry. More than nine-tenths live in one-room huts of corrugated iron, with as many as six persons to a room eight by sixteen feet, located in the filthiest parts of the cities and without a trace of sanitary provisions. "The general feeling of the mill owners," the Director of Public Health in the United Provinces stated, "is that laborers kept good health for about ten months... after which they show signs of breakdown, and unless they take rest they are seldom found satisfactory after that period.... One undertaking frankly admitted that they get rid of men as soon as they become unfit." This poverty has driven hundreds of thousands of parents to sell their children into semislavery.

Why have Indian workers not rebelled against this wretched system? First, they have been too weak and too downtrodden to have the energy and initiative for rebellion. Second, although they have organized unions—notwithstanding their illiteracy—and have staged immense strikes which paralyzed whole industries, the odds have been heavily against them. They have had to confront not only the employers but the whole imperialist administration as well. Irrefutable evidence was brought before the Royal Commission on Labor proving that the British authorities had been actively hostile to all labor organizations, crushing strikes with *lathi* charges and terrorizing workers into obedience. Chambers of commerce and manufacturers' associations have had not only economic power but, through the privilege to elect their own representatives in the legislatures, no small measure of political power as well. Need one be surprised if Indian workers solidly support the Congress Nationalists against the British rulers?

IMPERIALISM AND POVERTY

To explain India's immense poverty by the rapid growth of population as a result of the establishment of *Pax Britannica* and the high birth rate, as is frequently done, is absurd. No doubt, India's population increased very rapidly during the past two centuries. Official figures place the birth rate in 1936 at 35.6 per thousand; but a correspondent informs me that "a group of some four thousand people I had to do with, and for whom I had accurate figures over more than ten years, had a birth rate a little in excess of forty-four" per thousand. I am inclined to accept the figures of my missionary correspondent as being a closer approximation to the truth. However, it is sorry economics indeed which accepts the despairing theories of the late Dr. Malthus. The experience of Europe has demonstrated conclusively that increase in population, far from being necessarily a curse and a cause of poverty, can be a decisive spur to unprecedented increases in wealth. As Henry George has said, "Men and hawks eat chickens, but the difference between the two is this: the more hawks the fewer chickens, but the more men the more chickens." Growth of population *per se,* however rapid, is no evil. A high birth rate becomes a cause of poverty only—as was, unfortunately, the case in India—when it is not accompanied by a corresponding expansion of productive capacities.

And responsibility for this discrepancy must rest to a very large extent on the British. India was a country of small peasant holdings and flourishing cottage industries when the British came. But the servants of the East India Company set themselves to undermine the structure. Whether it was inability to understand the Oriental idea that land, belonging to God, can have no "owner" in the Western sense, or a far-sighted plan to create a class of feudal landlords who would be their allies, the British decreed that *zamindars,* hitherto merely village tax-collectors appointed by the government, should be the real and absolute owners. Thus with one stroke a class of parasites was saddled on the miserable cultivators, whose burden has increased with the passage of years. While the so-called Permanent Settlement of 1793 fixed for perpetuity the amount of taxes *zamindars* in a number of provinces have to pay, they have been free to exploit the great land hunger to raise rents, until at present less than a fourth of their income returns to the government in taxes.

Yet nothing has been done since to mitigate the evils of the system. On the contrary, "The introduction of more vigorous enforcement of civil rights," says Mrs. Anstey, the conservative historian of India's economic past, "strengthened the position of the landlords, and tended to facilitate the enhancement of rents and eviction of the tenants." *Zamindar* incomes have been exempted by the income-tax law from all direct taxation—on the theory, apparently, that they were poor peasants. Nor has the government ever attempted to force the *zamindars* to give some service in exchange for their annual drain. They have remained a class of parasites feeding on the helpless peasantry.

Unfortunately the government has not given much more service for the revenue it collects than have the *zamindars*. Security it has given; very little more positive. The Indian Civil Service has been innocent of all intentions to carry through a fundamental modernization of agriculture; nothing was done even in the way of agricultural research until an American, shocked by the miserable conditions, came forward with a generous donation. Only 4 per cent of the cultivated area is sown with improved seed; the irrigation system, which has become the standard example of the benefits accruing from British rule, has benefited only a small part of the agricultural population. Lord Curzon, during his viceregal reign at the beginning of this century, showed some interest in the agricultural problem and sponsored several laws to regulate peasant co-operatives; but the Civil Service was not overcome with enthusiasm for the idea of co-operatives and very little was done. The only other claim of the British authorities to progressive legislation is a group of laws to protect the ryots against usurers enacted in some provinces after peasant rebellions, which, even if they had been enforced vigorously, as they have not, would have left the basic problems hardly affected at all.

More disastrous have been the results of deliberate efforts during the eighteenth century to undermine the thriving native textile industry. Export duties on Indian textiles were imposed before the Industrial Revolution; afterwards, the competitive advantage having shifted in favor of England, free trade was decreed for India. What matter if hundreds of thousands of weavers, among the finest the world has ever produced but unable to compete in price with the machines in England, were left to starve? What matter if the native economy was upset and the standard of living of the masses sank to new depths so long as Lancashire could flood the market with its prints? The intention was clear: India was to be kept as a producer of cheap raw materials for British industry and as a vast market for the finished products of the latter.

The policy to discourage development of native industry remained unchanged as long as Britain could enforce it, which means until well after the World War. In vain did Indians appeal times without number for protection; free trade served as a convenient moral stick. Even under the reformed constitution during the twenties the Indian Legislative Assembly found that the only way to dissolve Britain's prejudice against protection was to grant preferential treatment to British industries. And when the rough old methods for keeping down industrialization became outmoded by the growth of nationalism, more refined methods were evolved, such as overevaluation of the rupee, which, in the words of one of the most prominent native financiers, "hit the Indian producer to an extent beyond his capacity to bear" by decreasing his power to compete against the relatively cheaper British goods.

What wonder, then, if, in spite of its wealth in natural resources, Indian industry has lagged far behind that of the West? Instead of leading India across the transition from handicrafts to modern industry, the British have killed the former and prevented growth of the latter. Even the appointment of an industrial adviser by a provincial government before the war was sufficient to horrify the central government, which obtained his immediate dismissal. The demands of Indian leaders for a positive program to establish village industries to relieve the horrible unemployment were met with a deaf ear.

The British have been no more progressive in the matter of labor legislation. The first Factories Act (1881), prohibiting employment of children below seven years of age and limiting the hours of children between seven and twelve years to only nine a day, was indeed a "triumph for conservative opinion" even if it had been enforced, as it was not. In 1922, however, the government decided to "make a decisive step in the protection of labor," as an official report puts it, by prohibiting employment of children below twelve years and limiting hours for adult workers to eleven a day or sixty a week. Applicable only to factories using power and employing at least twenty workers—a limitation which immediately placed the vast majority of workers beyond its scope—even this law has never been adequately enforced. No more revolutionary has been the Workmen's Compensation Act, employers still finding it cheaper to pay about seventeen dollars in compensation for each accident than to install expensive safety devices. And this has been about all the British have done to protect Indian labor.

Budgets for the "nation-building services" provide a reliable barometer of the interest shown by the British in constructive social work. Since the last quarter of the last century Indian leaders have demanded larger appropriations for those services, urging that, especially in so backward a country, greater outlay on education, agriculture, industrial research, and health is remunerative even from an economic point of view. The British, however, have had a different scale of values. In 1913-14 the central and provincial governments spent a grand total of fifteen million dollars on education out of budgets totalling two hundred eighty millions; seven millions on public health; while agriculture—which was supposed to give livelihood to nine-tenths of the population—received the munificent sum of $625,000. Not a cent was devoted to industry, while all the scientific institutions combined received rather less than two and a half millions. Contrast these niggardly sums with the one hundred twenty millions spent on the military establishments.

This scale of values remained unchanged as long as the British could help it. In 1925-26, for example, two hundred seventy million dollars out of budgets totaling five hundred forty millions—or exactly half—went for military and debt charges: agriculture was given six and one-half millions and industry rather less than five millions. A student of Indian agricultural economics has pointed out that the Punjab spent a total of seventy-nine rupees per thousand of the population on promoting agriculture, as contrasted with the one thousand twenty rupees a year spent by the United States and nine hundred sixty by England, although in neither does agriculture form so vital an economic enterprise as in India.[1] A better barometer of the interest shown by the British in

[1] M. L. Darling, *The Punjab Peasant in Prosperity and Debt.*

nation-building is provided only by a comparison of expenditures on education; and in such a comparison, they fare even worse.

AGINCOURT AND INDIAN GIRLS

I once visited a High School for Girls, very well conducted by an English mistress ... It was in the classroom devoted to geography and history that my doubts were aroused by two maps displayed on the walls, and pointed out, with no little pride, as the work of the girls themselves. One was a map of England, on which the principal products were shown by means of objects attached at the appropriate spots. Thus a toy motorcar indicated Coventry, a ship, Liverpool, a knife, Sheffield, a scrap of woolen cloth, Bradford, and so forth. In this there was no harm, if one had felt sure that the local products of India had been illustrated with similar care; but one or two maps of India, exhibited at the same time, showed no such elaboration of detail. The second map to which my attention was called belonged to the historical department. The reader would scarcely guess its subject, if he were to think for a year of the unlikeliest theme to propose to a class of Indian girls. It was a map of the battlefield of Agincourt, showing the position of the contending forces! The details of the battle of Agincourt may be of great interest from a strategic point of view, or from the point of view of a somewhat narrow British patriotism; but what have Indian girls to do either with strategy or the quarrels of the Plantagenets? [2]

William Archer, no anti-imperialist critic, has given these examples as typical of the Anglo-literary type of education imposed by the British on India. As in all other colonies, the British have not been interested in raising the cultural level of the masses; their one aim has been to train clerks able to transcribe the mountains of papers passing from one department to another. At a time when every effort should have been made to train Indians in the sciences—the fields of knowledge in which they were most deficient—literary education, which indeed was no education at all but merely a process of learning to draw characters in a foreign tongue and memorizing sets of unco-ordinated facts as inscrutable as the will of God, was emphasized to the exclusion of all others.

[2] *India and the Future*, p. 269.

Who can estimate how much this miseducation has cost poor India? Although only a fraction of boys and girls entering elementary schools ever reach the universities, a system of examinations leading to the entrance requirements of British universities was imposed like a strait-jacket upon the whole educational structure. Since Oxford does not require English entrants to have any special knowledge of India, children in the Punjab have had to learn a great deal about England but very little about their own environment and society, about India's political, economic, and cultural problems. Far from being a preparation for life and service to the community, schooling has meant swallowing meaningless facts, at least nine-tenths of which can be of no conceivable use; and the Indian university graduate has been an intellectual cripple and a parasite upon the body politic. Lawyers and clerks—that is all the machine has produced.

The civil service ideal has also made for a totally disproportionate emphasis on universities over elementary schools. No country in the world spends so large a part of its educational funds on the former as India. The two hundred thousand primary schools for the whole continent have been extraordinarily bad. More than half the teachers in boys' schools are themselves untrained; of those who have received some sort of training, only about two-thirds have completed high schools. The extremely low salary, averaging in Bengal less than three dollars a month, has attracted to the teaching profession only the most slovenly, incapable, and ignorant. What wonder, therefore, if fewer than one-tenth of the boys, and an even smaller percentage of the girls, who enter the first grade remain in school to reach the fourth grade? Education has simply not been made meaningful enough to attract anybody except the children of the wealthiest, who have the means to persevere until they get diplomas and eventually clerkships.

What these policies have meant in terms of Indian life can be seen from the dry statistics on literacy. In 1911—after more than two centuries of British rule and after almost a century since Lord Macaulay's famous Minute on Indian Education—only twelve men out of every hundred could boast of an ability to read and write, and only 1.2 of every hundred women! Subsequent years brought a slight improvement; even in 1931, however, 84.4 of every hundred men and no fewer than ninety-seven out of every hundred women were still completely illiterate. Even in 1935 the total school-going population in British India, from primary to university, was less than 13.5 millions, or about 4 per cent of the population; it should have been, if all children had been in schools, close to 30 per cent.

British apologists notwithstanding, the problem of abolishing illiteracy is not nearly as great as they pretend. "In England," writes Ernest Wood,[3] "it took twelve years from the date when free and compulsory education was established to raise the percentage of children at school from a low figure to nearly 100 per cent. In Japan it took twenty-four years to advance the percentage from twenty-eight to nearly one hundred." Iraq, too, has wrought miracles in less than half a dozen years. All that is needed is funds, a plan, and, above all, a real desire to solve the problem. In India, the first two prerequisites have not existed because the last was absent. The British have simply not been interested in raising the cultural level of the Indian masses or in introduction of a scientific civilization. Therefore, the total number of normal schools—the key plants in the production of teachers—was even in 1935 below six hundred; therefore girls' education received only about two cents per head of the population; therefore, the total cost to all branches of government for each scholar, from infant to university student, has been less than three dollars a year.

Indians smile cynically and bitterly when the British cite "good administration" in justification of their rule. The record, only an insignificant fraction of which has been reproduced here, tells a different story. And today, this enormous illiteracy not only clogs India's feet towards economic progress but constitutes one of the most serious impediments to political liberation. Democracy and self-government must remain a farce as long as more than nine-tenths of the population is completely illiterate; such a populace must remain a prey to medievalism, religious prejudice, and social conservatism. The British know this

[3] Ernest Wood, *An Englishman Defends Mother India.*

only too well; and even if their educational policy was not designed to keep India in subjection, today they point, with much truth, to the existence of this illiterate mass as the most convincing reply to the advanced nationalists who demand immediate dominion status.

ISLAM IN INDIA

Another great, and until now insurmountable, stumbling block on India's road to independence are the religious minorities. We can disregard the numerous faiths counting only a few million adherents, although they help make the confusion more confounded; but the Moslem community of eighty millions, or almost a quarter of the population of British India, cannot be disregarded. Fearing the Hindu majority, the Moslems have been violently opposed to complete self-rule unless they were to be granted extravagant guarantees which would give them an amount of power totally out of proportion to their numbers and which might make administration impossible. They have co-operated with the British authorities against the Hindu nationalists; and efforts by enlightened leaders in both camps to work out an effective *modus vivendi* have until now ended in complete fiascoes.

On the contrary, communal bitterness has mounted rapidly with the development of home rule. The reforms of 1919, the first step towards dominion status, brought in an era of riots and ceaseless conflict. Sixty-five distinct communal riots occurred in the eighteen months between April, 1926, and October of the following year, during which about three hundred people were killed and twenty-seven hundred were injured. In negotiations with the British Government for greater autonomy the two communities have invariably been at loggerheads. The reforms of 1935 marked a new stage in the conflict. Hardly a month now passes without reports of riots; for the Moslems have become increasingly restless. One does not have to be a prophet to foresee that major troubles will develop the moment full self-rule comes in sight.

The roots of the conflict are embedded too deeply in history to be affected by resolutions of good will. Much has been made of the eternal "cow and music" problem. It is the spark which usually sets off the powder barrel. Much more important are the economic and social causes. Traditionally the Moslems have constituted the poorer, less educated, and politically less advanced community. Prohibited by Islam from taking interest themselves, many are indebted to Hindu usurers; and the usurer is nowhere loved. Purely agrarian conflicts are transferred to the religious plane, since most of the landlords are Hindus, and thereby become more bitter and less soluble. Not until the agrarian problem is solved will the foundation be laid for religious peace.

The advance of education among Moslems has only intensified the conflict. Finding government jobs monopolized by the Hindus, who were the first to take to English education, the graduates of Moslem schools at the end of the last century raised the demand that a definite percentage of all jobs be set aside for them irrespective of merit. Government degenerated to rule by arithmetic, each community, having many candidates for each job, always on guard against infringement of its arithmetical rights. Even the admission of students to universities, not to speak of appointments to faculties, was to be regulated on a communal basis. Interpolations like the following became matters of daily routine in the legislative bodies: "Will the government be pleased to state how many Moslems are there, in proportion to their numerical strength in the population, among the Inspectors of the Police?" Of course, the interests of the great masses are not affected by these squabbles, for government employment is an upper-class affair; but these classes have been able to influence public opinion.

And it must be remembered that religion in the East colors the whole life of man. Philosophy, literature, law, political and social practices, even ordinary manners and ways of eating, sleeping, and drinking—all these are part of religion. Each community lives a self-contained social life; contacts between them after business hours are few. Dozens of Moslems visiting the holy places of Islam in the Near East have confessed to me that they feel much more at home among the Arabs, whose language and customs are strange to them, than they do in India, where religion divides them from the rest of the population. They have not forgotten that they once conquered India and held the despised Hindu idolaters in subjection; and they have no intention of being reduced to a helpless minority because nowadays it is the vote, not the sword, that decides issues.

It is true that the British have done nothing to bridge the gulf dividing the two communities; but it is slander to accuse them of consciously furthering the rift in order to rule. British officials have not had to pour oil on the flames; their role has been much more subtle. First, by maintaining an attitude of angelic passivity they have permitted the bad to become worse. Second, even if they would have been as moral as the angels, their mere presence could not but aggravate the problem. Being foreigners and Westerners, they have been eager to protect the "rights" of each community. But scrupulous maintenance of rights is impossible in the Orient without arousing extravagant hopes in one community and no less wild fears in the other. The Orient has known religious oppression, which it understands; the Hindus of Hyderabad, who form the vast majority of the population, do not expect absolutely fair treatment from their Moslem ruler. And it is only a short step from rights to privileges. What wonder if Moslems fear that majority rule by Hindus would make short shrift of the new standards introduced by the British?

THE PRINCES SUPPORT BRITAIN

Not so passive has been the British attitude towards the five hundred and sixty princes, chieftains, and feudal lords in India, whose domains range from states the size of Great Britain with populations of ten million or more to petty principalities of a few square miles with a few thousand inhabitants. Judged by Oriental standards, some have given fairly good administration; of the vast majority this cannot be said. They are autocrats of the worst kind; oppressive taxation has enabled them to maintain grand courts and to accumulate vast treasures. The Nizam of Hyderabad is reputed to be the richest man in the world. Illiteracy is higher in the states than in British India and economic progress has been even slower; public health facilities are distinctly inferior; their standards of justice are much below those prevailing in the British-administered territories.

That they have been able to survive to this day is due to a very large extent to the support they have received from the British authorities. Early in the last century the East India Company entered into treaties with the princes by which it assumed the burden of protecting their frontiers and maintaining law and order in exchange for control of their foreign affairs and other concessions. Since then the British have become the real rulers of the states, operating behind the native princes. Every succession must be approved by the British government before it becomes valid; the British depose rulers and assume direct administration during the minorities of heirs to thrones; and there seems to be no legal limit to their right of intervention in internal affairs. They may intervene whenever stability is likely to be threatened, to suppress rebellion, and to "prevent gross misrule." It should be added, however, that the last, though very apparent, has not usually been a cause for intervention.

The upswing in the nationalist movement has placed the princes more at the mercy of the British than ever. They watch with ill-disguised hostility the development of the democratic Congress movement, which aims to create a free self-governing India. Knowing that very little will be left for themselves if the Congress scheme materializes, they have opposed every attempt at reform and have mercilessly suppressed all Congress activity in their territories. The latest fast of Gandhi, staged in the spring of 1939, was for the purpose of winning mild reforms in one of these states. Later he presented an ultimatum to the princes demanding the following reforms: first, full civil liberty, including freedom for local and outside newspapers; second, freedom to form associations to educate public opinion in favor of responsible government; third, that Indians from outside receive the right to enter freely and to remain as long as they do not engage in activities intended to destroy the state; fourth, that the ruler's privy purse be separated from state revenue, and that the ruler's income be limited to 10 per cent of the state revenue if below a certain figure and in no case exceed $110,000; fifth, establishment of an inde-

pendent and permanent judiciary above executive interference. Characteristically, in making these demands Gandhi
placed special emphasis on the last, since justice "is the one
institution which the British have built up with special care."
However, none of the princes took the trouble to reply to him.

British concern for the welfare of the puppet native rulers
assumed many forms during the past two decades, since the
British had come to depend on the princes as a bulwark
against the nationalists. A press law was enacted "to prevent
the dissemination by means of books, newspapers and other
documents of matter calculated to bring into hatred or
contempt, or to excite disaffection against princes or chiefs
... or against the government or administration established
in such states"—a law which, in effect, has tended to prevent
unfavorable mention of the princes in all Indian newspapers
and, especially since the amendment of 1934, to limit dangerously criticism of maladministration. So important did the
British consider the law that they disregarded criticism by
the Indian Legislative Assembly and enacted it with the
viceroy's signature. The establishment in 1922 of a Chamber
of Princes has been of mutual benefit, since the native
potentates have thus been enabled to co-operate more effectively with the British by agreement on common lines of
action. The co-operation reached a new stage during the
Round Table Conferences in 1931-32, when Britain openly
played for the support of the princes, who in turn "were
engaged essentially in the business of securing a definite
position whence they could defy the introduction of any
form of democracy in their dominions," showing "that they
would act rather as a support for British control than as
furthering Indian autonomy." [4]

From a long range point of view, the rule of the princes
is no doubt doomed. Their estates are part and parcel of
British India, and their frontiers have no geographic, economic or ethnological justification. The growth of education,
development of railway, radio, and telephone communication,
as well as the existence of great universities attended by
youths from all over India—these are creating a feeling of
unity which sooner or later will sweep away the princely

[4] A. B. Keith. *A Constitutional History of India, 1600-1935*, p. 297.

autocracies. The Congress movement is also beginning to have an effect on the masses of the states, from whom faint rumblings have already become audible. Meanwhile the rest of India is beginning to exert an amount of pressure which will become increasingly difficult to resist as time goes on. Unlike the British, Indian nationalist leaders are not at all concerned with the treaty rights of the autocrats and very much concerned with the rights of the masses, who are not mentioned in the treaties between the rulers and the British.

At present, however, the states remain a very serious impediment on the road to independence and democratic federation. It is not only that they are willing to play the British game; rather, co-operation with Britain is to their own interests. An alliance based on mutual selfishness has thus come into being; and to defeat the two will not be easy. The princes have enormous wealth and armed might, both of which they are prepared to use in support of the paramount power and their own tyrannies. On the other hand, Britain's "loyalty" to the native autocracies has provided the progressive nationalists with another—and who can say unjust?—grievance. How in the face of this record, they ask, can the British claim to be a progressive force in India? Indeed, they have made ignorance, poverty, social and economic backwardness, religious fanaticism their allies—the only allies they have or can have.

THE BURDEN OF THE WHITE MAN

Indian nationalists add another grievance at least as important as all the preceding. Not only has Britain drawn immense wealth from poor India to build her empire; the nationalists maintain that imperialist rule has been too incompetent and too much of a luxury for so poor a country.

With the details of the economic grievances we need not concern ourselves. Many are imaginary; the burden of many more is exaggerated. The overwhelming part of the one hundred fifty million dollars India sends every year to England is in payment for services rendered. India would have had to pay interest on the capital invested in her railways and industries even if there had been no British; she would have had to employ foreign experts and pay good salaries.

Unfortunately this is not the end of the story. Indian nationalists distinguish between the direct cost of imperialism and the indirect, which, although rarely mentioned, far exceeds the first in importance. Under the heading of direct cost, the greatest drain has undoubtedly been the army establishment, which has eaten up half of the federal revenue. Would an independent India have needed so large an army for defending its frontiers and for maintaining internal security? The fact that her troops could be spared for fourteen different wars during half a century in areas far removed from her borders, without jeopardizing India's own security, shows that so large a military establishment was not necessary. Although in no case were India's interests involved, her troops were used by the British for imperialist wars in China, Abyssinia, Egypt, the Sudan, and elsewhere; even the Afghan campaigns were not launched solely for India's interests. Moreover, an army as large as the present one could be maintained for a fraction of the present cost if only native troops were used. The British force of sixty thousand men costs much more than the rest of the army, totaling one hundred sixty thousand. It costs four times as much to maintain a British soldier as a native one, and twenty-four Indian soldiers cost less than one British officer. India pays for the recruitment and training of soldiers in Britain before they set foot on her soil; she pays for their transportation back and forth; she pays their pensions on retirement from service.

No less costly has been the civil administration. Dr. J. T. Sunderland has shown that eight thousand European officials received in salaries a total of seventy million dollars, while one hundred thirty thousand Indians earned annually a grand total of sixteen and a half millions. India has had to pay the cost of administering Aden for the Empire; of maintaining imperial embassies in different parts of Asia. And natives shake their heads when they see the imposing public buildings constructed by the British. Does India really need —can it afford—railway stations and other public structures costing millions?

The diversion of funds from urgently needed productive schemes cannot be explained by any special depravity of the

British. Such management is inherent in the imperialist system; and the British have been no worse—probably a deal better—than other imperialist nations. Enlightened Indians emphasize that imperialism must maintain a pomp and extravagance to preserve its self-respect and, so the foreigners imagine, the respect of the natives. But for all that India must pay.[5] Besides, lacking direct access to the feelings and needs of the people, the imperialist rulers must maintain a huge and costly bureaucracy; before anything constructive can be undertaken, mountains of forms have to be filled out. Imperialist regimes grind slowly, and they are always behind the clock of history.

To cite examples of conspicuous waste is not difficult. One might mention the six hundred thousand dollars spent annually on Anglican bishops; or the incident, called by a former prime minister of England "the depth of meanness," when "we tried to charge India with ... the cost of the representatives and guests from India who took part in the coronation ceremonies of the late King."[6] But much more important has been the indirect cost of the imperialist administration. Who can estimate how much Britain's industrial and tariff policy has cost India? Because Lancashire brought very heavy pressure to bear, Lord Salisbury denounced in 1877 India's demand for duty on cotton goods as "at once wrong in principle, infamous in its practical effects, and self-destructive...." This policy has had disastrous effects on India's standard of living and has impeded social progress.

Obviously, under any circumstances India would have had to employ foreign officials. But, the nationalists ask, was it necessary to pay such immense salaries? Moreover, have the officials been wisely employed? There would be little objection if the officials were technical men. India needs science —needs it more than anything else. But the expensive British

---

[5] As to the value of India to England, it has been estimated that one out of every five persons in Great Britain depends directly or indirectly on India for livelihood. This calculation is borne out by a leading article in Lord Rothermere's *Daily Mail* (1930): "For us, India is not far from being all in all.... At least four shillings in the income of every man and woman in Britain is drawn directly or indirectly from the connection England has had with India."

[6] Ramsay MacDonald, *The Awakening of India,* p. 148.

officials have not been scientists and technicians; on the contrary, they have been political administrators who have actually retarded scientific and technological progress. The cost of the foreign officials, if seen from this point of view, vastly exceeds the hundreds of millions paid out in extravagant salaries.

Worse still: instead of providing healthy political training, the foreign political masters made Indians more incapable than ever of governing themselves. The centuries of sheltered existence did not demand of the natives that they develop their capacities by grappling with normal administrative questions; and submissiveness, docility, and acceptance of thoughtless routine became virtues prized above all others. All the while the administrative machine, far from providing constructive leadership, remained deadening, cumbrous, expensive. The following two experiences of C. F. Andrews[7] are typical of the wastage inevitable under imperialist rule:

At Chandupur, in the cholera camp, the clash came between the national workers and the officials.... The Government had sent down an array of sub-assistant surgeons and compounders of medicine with their regulation equipment, under an officer from the Indian Medical Service; but the poor people who were suffering would have none of them. They openly preferred the help of the national volunteers, who had come first to their aid in their distress. With incredible speed a makeshift for a hospital had been arranged with different sheds. Volunteers offered themselves up three times the number we required. A doctor, dressed in homespun, wearing a Gandhi cap, was in command. The work was brilliantly carried through, and the epidemic was stayed. But one could see in the midst of it all how the poorest of the poor clung closely to the national workers. One of the latter sacrificed his own life in the service of the poor, and others were very seriously ill. Some returned with health shattered.... Meanwhile the Government medical officer and his staff were stranded. They had no patients. By the greatest effort of conciliation I was able to get the Government officials taken into the national work for a few days. But the scheme broke down.... Their methods were entirely different. But the experiment proved how cumbrous and expensive the Government scheme was, and I saw at the same time how re-

7 *India and the Simon Report,* pp. 60-63.

markably cheap and efficient the National Congress organization had become.

Or take his experiences at the Orissa floods of 1927, when eighty thousand houses were washed away:

Here again the national workers...came as volunteers and risked their lives in one of the most malignantly malarial parts of India....The clash came almost immediately between the Government subordinates and the nationalists....With the Government subordinate officers everything was done with an air of compulsion. People were ordered here and ordered there. The equipment required was extravagantly expensive compared with the methods of the volunteers. I tried my very hardest to work with both sides; but it was almost impossible. It was like mixing oil and water.

It is this aspect of British rule that undoubtedly constitutes one of the most serious grievances of the Indian national movement. The plain fact is that India is far too poor to support the expensive, cumbrous, unwieldy administrative apparatus set up by the British—too expensive in its direct monetary costs and, what is even more basic, acting as an insurmountable bar to progress. The British, as pointed out above, are not to be blamed for it; the defects are inherent in the imperialist system. Lacking contact with the people, ignorant of the basic springs of their being, and commanded by officials who are birds of passage, how can it appeal to the finest instincts of the people and lift them to the heights of self-sacrifice and devotion necessary for great national tasks? It cannot do it. It has to appeal to the lower instincts of its servants—to their selfishness, to their desire for honor and financial aggrandizement. It corrupts the people, and leaves urgent tasks undone.

FROM REBELLION TO REVOLUTION

Only in the light of the conditions described above is it possible to understand recent political developments. During the last century a number of British statesmen hoped to establish relations between Britain and India based on trust and mutual interests rather than on domination and exploitation. "Let us so conduct ourselves in our civil and military operations," Sir Henry Lawrence wrote in 1844, "that, when the connection between India and Great Britain ceases, it may do so, not with convulsions, but with mutual esteem and affection"; and Lord Macaulay contemplated a friendship becoming stronger and stronger. However, narrowness of conception no less than greed stood in the way. "There is only too much to fear that the English, unless held in check, exhibit a singularly strong disposition towards cruelty, whenever they have a weak enemy to face," Sir Charles Dilke, one of the outstanding imperialists of the century, admitted. "I noticed in all the hotels in India the significant notice: 'Gentlemen are earnestly requested not to strike the servants.'"

Like Pooh-Bah, Indian nationalism was born sneering. Imperialist selfishness was its nourishment from the early days of childhood; relentless opposition, its birthright. The National Congress, born in 1885 at a meeting in Bombay of a few scores of educated young men, has carried on the struggle with a tenacity, courage, and intelligence shown by very few other nationalist movements. Since then, a complex and highly efficient organization has come into existence, with branches in all cities and towns, and counting about five million members.

Until well into the World War, however, the nationalist movement was almost exclusively a Hindu affair; more important, it was the business of a small class composed of educated men, mainly Brahmins, and touched the great masses hardly at all. Leaders in the Congress were the Chitpavan Brahmins of the Deccan and the Parsees in the city of Bombay, who saw their hold on India disappearing—the former displaced by British officials from all positions of prominence, while British traders had taken away the monopoly of the latter. The Bengalis became interested when government jobs could no longer be found for all school graduates. Those nationalists could not forgive the British Raj for monopolizing the best and most lucrative positions in the government and all they asked was a larger share of the spoils of exploitation. Since their share could be increased only at the expense of the foreigners, they were anti-British.

From Bengal the nationalist movement spread to the

Punjab and then into the interior, without however, broadening its base. It was driven by measures which seemed to threaten the interests and influence of the educated Brahmin and professional men. Lord Curzon's decision to tighten government control over the universities evoked an avalanche of criticism, as did his policy to divide Bengal into two provinces. From an administrative point of view the latter measure was probably justified; the Bengali Hindu intelligentsia, however, saw in it a scheme—which it probably was—to counterbalance their influence by setting up a predominantly Moslem area with its own bureaucracy, thus taking away a mass of potential jobs. In the Punjab, a policy of appointing rural men to government positions evoked the bitter ire of the city intelligentsia; the laws protecting the ryots against usurers, although very mild, further incited the business classes and lawyers. Discontent was increased by laws tightening control over the press; while the growing power of the British bureaucracy through centralization and surveillance over teachers and other educated Hindus was bitterly resented. Meanwhile cultural movements had been at work: Western ideas on liberty, democracy, and self-government appeared, and Hindus created an extraordinary cultural revival to counteract the hated foreign arrogance.

For a long time the British did not take the nationalists seriously. They paid little attention to the political speeches of the intelligentsia; the Congress was allowed to continue with little official interference. Having sized up the so-called nationalist movement, they saw that it was in no way a serious menace to their rule. The few thousand intellectuals could be curbed whenever the need arose; should strongarm measures prove impolitic, a few crumbs from the imperial table would quickly silence the eloquent nationalist mouths.

Towards the end of the first decade of this century, which saw an upswing in nationalist activity, the British began to implement both sides of this policy. A number of agitators and terrorists were hanged; many more were imprisoned and exiled, while stricter control was imposed on the native press. Outbreak of the war and a rise in anti-British sentiment intensified the official terror. The Defense of India Act of 1914 legalized internment of suspicious characters without trial, and ordinary officials were given the right to determine who was a suspicious character; special tribunals were set up to hand out summary justice. And these fascist laws were used ruthlessly. In the Punjab alone one hundred and seventy-five persons were tried by these Tribunals, of whom twenty were hanged, fifty-eight were transported for life, and an equal number were transported or imprisoned for various periods. Thousands of "suspicious characters" were jailed.

Long before the war ended, however, it became obvious that mere repression would not bring peace to India. Nationalist activity continued, forcing the British to consider how to come to terms with the leaders on the basis of a fairer distribution of spoils. That they would try to retain as much of their power and spoils as possible was to be expected; and the most reactionary elements in the Civil Service used the war in Europe as an argument against concessions. Announcement of the concessions in the form of the Montagu-Chelmsford Reforms, showed that the voice of die-hards still determined policy. The so-called "dyarchy," or dual control by British and natives, granted in the Reforms was a misnomer. There was no dual control: all power remained as before concentrated in the hands of the British, the natives receiving nothing more than high-sounding titles. It was a plain attempt at bribing the Indian nationalist leaders to stop agitation for the price of the honors and emoluments of office.

The details of the absurdly complicated scheme need not detain us. Administration of provinces was divided between native ministers responsible to elected bodies, who assumed charge of transferred subjects, and the British Governor in Council, who retained control over reserved subjects. Finance, justice, police were of course reserved to British discretion; how the other subjects were transferred to native control can be seen from a statement by Sir K. Venkatta Reddi, Minister of Development for the Madras Presidency: "I am Minister of Development," he explained with fine sarcasm, "minus forests, and you all know that development depends a good deal on forests. I am Minister of Industries without factories, which are a reserved subject,

and industries without factories are unimaginable. I am
Minister of Agriculture minus irrigation. You can understand what that means. . . . I am also Minister of Industry
without electricity, which is also a reserved subject. The
subjects of labor and boilers are also reserved. But these,
after all, are some of the defects of the reform scheme."

A similar division was effected in the central government.
The elected representatives represented a small class only,
not the people. The Council of State was elected by thirty-
two thousand voters in 1925-26 out of a population of two
hundred and forty million; 1.1 million were qualified to vote
for the Legislative Assembly, and no more than 8.3 million
for the Provincial Legislative Councils. In addition, all these
bodies were packed with nominated members who voted as
ordered. If by chance a bill not desired by government went
through, the provincial governors and the governor general
had the power of final veto. On the other hand, their signatures were sufficient for enacting a law thrown out by the
legislative bodies, where some subjects could not even come
up for debate. The reforms were certainly not democratic
and were not intended to make even a beginning in representative and responsible government. What was intended
was class government—to win the propertied and moneyed
classes to support Britain.

A dozen years before, the "reforms" might have satisfied
the nationalist leaders. As usual, however, imperialism was
too late. One of the chief defects of foreign rule is its inability to read the clock of history; it is always late. The war
had made a profound impression on India; new social classes
had emerged; and for the first time, the nationalist movement was ceasing to be a movement of leaders—even a movement of intellectuals. Millions of people had entered the
arena, and to those millions a few high-sounding jobs meant
nothing at all. At first those millions had been used by the
leaders; now, having had some ideas put into their heads,
they came forward with demands of their own, and found
new spokesmen. And they became a threat to the Empire;
for to them there could be no compromise on the basis of
dividing the spoils. They were the despoiled; and compromises to them meant the end of exploitation.

V

THE GREAT DOMINIONS

WITH NO LITTLE PLEASURE does one turn from the sordid story of British negligence, incompetence, and selfishness in the management of areas inhabited by darker races to the heroic tale of British colonization. Popular impressions notwithstanding, the highest accomplishment of the British has not been in the field of colonial administrators, though in this, too, I believe, they excel all other European peoples; their greatest achievement has been, rather, as colonists, as conquerors of vast spaces for settlement.

So smug and self-satisfied at home, they have nevertheless shown the highest ability at adapting themselves to types of climate, geographical conditions, and environments totally different from those prevailing in "old England." Their individualism has stood them in good stead. Whether in the wilds of North America or under the no less difficult conditions of Australia, the settlers learned quickly to extract a livelihood from the virgin earth and to exploit natural possibilities. They were industrious, courageous, and devoted themselves to the task with single-minded devotion. Hardships offered no obstacle; and their adventurous spirit drove them to extend constantly the bounds of settlement.

When Englishmen of the last century spoke of the "colonies," they had in mind not Ceylon, Jamaica, Fiji, or any other of the areas now called colonies, but a few vast territories which were being settled by Englishmen. There was, first of all, Canada, stretching over 3.7 million square miles and almost forty times the size of England; there was the Cape Colony in Africa; and finally, the islands of Australia and New Zealand with a combined area of 3.1 million square miles. Those territories were most in the mind of English

people and in the eye of Whitehall. They were always making demands on the mother country, if not for money then
for political concessions; and, though Englishmen felt that
the colonies were asking too much and were a nuisance and
a waste, they were proud of the "little Englands" springing
up on all the continents.

This is not the place to tell how the small British Isles
came to expand over America, Africa, and the Antipodes.
More to our purpose is to see what position these colonies—
now, having grown to full-fledged nations, called Dominions
—have come to occupy in the imperial scheme, and what
forces keep them there. The six Dominions—Australia, Canada, Ireland (Eire), Newfoundland, New Zealand, and the
Union of South Africa—are not kept in the Empire by means
of military might. Britain withdrew her troops from these
areas during the last century, and no one imagines that she
would send her navy if any Dominion were to sever tomorrow the imperial connection.

Until 1913 the situation was fairly simple. Although the
Dominions had long before been given complete autonomy
in internal affairs, a number of legal ties still bound them
to the mother country. Plain self-interest also prompted them
to maintain the connection. With the exception of Ireland,
whose presence in the imperial family is due to unique causes
which need not detain us, all were dependent on British
capital for the development of their primitive economies;
their small population totaling about fifteen millions forced
them to rely on the British navy for protection against
aggression; they relied on British immigration to fill their
vast empty spaces. These material ties were re-enforced by
cultural bonds, the influence of which it would be folly to
underestimate.

Unity of language, cultural traditions, and race forged a
bond between England and the Dominions such as could not
possibly exist in connection with the parts of the Empire
inhabited by the dark races. It is difficult to explain in hard
words so ethereal an entity as "British traditions"; yet one
needs only to live in a British community, whether in England, Australia, or Canada, to see its reality. There is a peculiar attitude toward life and the world; there are certain

manners and even mannerisms; more important, there are certain underlying ideas which are assumed as maxims. Whether in England or in the colonies Britons have had a pragmatic attitude to life; their thought has generally moved along practical channels; they have had strong ideas on individual liberty, a definite attitude on law and justice. Above all, since the days of Queen Elizabeth at least there has always been that peculiar pride in being "British." Australians still bid the world remember that they are "ninety-eight per cent British." Immigration, although dwindling, helped much to keep alive the cultural bond.

The first serious blow to the system was delivered by the World War, when the Dominions discovered that the imperial connection also entailed responsibilities and great liabilities. Although in no way responsible for the war, they were called upon to send hundreds of thousands of men and to supply hundreds of millions of dollars; and a great wave of anti-imperial sentiment swept over all the territories. Other factors tended to add momentum to the centrifugal forces. While the strength of Britain declined, their own importance and power rose steadily, which made them less willing to accept any kind of British superiority. The Dominions suddenly discovered that they were great nations in their own right. Their trade expanded greatly; their wealth multiplied rapidly; their population increased.

Profound changes in the structure of these parts of the Empire became inevitable as soon as the war ended; and they will be examined in a later chapter. Suffice it to say that so fundamentally were relations transformed that the complete separation of the Dominions from the mother country appeared unavoidable even to British statesmen. But those gloomy prophecies were not realized, and to understand the causes which drove history to follow a different course, must be our first concern. Here, then, must be examined the factors operating toward unity and, alternatively, toward separation in the various Dominions. Only such an analysis can make the past intelligible and furnish a clue to the future.

RACE AND UNITY

If racial homogeneity has cemented relations between England and certain Dominions, the racial factor could not but operate in the reverse direction in other areas. There are large communities in some Dominions which are not of British descent and which do not partake of the English tradition. Some of those peoples have been conquered by the British; and the Empire, far from being a source of pride, is the object of their sincerest hatred. The importance of the non- and anti-British communities in some of the Dominions cannot be overestimated, forming as they do one of the most important centrifugal forces in the imperial framework.

Turning our attention first to Canada, we find that the French community numbers more than 3,000,000 souls, who constitute 28 per cent of the population. Three-quarters of the French live in the province of Quebec, which in many ways has retained more of the characteristics of eighteenth century France than the most backward French province. They have been assimilated neither mentally nor emotionally. Their literateurs look to Paris for recognition; their civil code is derived from the pre-Revolutionary *Coûtume de Paris;* Catholicism plays an immense role in their lives, and is certain to come to the foreground in crucial issues, when Quebec presents a united front in opposition, frequently, to the other provinces. During the Abyssinian war, for example, Catholics generally sympathized with Italy against the League, and in the Spanish civil war the overwhelming opinion in Quebec was pro-Franco.

It is true that the French Catholics do not look with hostility upon the imperial connection. They realize that since 1763, when Canada was ceded to Britain, London has been doubly careful to safeguard their rights and privileges. French has been placed on par with English as the official language in Dominion parliament and courts, not to mention those of Quebec; and their privileges have been upheld in numerous judicial cases tried in London involving sovereignty of the Dominion parliament. For the same reason they are solidly opposed to union with the United States, as they consider the British more tolerant than Americans. But if not antagonistic to the imperial connection, neither do they feel bonds of close sympathy with the rest of the Empire. They champion local nationalism as a bulwark against both British influence and American domination, and they are bitterly opposed to Canadian participation in imperial wars.

Extremely important to the future of the Empire is the fact that the proportion of French Catholics to the general population is gradually increasing. Their birth rate has always been higher than that of the British. The uneven increase has become greater since 1930, when, due to the onset of the world economic depression, immigration from the British Isles came to an end, while, on the other hand, emigration of French Catholics to the United States, which attained considerable dimensions during the twenties, almost ceased. Nothing has so far come of the plans to resume large-scale British immigration to redress the balance; and, as can be imagined, the idea did not find much favor in Quebec. The power of the French Catholics is enhanced by large groups of other peoples, notably Germans and Irish, which have immigrated since 1920, and which do not look with favor upon imperial connection. Although the influence of these groups, or of the Italian, Polish, and other European immigrants is very small at present, it is bound to increase in the future; and antagonism to the Empire is sharpened among these peoples, most of whom follow agrarian occupations, by economic rivalry with British-Canadian manufacturers and bankers who are identified with imperial control.

In South Africa the racial factor is of even greater political importance. Settled by the Dutch in the early years of the seventeenth century as a "tavern of the Seas" for Dutch traders with the Far East, the colony was occupied by Britain in 1814. Friction was not slow to develop between the new rulers and the Boers. The latter were intensely nationalistic; also, they violently disliked British ideas on slavery and resented British tolerance of the natives. The Boer farmers—Afrikaans, as they called themselves—would not acknowledge even theoretically the humanity of the blackmen, who appeared to them as slightly, if at all, more advanced than cattle. The Boers were then, as they have remained ever since, a reactionary, cruel lot, whose economic exploitation is not mitigated by any ethical considerations. Trouble developed as early as 1815, when two European officers with a dozen Hottentot soldiers were sent to arrest a frontiersman who had consistently refused summons to appear in court on charges of cruelty to a colored servant. The frontiersman resisted arrest by firing on the military party, and when he was himself shot his friends tried to raise the frontier to revolt. Enactment of the famous Fiftieth Ordinance, which canceled all restrictive laws of earlier years, assuring civil rights to the free colored population, and finally the emancipation of slaves in 1834, proved too much for the Boers, who began their "Great Trek" into the interior to escape British "tyranny."

The British followed also an enlightened political policy. Hardly a decade after the final secession, a Council of Advice, consisting of three official and three nominated members, was established; in 1833 the governor's power suffered diminution with the establishment of a legislative council; twenty years later the colony obtained a very liberal constitution, which provided for an elected parliament, and the franchise—to the eternal credit of the British Government—made no distinction on the ground of race or color. Only a low property or salary qualification, which many natives could meet, was imposed.

There is no need to detail the events leading to the Boer War at the end of the century. Too many liberal tears have been spilled for the allegedly innocent victims of perfidious British imperialism. The war, and the Jameson Raid which preceded it, was not the result of might against right. There was very little right on the side of the Boers. It was a case of one might against another, one imperialism against another imperialism. Eager to avoid a bloody conflict, the British held the door open for a negotiated sensible peace until the last moment; President Kruger, however, and his fanatical patriots refused to grant the legitimate demands of the non-Boer settlers.

What is important to us is that the war immensely exacerbated bitterness between the two communities. Memory of the defeat and a lively consciousness that a great injustice had been done to them have made the Afrikaans intransigent; and oddly enough the British have helped increase the power of the Boers. Eager to conciliate the vanquished foe, Lord Milner, an enlightened imperialist, granted them responsible government almost as soon as hostilities ceased; formation of the Union of South Africa on the eighth anniversary of the peace of Vereeniging placed the whole area under Boer control. By uniting the Boer territories with the predominantly British provinces, the Boers became the majority population in the new Dominion.

Having won the war, the British thus lost the peace. Today the Afrikaans rule not only themselves but the British population as well. The census of 1927 showed that only 33 per cent of the white population of the Union was of the British origin, while the Dutch constituted no less than 57 per cent. The proportion has changed in favor of the latter since 1930, when British immigration gave place to an annual emigration. All prime ministers of the Union have been of Dutch descent: all, moreover, have been military leaders who had fought against British troops and the crown.

Some of the Boer leaders of course oppose the imperial connection less than others; General Smuts, for example, has been more moderate than General Hertzog; important, however, is the fact that the Afrikaans have been able to assert their predominance. The Minister of Defense recently stated that "sentimental appeals to support Britain would be meaningless" since 60 per cent of the population has no British blood in its veins. It is no accident that the Union has advanced the doctrine of the right to "immediate secession" from the Empire in opposition to the other transoceanic Dominions, and that at every imperial conference the Boer spokesmen led the vanguard toward abolition of every legal tie. According to Dr. Bodenstein, Minister for External Affairs, the Union was fully entitled to remain neutral in a British war and could "walk out of the Commonwealth at any moment without even notice."

Even the British population in the Union has not escaped Boer hostility. "There are many English people in this
country who have their reasons for fear," the Bishop of
Johannesburg said in a sermon on a solemn occasion in
1930. "We hear rumors...that in the Great Civil Service
...Englishmen are not always welcome. And we wonder,
some of us, whether we are wanted here....And again,
there are those of us who are married and have children,
and have fears clutching at their hearts. What is to be the
future of the descendants of English people in this land?"
In mentioning the Civil Service the Bishop was referring
to the consistent policy of the Boer-controlled governments
in filling all vacancies with Afrikaans-speaking whites. Petty
incidents are sufficient to blow the smoldering embers into
open flames. The flag controversy, when the Boer nationalists demanded that the Union Jack should not form part
of the South African flag, aroused passion; and, more recently, celebrations of the hundredth anniversary of the
Great Trek were exploited for propaganda against the British and for starting riots against blacks.

On the other hand, unity of race has been one of the
strongest ties binding the British peoples to the Empire.
The British of Natal, whose very existence is threatened by
the Boers, have naturally used all their power and influence
to prevent a break. Natal cities have given contracts to British firms charging a third or more as much as German or
other firms had asked.

Though less devoted than the British of the Union, because less in need of English support, the British in Canada
have also generally favored co-operation with England, especially when the mother country seemed to be threatened
by foreign enemies. Inevitably, however, it has been Australia, Newfoundland, and New Zealand, almost solidly
British in their population, that have stood for the strongest
co-operation. Both the first and last have co-operated actively with England in facilitating British immigration during the postwar years; and it was an Australian statesman
who uttered the classic statement that his country would
fight with Britain "to the last man and the last penny."

CONFLICTING LOYALTIES

There is no denying that nationalism has become, even among Britons of the Dominions, a centrifugal force with which every imperial political engineer has to reckon, and in a Dominion like Ireland an uncontrollable explosive force. Deeply rooted in all social classes, Irish nationalism has been strong enough to foment innumerable rebellions; and British bayonets, far from quenching the burning flame, have only made it blaze more fiercely. Nationalism to the Irish has meant complete severance of political ties with the United Kingdom, even if a tremendous economic price had to be paid. To them there is only the "bloody Empire."

Economic, racial, religious, and political factors have combined to make Ireland one of the most explosive forces in the Empire. Since 1921 "the rape of Ulster" has ranked first among Irish grievances; and it is certain that until a new solution is devised for the Ulster problem Ireland will not be appeased. But behind this issue lie hundreds accumulated during centuries. No other part of the Empire has so many just grievances against Britain; no other people has suffered so much persecution from British officials. With a cruelty rarely found even in the annals of British rule in India and Africa, the British tried to crush the native faith, the Irish language and culture. Economically, the British ruined Ireland not once but many times. Irish industry was annihilated; later one form of agriculture after another was purposely undermined, till the country was reduced to semi-desolation and its people to starvation. Britain must carry responsibility for the death of tens of millions of Irishmen.

What wonder if the Irish since gaining autonomy in 1921 have overlooked no opportunity to weaken Britain and the Empire? The bitterness engendered during the long struggle for self-determination went too deep to be easily forgotten. Sinn Fein and the Republican Army are still powerful factors. Burning with fiery nationalistic zeal, the latter has continued its terroristic struggle against Britain; but even the moderates and official spokesmen, who cannot permit themselves the freedom of action of the Irish Republican Army, have made it a point to annoy the British whenever possible. In December 1937, for example, Premier De Valera decided to send a Minister to the "King of Italy and Emperor of Ethiopia," thus recognizing the Ethiopian conquest, to accentuate, as A. B. Keith says, "the sovereign independence of Ireland and the purely subordinate position of the Crown, the King being compelled to appear in the role of a King with Two Faces, recognizing, for Ireland, the King of Italy as Emperor of Ethiopia, and, for the rest of his Dominions, the exiled Emperor as sovereign *de jure.*" The new amendments to the constitution passed in 1937 practically eliminate the Crown from Irish affairs, the government being left free to function as a republic should it so desire. Even the abdication of Edward VIII was exploited for pricking the British. In the United Kingdom, Canada, New Zealand, and the Colonial Empire, Edward VIII ceased to be king on December 11, but he remained king in Ireland till the following day. Appeal to the Privy Council, one of the last vestiges of the imperial connection, has been abolished. "Nothing can be more humiliating than the position of the Governor General"—the one remaining symbol of imperial unity. "Debarred from participation in any State ceremonial, his one function is on instructions to sign bills." To add insult to injury Mr. De Valera appointed to this exalted post an obscure Irish citizen, who lived in a suburban villa and never appeared in public.

More interesting is that local nationalism has been pitted against the more embracing imperial loyalty even among such a purely British population as that of Australia. A stream of nationalist pamphlets began to appear during the last quarter of the nineteenth century, all aiming to bolster up local patriotism, and to make the populace conscious that they had become "independent Australian Britons." "There is a note of self-assurance in the very titles of their pamphlets," as Professor Hancock has remarked, quoting the following interesting specimen: "AUSTRALIAN NATIONAL-ISM: An Earnest Appeal to the Sons of Australia in Favour of Federation and Independence of the States of our Country. By Robert Thomson, a son of the soil, who fervently loves Australia, and whose highest ambition and aspiration is to be true to her and to serve her cause." To this son of the soil imperial loyalities are a poor substitute for local nationalism. The spectacle of "the rising tide of self-reliance on the broad breast of Young Australia" gives joy to his patriotic spirit; and he advances the slogan "Australia for the Australians," meaning "that Australia should be devoted solely to those who are devoted to her."

Australian nationalism is also "the child of Australian democracy, and grew to be an untidy, vociferous urchin in that bitter period of democratic bluster and bungling over the land problem." The large landowners did not look upon Australia as their home. They came to the new country to advance their fortunes, and shuttled back and forth between the new and the old countries. "Behind them stood the powerful financial houses, controlled from London and controlling the economy of Australia; they were welcome at Government House, and met there officers of His Majesty's Navy and journalist-politicians who argued for imperial federation." What more logical than that the common immigrants, landless and with strong trade-union proclivities, should make nationalism part of the struggle for free land, better wages, and a democratic society free of the class domination? Labor, determined to obtain a "fair and reasonable standard of living," fought for protection against the imperial free trade; in the struggle for union rights and later for socialization, London finance was equated with the local moneyed interests.

Pride and boundless optimism have been characteristic of all the dominions. What do they care for the Old World's values and its atrophied civilization—they who waited impatiently to "become ourselves, distinct"—

"Product of the present only,
Thinking nothing of the past."

Literature stimulated and reflected the nationalism of the young Dominions, which became wider and embraced more than merely political independence. Neither Australia nor New Zealand had to fight against a conservative metropolis to attain autonomy; indeed, England was only too glad to bid her Far Eastern offspring good riddance and did her best to advance Australian federation, which alone could give meaning to the nationalist aspirations. But nationalism took the form, of reaction against the whole set of social standards, conventions, and *mores* of the mother country. If the first Australian writers looked upon the country as "a fantastic land of monstrosities," and sent their heroes to England to spend their declining years and mounting fortunes, it was not long before a typically Australian literature sprang up with heroes of undaunted frontiersmen, who consciously repudiate the genteel British tradition and assert a new democratic virulence. A vision arose, not of a colonial Australia, but of "A new Britannia in another world."

More fanatic has been the nationalism of non-British communities. Boer nationalism has its origin in anti-British sentiment, which has been its justification. It is not carried along by lofty social ideals as the nationalism of the British communities, and seeks no cultural values in justification. On the contrary, the nationalism of both Boers and French, to mention only the largest communities, has been culturally barren and socially reactionary, which has not, however, prevented them from becoming political forces of the first magnitude, boring from within to undermine the imperial structure.

Cast adrift from their own mother country, the French in Canada have focused all their loyalties on the new land. They have evolved the concept of *Canadien* as opposed to loyalties to overseas powers, upholding in every crisis local particularist interests. All the French newspapers and political parties are strongly *Canadien* in character; laudatory mention of the Empire in a political speech does not evoke much applause. Even the Commonwealth parties, whether the Liberal or Conservatives or Socialists, sport a local patriotic flag. Canada being the oldest, largest, and most densely populated Dominion, its nationalism is self-conscious, virile, and active, even if it lacks the bitterness of the Irish and Boer movements.

Recent years witnessed an increase in the influence of the extreme Afrikaans nationalists, who advocate complete separation from the Empire and the establishment of a republic. The decline in the power of British elements has driven even moderate Boer politicians to flirt with the extremists

who now form the second largest party in the Union and
who have succeeded in forcing on the moderate coalition
government many anti-British measures. For the first time
the speech of the governor general was read in Afrikaans
as well as English at the opening of the Union Parliament
in February, 1938, when also *"Die Stem van Sud Afrika"*
was sung after the national anthem. To emphasize their independence the Boers now insist that only *"Die Stem"* shall
be considered the national anthem. The future is made the
more precarious by the growth of fascist parties among the
Boer youth, marking a new stage in nationalist extremism.

ECONOMIC FORCES

Economically, too, the Dominion Empire presents a conflicting picture. Both centripetal and centrifugal forces have
been at work, with the former definitely gaining over the
forces of unity. On the one hand, trade with England, if not
as important as before 1913, has remained as an effective
unifying force; on the other hand, developments in the internal economic structures have done much to push the Dominions away from each other and from the mother country. Instead of adjusting the economic potentialities of the
various parts to produce a unified whole, each part, racing
towards industrialization and self-sufficiency, has developed
along independent lines without regard to the interests,
needs, or potentialities of the other. The economy of Canada, for example, does not supplement that of the United
Kingdom, Australia, or other Dominions. Rather, Canada
competes with the United Kingdom in some essential respects and to an even greater extent with Australia; trade
with non-imperial countries is more important to every Dominion than trade with the whole Empire.

The laissez-faire economic theories in vogue during the
last century ruled out, of course, planning even on a national scale, not to speak of imperial lines. Yet the Commonwealth's economy might have been less of a chaos had
Britain's efforts at imperial unity been of the type to inspire
confidence among the Dominions. Except under the influence of mercantilism in the early part of the eighteenth century, and then only half-heartedly, Britain never evolved an

economic plan for the Empire which would leave room for ample development of each part while making for greater unity among all. Hoping to restrict the Dominions to the production of industrial raw materials and agricultural products and to make each in turn dependent on her own industry, the mother country never offered to relinquish any industrial branch which could better be developed in another part of the Empire. Not till after the World War were attempts made to study the resources—and then mainly the agricultural resources—of the Empire; and very little has come out of those late studies. As in so many other respects the Empire has developed without a head and without a central nervous system.

The movement towards individual economic development was in full swing long before 1914; the war and subsequent years intensified the process. Britain lost direct control over the trade and industrial policies of the Dominions by the middle of the last century, when Australia won full financial autonomy; in 1859 Canada imposed the first anti-British protective tariff in the Empire. "This," mused John Bright, "is the first step towards separation of Canada from Great Britain." Before long the Dominions won the right to adhere separately to trade treaties negotiated by Great Britain or to refuse adherence; finally in the seventies they began to negotiate their own trade agreements in co-operation with a British representative. But even this slight vestige of British control was not to last long. The blow came from Canada, which in 1907 negotiated a trade agreement without the intervention of a British representative. The slight concessions to imperial unity in the form of preferential duties on imports from Britain were not sufficient to counteract the main tendency, which was in the direction of protection and atomization.

Momentous intensification of this tendency has taken place since 1914. Customs walls have risen everywhere to unprecedented heights. Lord Balfour's committee noticed in 1924 "the remarkable fact that the main increase of tariff rates on British exports has been within the British Empire, where the average *ad valorem* incidence has risen by nearly two-thirds, while in foreign countries, despite the great in-

crease in the United States tariff, the average *ad valorem*
incidence has decreased by one-fifth." In Australia, to cite
one example, tariff duties increased by 145 per cent between
1913 and 1925—"an increase with which no other country
can compete." In 1908 Australia had eight items protected
by duties of 40 per cent *ad valorem* or over; by 1928 the
number had increased to 259.

Protected by tariff walls, industry developed in every Dominion without regard to inherent local conditions. The
World War provided the Dominions with unlimited opportunities. Cut off to a large extent from British industry,
they concentrated on developing local industrial plants,
which could not be dismantled when peace came. Instead,
higher tariff walls were erected to protect them. Between
1925-29 Canada's industrial production increased by no less
than 40 per cent—one of the highest figures on record, making her the fifth largest manufacturing nation in the world.
Increases almost as great took place in all the other Dominions. Australia, New Zealand, and the Union of South
Africa became almost self-sufficient in numerous manufactures for which they depended on Britain before 1914 and
have even begun to compete with her on foreign markets
in some. Great textile industries have risen everywhere;
metallurgical plants have developed; shipbuilding is no longer
a British monopoly, and notable progress has been made in
all engineering fields. What matter if British industry—
not to mention that of the rest of the Empire—suffer from
their artificially stimulated development? The Dominions
compete with each other and with England also in industrial
raw materials, the production of which is in no case regulated on an imperial basis.

No greater co-ordination has been introduced in agriculture, which provides the bulk of Dominion exports, and all
scramble for the British market. They compete with each
other in wheat, meats, wool, dairy products, and in a long
line of other agricultural goods. On the other hand, they
all depend in varying degrees on non-imperial countries
for numerous agricultural products which, with planning,
could be produced in the Empire.

What parallel development has meant became evident during the Imperial Economic Conference at Ottawa. Great Britain and the Dominions found it almost as difficult to harmonize their economies, even to a very limited extent, as if each had been completely unrelated to the other. Dominion spokesmen found it extremely difficult to be "rational" and to adopt "a scientific tariff," as the British delegation asked. They made it clear that Manchester's cotton goods, among numerous other manufactures, could no longer find a welcome in their territory. Instead, the leader of the Australian delegation put forward the view "that if Great Britain is to retain this position" as a large exporter, "she must become to an increasing extent the industrial specialist."

Trade, however, continues to provide one of the strongest of imperial bonds. More than 40 per cent of the exports of every Dominion still goes to the Empire; and this factor undoubtedly explains in a large degree the failure of, say, the militant nationalists of the Union to win the support of all Boers for their radical anti-Empire program. The Union would be hard put to find a market for her large exports if the Empire, which has always taken about half of her total exports were closed to her. Eire, too, sends more than 90 per cent of her exports to the United Kingdom, whence comes only about half of her imports.

TAKING TO WING

Maturity produced new problems for the Dominions. Until the last World War the Dominions accepted inferiority as an inevitable by-product of imperial unity. They were content if the British Government associated them in negotiations involving their specific interests. Canada, it is true, had negotiated a treaty with the United States without a British representative; but the treaty was of little importance and did not set a precedent. The Dominions did not conceive of their foreign interests as apart from those of the mother country. At the Imperial Conference of 1911, when the Empire's diplomatic position and problems were reviewed for the benefit of the assembled Dominion prime ministers, Mr. Asquith made it abundantly clear that there could be no question of joint control of high policy.

Then came the war, and the Dominions discovered the consequences of leaving control of their foreign relations with the imperial government. Although they had not been consulted and were only partially informed of the trend of diplomatic negotiations, they automatically became involved in a great war far removed from the spheres of their immediate interest. They discovered that although Great Britain was a world power, in the fullest sense of the word, with vital interests from the Mediterranean to the Arctic, she was above all a European power, and European affairs were and had to remain in the future her main concern. Yet to them, European affairs were only of secondary importance.

The war taught the Dominions a lesson and they decided to exploit the opportunity, when Britain was engaged in the greatest struggle in her history, to complete their independence by breaking her monopoly on their foreign relations. They were determined never again to be in the position of 1914. They demanded, therefore, and obtained an "adequate voice in foreign policy" through "effective arrangements for continuous consultation in all important matters of common imperial concern, and for such necessary concerted action, founded on consultation, as the several governments may determine."

The creation of an Imperial War Cabinet, giving an opportunity for the first time to the Dominion premiers to deal with questions of high policy, marked an important stage in their development. Before long, however, concerted action ceased to suffice, and the cry arose for full diplomatic independence. Of no avail were London's pleas that imperial unity would lose all meaning if each were free to conduct its own foreign relations. The clamor could not be silenced; and when the time for signature of the peace treaties arrived, each Dominion and India signed on its own behalf. Their new status received symbolic expression when they became, by own right, original members of the League of Nations.

The Dominions' special foreign problems have since come to the forefront, especially during the past few years which

witnessed the decline of the prestige of the Empire. Britain
of course is still a world power; more and more however
her interests tend to be centered on the European continent
and on its immediate vicinity. On the other hand, the parochial interests of the Dominions have vastly expanded, while
their concern with Europe has contracted. Canada's main
interest is obviously the United States, where she has been
represented since 1926 by a Minister. Relations between
these two countries have constantly become closer. During
the postwar years old economic ties were strengthened and
new ones forged. Canada became dependent on New York
for capital. Ottawa welcomed Washington's unilateral decision that, by virtue of the Monroe Doctrine, Canadian independence would be protected if threatened by foreign
aggression. More and more Canada has tended to think of
herself as an American power. There has been a steady
increase of interest in South America, with which until recently there had been little concern; and the number of
Canadians in favor of joining the Pan-American Union has
grown rapidly. Recognizing the special interests of Canada
in all matters pertaining to the United States, the Imperial
Government has permitted her to deal separately even when
joint British-Canadian interests were involved. Thus negotiations for reparations after the sinking of the vessel *I'm
Alone* were left entirely to the Canadian Minister at Washington.

Parochial interests loom even larger in New Zealand,
Australia, and the Union. In the first two, affairs in the
eastern Pacific occupy the center of attention. Japan's advent
as the first power in the Far East has produced much misgiving there. Reconstruction of the Singapore fortifications,
undertaken chiefly at their promptings, has reassured them
only slightly, and they no longer feel as secure under the
shadow of the British navy as they did during the last century. The Union government, too, is disturbed by Japan's
known ambitions for a foothold in Africa. The Union con-
siders its future in terms of Africa; interest in Europe is
limited. More diversified distribution of their trade has also
given the Dominions wider political interests. The share of

non-imperial countries in their total foreign trade has increased since 1914.

As a result, the diplomatic atomization of the Empire has proceeded apace since 1920. Ireland was first to avail itself of the newly-won right to separate diplomatic representation when it appointed a Minister to Washington in 1924. Since then, three Dominions have appointed diplomatic representatives in about ten capitals of special interest to them. The foreign ministers of the Irish Free State and the Union now issue their own letters of credence to their envoys, instead of through the British Foreign Secretary; foreign envoys to the former are no longer received by the Governor General as personal representative of the King, but by the President of the Council; and these Dominions have now provided themselves with seals of their own for ratification of treaties to avoid resort to the Great Seal of London. Important international treaties requiring unified action by the Empire are now ratified separately by each government. "It is not necessary even that ratification should be expressed in one instrument; in the case of the Paris Pact of 1928 separate instruments were preferred."

The sole limitation on Dominion sovereignty that has remained, which distinguishes them from completely independent states, is the requirement not to engage in foreign negotiations on matters of common interest without advance notice to the Commonwealth, thus enabling members to express their views whenever their interests are affected. But the Dominion in question is not bound to accept the views of the British government or its sisters in the Commonwealth. The Union disregarded the protests of the whole Commonwealth against a clause in the commercial treaty negotiated in 1928 granting Germany all privileges accorded to members of the Empire, although the clause tended to invalidate the basic doctrine of special inter-imperial relations.

The rights and powers won by the Dominions since 1919 have been more than sufficient to break up the Empire. Australia would have been within her rights had she chosen, say, to declare war on Japan; what such an event would have done to imperial unity if other members of the

Commonwealth had not followed her example, as they probably would not have, is obvious. One or two Dominions actually created extremely awkward situations, though falling far short of war, when they branched out on their own into the foreign field—as when Eire recognized the Ethiopian conquest before the rest of the Empire was prepared to do so.

Nevertheless, history since 1920 shows that the Dominions have been more interested in obtaining the abstract right to pursue foreign policies of their own than in utilizing it. Generally speaking they have not been unwilling to follow a British lead. First, collective security under the League of Nations gave the Commonwealth a policy in the pursuit of which they could tacitly co-operate. The mere fact that all had been extremely eager to avoid war ruled out major disagreements. Second, the newly-won rights had to remain largely on the theoretical plane, because not one of the Dominions has had the necessary military strength to execute a foreign policy of its own without the co-operation of Great Britain.

No less important, the Dominions soon recognized the wisdom of relying on the British Foreign Office for diplomatic information and for the conduct of normal business relations. They recognized that the British Foreign Office with its immense and highly trained staff all over the world was obviously a far better organization than any which they themselves could afford. It has therefore become the practice that in negotiating with countries where the concerned Dominion has no diplomatic representative the authorities communicate directly with the British minister or ambassador, who carries out Dominion instructions without consultation with London. Only in cases affecting imperial interests does he seek London's authority. The Dominions also began to receive most of their information on international political developments from the British Foreign Office, which transmitted to them, via the Dominions Office, the stream of diplomatic reports constantly arriving from all over the world.

Yet all this could not hide the extreme precariousness of the situation. Britain's monopoly on foreign relations was broken; and there could be no telling when a Dominion would decide to adopt a policy which would not have the support of the rest of the Commonwealth. Even their common pursuit of collective security was not unaccompanied by serious friction. True, the Dominions lost no opportunity to emphasize that they were more enthusiastic adherents of the League of Nations than Britain; illogically enough, however, they resisted even more than the latter all obligations resulting from collective security. The Dominions were much more responsible for Britain's failure to check aggression in Europe and Asia than is usually supposed. In this field as well, the Empire developed without a central brain.

DEFENSE AND UNITY

Theoretically, since the latter part of the last century each Dominion has been responsible for its local defense. Resenting the presence of British garrisons, the Dominions announced themselves willing to assume full responsibility for the protection of their frontiers and proceeded to set up defense forces free from all "outside meddling" by Britain. Each parliament became the sole authority in the determination of the size of the armed forces; local laws were enacted to govern recruiting and training of personnel. The postwar years completed the process of Dominion independence in all matters of defense, and it is difficult to conceive how, short of complete disintegration of the Empire, disintegration of control could have been carried further. Eire enacted a military oath which, symbolically enough, completely ignores the Crown; and notwithstanding Britain's protests, the Dominions assumed for the first time effective control of their naval forces outside their territorial waters.

So far did atomization go during the postwar years that all except two Dominions unhesitatingly turned down British schemes for co-operation in defense of common imperial interests and trade routes. The Union government discontinued in 1921 a very modest subsidy to imperial defense inherited from the Natal and Cape territories. Australia canceled an agreement to contribute about a million dollars a year toward the maintenance of a British squadron in Australian waters and to raise the crews for four British vessels. Suspicious lest common action involve their country in foreign entanglements, Canadian statesmen rejected with singular unanimity many "rather pointed suggestions" from Britain that their country contribute towards the protection of the imperial trade routes which are so profitable to her, and they refused to listen to the appeals from Australia and New Zealand to show a more lively concern in the defense of imperial interests in the Pacific.

However, the great expansion in the foreign interests and responsibilities of the Dominions was not accompanied by a proportionate growth in their military power. Although full-grown nations, they refused to provide sufficient funds and men for safeguarding their territorial integrity against aggression. Until 1914 the Dominions had practically no armed forces of any kind; and the World War, which had such far-reaching effects on all other fields, did not produce notable changes in this. None of the Dominions spent on all types of military establishments a percentage of its budget comparable to that expended by third-rate European powers which possess a fraction of the interests the former have had at stake. Everywhere military budgets were cut down to the barest minimum. Even as late as 1937-38, when a rearmament campaign was launched, Canada spent less than thirty-five million dollars on all types of defenses, and this represented a large increase over expenditures in the previous years; Australia, which had done more in this respect than all the other Dominions, spent a total of fifty-five million dollars; the Union actually appropriated less than $8,350,000. As a result, not one Dominion has been in a position to defend itself against a foreign invasion; not one has been able to protect its sea routes. In various degrees, all have had to rely upon the British navy and the British air force for protection.

Nor was Britain in any way responsible for the defenselessness of the Dominions. On the contrary, she was willing to run the risk of further weakening imperial relations and pleaded, at one imperial conference after another, that more substantial military machines be constructed. Britain went so far as to make monetary contribution to help the rich members of the Commonwealth pay for their defense. Loans for defense purposes were made to New Zealand on extremely generous terms, and airplanes were sold to the Union for a nominal sum. But the Dominions preferred to use their resources for constructive social purposes.

Yet all the Dominions, with the exception of Canada, which is fortunate in having the United States as neighbor, could ill afford to overlook the possibility of a foreign attack. Australia and New Zealand have been in the most vulnerable position. Asiatics could utilize to good advantage their vast uninhabited spaces; their colonial possessions and their rich wool and wheat yields make them highly attractive prizes for such a country as Japan, which has a large fleet and a tested modern army. The Union of South Africa, with gold and diamond mines, has offered no insignificant inducements to a "have-not" power. Japan has thrown covetous glances at the Union; Italy, especially since she established herself on the mountains of Abyssinia, could swoop down upon the neighboring territories, and the Union has been a far more attractive prize than Abyssinia will ever be.

A strange and wholly illogical situation thus developed. On the one hand, each Dominion has been theoretically responsible for its own territorial defenses and for protection of its vital interests; on the other hand, not one was able in practice to fulfill its responsibilities, or indeed, showed any inclination to do so. Having expelled British "meddling" as incongruous with complete independence, each and every Dominion promptly fell back upon the protection given gratis by the British military and naval establishments. In practice, therefore, they all have had to rely on Britain for the active protection not only of their vital sea communications but, were the necessity to arise, of their own territories. Of course, in normal times no such necessity was likely to arise. The mere existence of the British navy and its army acted as sufficient deterrent to potential enemies. Japan has been kept away from Australia's shores not by Australia's three cruisers and her badly trained land forces. It has been the armed might of Britain, which is always present on the horizon, that has kept Japan away and protected imperial shipping. Only in the British system with its anachronisms, incongruities, and muddle-headedness could such confusion exist.

But if this system worked havoc with imperial defense, dependence on Great Britain for the protection of territories and vital interests, more than any other single factor, forced the Dominions to abide by the imperial connection. The security which Britain has given since their infancy has undoubtedly been one of the most important factors neutralizing the effects of the numerous centrifugal forces. In the last analysis, as Gladstone declared in the middle of the last century, "No country which is not charged with the ordinary business of its own defense is really or can be in the full sense of the word a free community. The privilege of freedom and the burden of freedom are absolutely associated together...."

The importance of this service which Great Britain has rendered cannot be overestimated. The knowledge that in the last resort the mighty arms of England were their only protection against aggression stopped many a nationalistic Boer statesman from taking the final step of severing the connection with the Empire. And all those who talk about the Antipodes Commonwealths veering towards the United States would do well to ask themselves whether the American navy could keep open in case of hostilities the Red Sea, the Suez Canal, and the Mediterranean, through which flows the bulk of their trade.

Such, then, have been the forces which have operated in the Dominion empire. First, in Australia, New Zealand, and among the British communities in the Union of South Africa and Canada, culture, religion, and common ancestry have operated as powerful unifying factors. On the other hand, these bonds have not only been lacking in Ireland and among large communities in the Union of South Africa and Canada, whose importance has constantly increased; but differences in culture, religion, and ancestry have been among the chief forces making for imperial disintegration. Second, local nationalism and parochial interests emerged everywhere. Third, the World War stimulated in all the Dominions powerful groups whose economic interests came to be vested in separation, while the importance of trade with Britain declined. Fourth, all remained dependent for security on the military might of Great Britain, despite the emergence of the League of Nations which temporarily tended to diminish the value of this service. A subsequent chapter will show how these forces worked themselves out during the postwar years.

VI

THE OUTER EMPIRE

NO STUDY OF THE British Empire can be complete without an analysis of its "Spheres of Influence"—the areas lying in the shadow of the British Lion. Although not colored red on any British map and legally in no way part of the Empire, nine states with a total area of almost four and a half million square miles and more than a hundred million inhabitants have been in reality an integral part of the Empire and have contributed greatly to its strength. The extent of Britain's influence or power has varied, of course, from area to area and from time to time. British influence has traditionally been greater in the Arabian Peninsula than in Portugal, and greater in the latter than in Tibet. In some of the spheres of influence Britain has had more direct power than in any of the Dominions and almost as much power as in her colonies; in other spheres her preponderance was occasionally challenged. Indeed, the extent and solidity of this part of the imperial structure served as the best meter for measuring Britain's power at any given time. In the days of the Empire's greatest glory—until 1920, that is—those territories were so closely connected with Britain that they constituted a distinct category which I label the "Outer Empire."

That membership in this imperial category should change from time to time was inevitable. For not only the amount of force London could muster at any given time determined the extent of this empire. Although military might was always in the background, its chief usefulness was as a potential threat, which, like Jove's thunderbolt, the rarer used the better. Normally Britain relied on different bonds. Prestige played an immense role, and tradition, too. More important, Britain generally tried to identify her own interests with those of the peoples in her shadow. In many cases the people of a sphere of influence saw that retention of the closest possible relations with the British Empire was to their own best interest, especially, as often happened, the only other alternative was subjugation to another power; and centuries of experience taught the British that the best way to retain this "empire" was to moderate their demands and to make at least a superficial show of respecting the independence of the various states. Until 1914, therefore, the boundaries of the Outer Empire constantly expanded, and there was a steady upswing in Britain's power in various territories.

The value of this empire to Britain can only with difficulty be exaggerated. Its military value is too obvious to need laboring. The campaign against Napoleon would have been much more difficult had Wellington not been able to use Portugal as if it were an English county. But for British power in Constantinople the history of the Near East —and possibly of the Far East as well—would certainly have been very different. Would England have retained control over India had Egypt, instead of becoming a British sphere of influence, fallen into the hands of a rival power?

Nor was the usefulness of the Outer Empire limited to times of war. Its economic contribution has been immense. More even than the colonies, the states of the Outer Empire helped to make Britain what she became during the last century—the world's greatest industrial and financial power. Britain owes her wealth almost as much to the Ottoman Empire as to India, and Portugal became early an important stimulus to Britain's industrial development. The diplomatic contribution was also of no small value. Not only did the satellites reinforce British diplomacy at almost every important diplomatic conference; influence in these countries gave Britain a very advantageous bargaining position in negotiations with neutral powers. To realize the vast significance of this factor, one needs only think how much "concessions" in her spheres of influence did to bring about the alliance with Russia in the early years of this century.

The spheres of influence were of course not established

fortuitously. Very good reasons explain why Britain did not attempt to involve, say, Rumania or Paraguay in the system. The first principle governing the selection of spheres of influence was imperial defense. Like the Romans, their great imperial predecessors in ancient times, the British early recognized the importance of a wall around the Empire as a protection against aggression from without; and since the British Empire was too large and too far-flung to be protected by a wall of steel and concrete, the British saw that the only other alternative was to establish around the Empire's strategic corners and around the most important routes of imperial communications a system of buffer states which should be friendly to the Empire and under its control. These states came to act as outposts of the Empire proper, and as the line dividing it from the outside, frequently hostile, world. The second consideration was ability to give protection against foreign aggression. Britain could convert Greece or even Persia into spheres of influence because she could protect them against foreign aggression; but her navy would be of small use in defending Finland or a South American state.

A cursory glance at the traditional British spheres of influence will show how well they conformed to these principles. Every one was either necessary for the protection of important routes of communication or for the defense of the Empire. The defense of India both from land and sea loomed very large in this scheme; with the emergence of the Mediterranean as one of the chief imperial arteries during the latter half of the last century, Britain spared no effort to surround her shores with states under her influence and control.

THE FOOTHOLD IN EUROPE

Located on the bump where the Iberian Peninsula begins to swing from the Atlantic into the Mediterranean, which places her on the junction of two of the most important trade routes of the world, Portugal was singled out by geography for special importance. Either she would be a great empire in her own right; or, failing that, her strategic location would make it inevitable that she fall under the control of a power stronger than herself. Like the possession of rich oil deposits, strategic location is a blessing to a country which can defend its advantages by force; but woe to the nation thus situated that lacks the necessary military might!

During the past five hundred years history realized both of these alternatives. Portugal entered modern times as the greatest empire of Europe with possessions ranging from the far end of Asia to the American Hemisphere. Her career was, however, meteoric, and the next great empire, Spain, realized Portugal's strategic value and conquered her. But the lingering memory of erstwhile greatness made her nobles too proud to submit to Spanish arrogance and a revolution in 1640 brought to an end the "Sixty Years Captivity." Unfortunately, no revolution could undo the disastrous events of preceding years, when, as part of Spain, with whom Britain and Holland were at war, Portugal was despoiled of her vast colonies, her navy and trade ruined. Weak and torn by dissensions, it was only a question of time before a great naval power would come to dominate her. France vainly tried to gain supremacy; but England's fleet was beginning its long reign, and the Earl of Clarendon's far-seeing eyes perceived the advantages of gaining a foothold in this highly strategic peninsula. In 1662 Charles II married the daughter of Portugal's king, thus beginning a connection that was to persist to this century.

It was no accident, then, that made Portugal Britain's sole sphere of influence in western Europe. British power has been very great in numerous Baltic, Balkan, and central European states; nowhere, however, have the British been so eager to establish permanent domination as in Portugal. Control of that kingdom of only thirty-five thousand square miles and seven million inhabitants gave them not only an easily accessible base for military and political operations on the continent. The Portuguese ports enabled them to dominate the trade routes to the Far East, the Mediterranean, and Africa, while domination over Portugal's African empire, both economic and political, proved of no slight value.

Conclusion of the famous Methuen Treaty of 1703, by which Portugal granted tariff preferences to British imports

in exchange for similar concessions on her wines, was to
have immense political and economic consequences. British
ambassadors attained a position of power second only to that
of the king; it took an exceptionally strong premier, like
the great Pombal, to resist them. Economically, the consequences were disastrous for Portugal. The demand for her
wines having been artificially stimulated in Britain, Portugal concentrated all her energies upon wine and cork production. Her industry declined; even her agriculture was
ruined and food stuffs were imported from England. A
regular British "factory" was set up at Lisbon; a large British trading colony settled at Oporto; British capital began
its steady influx that was to make the country as dependent
on the London money market as India.

British history—and therefore the history of Europe—
might have been considerably different had Portugal followed an independent national existence. Its supreme strategic importance was to be demonstrated again and again.
Hardly had the Methuen Treaty been signed than Portugal
was called to do yeoman service for Britain in the war of
the Spanish Succession then rocking Europe. Pedro II had
recognized the grandson of Louis XIV as king of Spain, much
to the disgust of Britain, which did not relish a French kingdom on both sides of the Pyrenees; and he had protected a
French fleet against the British. Signature of the treaty
turned the tables, and Pedro entered the war on the side
of Britain.

During the eighteenth and nineteenth centuries Portugal
"remained in a political sense"—certainly economically—"a
mere province of England, and was bound by the Methuen
Treaty to take part in all the wars in which England was
engaged." Her importance again became evident during the
Seven Years War, fought by England to preserve her delicate
balance of power. But it was during the mortal combat with
Napoleon that the strategic value of this sphere of influence
became most evident. Portugal became one of England's
most important bases on the continent; her fleet and ports
helped solidify Britain's domination of the seas; her troops
participated on many fronts and won the praises of Wellington. It was during this period that the tradition of British

hegemony in the army and navy was established—a tradition that was to endure till the first years of this decade. British military and naval missions became all-powerful, and Portugal's armed forces modeled themselves after England's.

Probably the best indication of the power Britain had come to wield was afforded by the appointment in 1808 of Sir Charles Stuart to the regency formed after the flight of the Portuguese king to Brazil. Sir Charles did not wait long before making himself master of the council, ruling Portugal as if it were a British colony. His tyranny, endured as long as the Napoleonic wars lasted, was only brought to an end by outbreak of revolutions. It should be added, however, that on the whole Britain acted as a progressive force during Portugal's tumultuous history in the last century, supporting the liberal constitutionalists against the absolutist and reactionary triumvirate of king, nobility, and church. A clash in Africa between British and Portuguese troops had no permanent effect on relations between the two countries; during the Boer war Portugal gave valuable assistance to the hard-pressed British, as it did again during the first World War. Rarely indeed has a sphere of influence been politically more valuable, strategically more useful, and economically more profitable than Portugal from 1703 to about 1920.

BRITAIN'S MEDITERRANEAN LAKE

Who could have foreseen in 1583 on the establishment of permanent relations between England and the Ottoman Empire that a day would come when the mighty Turk would depend for his existence on the power of Britain? For two centuries Britain remained, outwardly at least, the weaker of the two. Englishmen were imprisoned on the slightest pretext, or on no pretext at all; even ambassadors were insulted, humiliated, and the face of more than one was wetted by the expectoration of Sublime Sultans. Then, at the end of the eighteenth century, fundamental changes which had taken place came to the surface; and the Ottoman Empire became a British sphere of influence. In 1790 the brilliant Pitt laid down the policy that maintenance of the integrity of Turkey was a vital British concern.

More than economic interests, great though they were,

were responsible for this policy. Political and strategic considerations were decisive. Recognizing the value of the Inland Sea in any imperial scheme, Britain spared no efforts to assure her domination over its waves and over all the surrounding territories. Control of the western terminus at Gibraltar was not sufficient. She did not relish the idea of a Russian Stambul with control over the Dardanelles and eventually over the excellent Greek harbors; nor could she afford to allow the Near East—the land bridge to India and other Far Eastern possessions—to fall into the hand of a strong power which might use it as a springboard for attacks on the Empire. There was no need to worry as long as Turkey exercised nominal control: itself impotent to threaten the Empire, its control would prevent more dangerous rivals from establishing themselves, while leaving Britain free to forward her own interests and influence.

If Britain profited greatly from her power in Constantinople, economically no less than politically and strategically, the arrangement was, however, by no means one-sided. True, Turkish diplomacy became an appendage to that of Britain; on the other hand, but for Downing Street the Ottoman Empire would have been dismantled more than once. Britain intervened with force on numerous occasions to drive away the wolves who had come too close to the gates, while knowledge in St. Petersburg and numerous Balkan capitals of Britain's avowed policy prevented wars without resort to force.

Gradually during the last century England came to control Turkey's foreign and even internal affairs. A series of British ambassadors became the rulers of the Ottoman Empire. Lord Stratford de Redcliffe exercised for long years almost unchallenged sway. "Our own government occupies a peculiar position," in Stambul, he wrote in an article. To prop up the shaky foundations of the Empire, he pushed through innumerable schemes of reform; he tried to alleviate the lot of Christian subjects to remove the excuse for European intervention. In him "the Turk found a friend, counselor, and schoolmaster ever ready to chastise them for their own good. The reforming Sultan Abdul Majid and his well-meaning Grand Vizier Rashid Pasha allowed themselves to be driven by him where they would not have been led by others; he was their *Elchi*—The Ambassador. So great was the Englishman's influence in Stambul and so unremittingly did he exert it to shield Turkey from Russian hostility and intrigue, that the Tsar regarded him rather than the Sultan as his adversary. Whatever the Sultan did, whatever he said, was received in Petersburg as an expression of English thought translated into Turkish." [1]

Typical of the regard with which Britain came to be held are the words spoken to a Turkish officer by his father: "Know, my son, that we have two kings: one is the Padishah in Stambul; the other lives in a far-away island called England." Turkish finance fell under the domination of London; the Turkish navy came under the unchallenged control of British officers; provincial governors looked to the British consuls rather than to Stambul for guidance and instruction. Even the Young Turk Revolution of 1908 brought only a minor change in Britain's position. Although some of the new leaders were not averse to flirting with Germany to counteract Britain's predominance, it was not German propaganda, or commercial interests or the Berlin-Baghdad railway that forced Turkey into the war against the Allies. As late as 1913 the Turks begged Britain for money and officials to reform the Asiatic provinces, "offering to invest the English officials with full executive powers," and "practically invited England to take Asia Minor under her tutelage."

What had changed was British policy, which had become willing to sacrifice part of this sphere of influence to win Russia's co-operation against Germany. Not till Russia actually entered the war were the scales in Stambul tipped decisively in favor of Germany. Yet the end of the war found everything as it had been before, except that Britain was now more than ever entrenched in her traditional sphere of influence. The Ottoman Empire had become a British colony. A British fleet lay anchored in the Golden Horn; British troops were stationed in Constantinople, where a British high commissioner was the real ruler and the Sultan-Caliph his ward. The British writ was law; and the Turkish

[1] J. F. Abbott, *Turkey, Greece and the Great Powers.*

authorities, their army and navy shattered, merely executed British orders.

Control of the Inland Sea could not, however, be complete without the excellent and numerous Greek ports and naval bases; and this too was accomplished. Nominally independent, Greece remained for all practical purposes a British colony. She had begun independent life under the tutelage of England, France, and Russia; but it was not long before the British Resident became the most powerful of the three. A chancellor lacking his support could not retain office for very long, as Chancellor von Rudhart and others learned to their great sorrow. When the Greeks sought to establish a constitutional monarchy, it was to Downing Street that they turned for approval; and Greece entered in 1843 the list of constitutional states.

Britain's naval supremacy in the Mediterranean had of course a determining influence on relations with Greece; yet this was by no means the whole story. Greece, indeed, has been an excellent illustration of the peculiar structure of the British Empire, whereby its power in one area was due to and dependent on its power in others, while its power in the latter was to some measure dependent on the former. Because of her supremacy in the Ottoman Empire, Britain, better than any other power, was able to protect the large Greek communities strewn from Constantinople to Alexandria, which in turn did much to support British political and financial hegemony in the Ottoman Empire.

No less important a factor in assuring British supremacy has been the immense esteem and love of the Greek people for Britain. The devotion of Greeks to Britain's cause is not easy to explain. Many a Hellenic national aspiration has been frustrated by the British policy of maintaining the integrity of the Ottoman Empire; Crete was kept in subjection to the Turks for almost a century, although it revolted constantly and invariably succeeded in teaching the Turks a humiliating lesson in the art of war. Yet the reality of the devotion has been beyond doubt, and at every decisive moment it appeared to tip the scales in favor of England. Greeks rejoiced over British victories as if they were their own; nearly every educated Athenian learned English; and

British liberal individualism threw a spell over all classes.

It was inevitable therefore that when a revolution brought to an end the Bavarian dynasty, the Greeks, in their devotion to England, should turn to London for a king. The Russians and other European powers, jealous of England, spared neither money nor efforts to popularize their candidate, the Duke of Lichtenstein. The Greek people, however, staged immense demonstrations before the British Legation to petition for Prince Alfred, and at a plebiscite gave him ninety-six votes for every one cast for the rival candidate. As the three protecting powers had entered a self-denying agreement against acceptance of the Greek throne, "Britain's passive acquiescence in the movement which resulted in the election of Prince Alfred was a mere diplomatic maneuver intended to let the world know how the three powers severally stood in Greek esteem." This object accomplished, the British government began to page through the *Almanach de Gotha,* that hoary register of royal heads, and its choice fell on Prince William of Denmark. Again, the mere knowledge that Britain sponsored this candidate was sufficient to gain his acceptance by the Greek people, and in 1863 Britain's nominee ascended the Greek throne as George I.

Not that estrangements and even bitter disagreements were wholly lacking. England's unkindly policy in championing Ottoman integrity produced bitter feelings more than once, as did her occupation of the Ionian Islands. But the periods of bitterness passed without leaving a permanent scar on British prestige and power; and the Greeks were quick to acclaim England's justice, when, in 1864, her High Commissioner laid the Ionian standards at the feet of the King of the Hellenes. The King invariably turned to Britain for advice on all matters; and a premier lacking the goodwill of the British Legation could not long remain in power. The sinews of Greek economic life came to be concentrated in London. During the Boer war, "while the press of every other country poured forth rivers of hate upon the British Empire... Greek newspapers mourned England's losses, young Greeks offered themselves as volunteers to the British Minister and consuls, and even humble Greek bootmakers, unable to contribute anything bigger to the fund raised for the English wounded, contributed boots made with their own hands."

Every war fought since the first part of the last century demonstrated the value of control of the excellent Greek naval bases, which the British navy was free to use. Their importance was fully recognized by Germany before the last World War, and she did her utmost to assure Greek neutrality. As the Italian naval expert Fioravanza wrote in a work on *World Naval Bases,* "any grouping of powers which gave Britain and France the use of the Grecian bases would mean the complete strangulation of Italy." Without control of those bases during the World War the British navy would have suffered much greater losses from German submarines than it did. Nor should the diplomatic and economic profits from this control be overlooked. The Greeks furthered British diplomatic interests in the Balkans, and London drew large profits from Greek insurance, banking, and trade.

While the traditional pro-Turkish policy was sufficient to assure British interests over the vast Ottoman dominions, opening of the Suez Canal in 1869 in the teeth of British opposition created new problems which demanded a new settlement. The British had sabotaged the scheme, persuading themselves of its impracticability; but again, as in the days of Napoleon, a Frenchman taught them a few lessons. Not only was the canal constructed; the number of steamers using it as a short cut to the Far East increased rapidly, and within a few years half of the European trade with the Far East went through the Suez locks. What a military genius had failed to accomplish was brought about by the diplomatic and scientific skill of Ferdinand de Lesseps. The threat to India was now greater than ever; and Egypt increasingly became a French colony.

The British were destined to lose every battle except the last; and a series of extraordinarily happy accidents—some of which may have been less accidental than they appeared—played into their hands. No one can say that the British government decided to reassert mastery over the Inland Sea and all its gates by occupying Egypt; yet this is exactly what happened; and it is not without interest to note that almost half a century before the opening of the Suez Canal, Mohammed Ali, the founder of the present Egyptian dynasty, foresaw Britain's occupation, and fearing it tried to forestall it. The chain of circumstances which made Britain master of the new gateway is far too complicated to unravel here. First Britain became the largest single shareholder in the canal company when the ruler of Egypt, Khedive Ismail, was compelled to raise cash to meet pressing obligations; then outbreak of disturbances in Egypt created new opportunities for intervention. By incredibly bad diplomatic maneuvering France and Turkey forfeited a glorious chance to undermine the growing British influence. In 1882 Egypt was occupied by British troops—and the Suez Canal, the most important gate to the Far East and India, passed into British hands.

Britain pledged herself "to seek no territorial advantages, nor concessions of any exclusive privilege, or any commercial advantage"; on August 19, 1882, General Wolseley proclaimed that "Her Majesty's Government have sent troops into Egypt with the sole object of restoring the authority of the Khedive." The Khedive's authority was restored quickly, yet Britain refused to leave the country. On the contrary, Lord Cromer was sent to take Egypt into his hands—and powerful hands they were. A cadre of British officials took charge of every branch of government, and reduced the authority of the Khedive to a shadow. Domestic and foreign policy was determined by England; the army came under the control of Englishmen; and British troops were stationed to be at the bidding of the Residency.

Legally, Britain's position remained an anomaly. No valid document justified Britain's presence in the Valley of the Nile: Egypt did not sign away its independence, and for a long time European powers refused to recognize Britain's domination. France did her utmost to make Britain's position in Egypt as difficult as possible. Far from being deterred by these handicaps, Britain constantly strengthened her control, and in the end even France had to recognize that Egypt had definitely entered the British orbit. British troops were at hand to protect the canal against any enemy; Egypt's riches flowed to England in an uninterrupted stream.

Outbreak of the war in 1914 demonstrated how useful this sphere of influence had become. Although not at war with anybody, Egypt made immense contributions to the Allied victory. Egypt was forced to give men, money, natural resources, and beasts; and she made possible Lord Allenby's campaign in Palestine and Syria. Not a single German ship went through the canal, where British men-of-war were always on guard. Egypt's whole cotton crop was taken over by the British at a nominal price; her food helped feed the large British army in the Near East, and she served as the base of operations for all campaigns in the Mediterranean. It is more than doubtful whether Turkey could have been defeated without control of Egypt. No more part of the British Empire than any other sphere of influence, Egypt yet contributed more to England's prosperity and might than many a crown colony.

IN ARAB WATERS

Nowhere did the British enforce their own Monroe Doctrine more stringently than in the Persian Gulf, the Red Sea, and the adjoining territories, which form the highway to India and her first line of defense against European powers. From the end of the eighteenth century till after the World War, British statesmen followed a consistent policy of brooking no rivals in this part of the world; and they could have said in 1800, as Lord Lansdowne said a century later, that "We should regard the establishment of a naval base, or of a fortified port on the Persian Gulf as a very grave menace to British interests, and we should certainly resist it with all the means at our disposal."

British domination began unostentatiously but grew rapidly. The first political agent in the Persian Gulf was appointed in 1763; twelve years later the Arabs saw for the first time ships of His Majesty's Navy. Since then, there has been no time when the gulf was without British men-of-war. The East India Company dotted the whole area with trading agencies, which, however, did not limit their interests to commerce any more than did the agencies in India. Domination over all local chiefs was established; France, which had come first to these waters, was gradually expelled; even Turkey's interests had to be sacrificed. Extension of the Indo-European cable from Jask to Moscat materially strengthened Britain's position; even the outbreak of a plague was turned to good advantage, for it provided the needed excuse for assuming sanitary supervision over the gulf.

The test was not slow in coming. When an Egyptian conqueror of the Arabian Peninsula in the second decade of the last century rejected British advice to keep away from the shores of the gulf, a powerful fleet was dispatched to shell and to occupy Arabian ports. After that British preponderance in these waters required no further emphasis. The Sheiks of the Trucial Coast hastened to conclude treaties giving Britain the right to search all vessels for the purpose of suppressing piracy and slave trading; the Kuria Maria Islands, with their deposits of guano, were added as "a free gift" to the Crown; the strategic island of Perim, located at the center of the narrow Bab-el-Mandeb strait, was occupied and fortified. To cut the last cord binding these territories to foreign powers, Britain decided to exclude French guns under the pretext that the warring natives had to be pacified—a noble motive which, however, loses some of its nobility if it is recalled that the only result of the edict was the substitution of British for French guns. Bahrein, another highly strategic island, was detached from the Ottoman Empire under the pretext of self-determination. The local sheikh agreed to place himself under Britain's management by submitting all disputes with neighboring sheikhs to Britain's arbitration and to allow British subjects to live and trade in his petty dominion. In another agreement concluded at the end of the century the sheikh agreed not to "cede, mortgage, or otherwise give for occupation" a part of his domain to any foreign Power except Britain or to accept diplomatic representatives except from the Court of St. James.

The identical story repeated itself in other islands; for the men-of-war made it obvious who ruled the waves. Aden was occupied and administered by the Bombay Residency; Moscat came into the British orbit; the temporary conquest of the Arabian Peninsula by the Sauds, an ancient ruling

house, immediately brought a warning from the British not
to stare covetously upon the Red Sea and Gulf shores. And
when the Sheikh of Kuweit was murdered by his brother,
who coveted his throne and harem, the British lost no time
in recognizing the new ruler, who hastened to sign an agreement placing his sheikhdom under Britain's exclusive protection.

Thus it came about that when the Germans, dreaming
of Empire, tried to gain a foothold in these strategic areas,
they found themselves completely forestalled. A German
mission which appeared in Kuweit in 1900 to explore for
oil and to undertake other development projects, had to
beat a hasty retreat. The Berlin-Baghdad-Basra railway
scheme was an obvious threat which Britain could ill afford
to overlook, and she did not. It was sabotaged as long as
possible; later, attempts were made to assume control over
it; but by 1914 the project had been realized only over a
small part of the way. At the outbreak of the World War
the Gulf and the Red Sea, although never part of the Empire, were British lakes, with Britain's flag supreme, her
political agents the real rulers behind a façade of native
chiefs; and no rival power could hope to gain a foothold.

Unchallenged control of Arabian waters inevitably resulted in British supremacy in the Arabian Peninsula. A
huge desert, the peninsula offered no economic advantages
to justify direct penetration. The existence of invaluable
oil deposits was not yet known. Britain's one interest was
to gain strategic footholds and to prevent European competitors from establishing themselves. Both ends were accomplished without great difficulty. Aden was occupied;
Oman and Hadramaut fell under British influence; and
every ruler of the interior of the peninsula learned to beware of the British, who cared not whether Turkey or a
dozen petty sheikhs misruled it as long as no powerful
centralized government assumed control. When Ibn Saud
seized Riyadh at the turn of the century and began to consolidate the sheikhdom his ancestors had lost, he found it
convenient to get in touch with the British and to assure
them of his immortal friendship. Years of residence at Ku-

weit had taught Ibn Saud the silent power of the British
navy.

Britain's influence and power in the Eastern part of the
Ottoman Empire expanded at the same time. Maintenance
of the territorial integrity of the Ottoman Empire was naturally not intended to prevent the East India Company
from extending its influence around Basrah and further
inland in Mesopotamia, or from becoming the effective
power behind the paralyzed Turkish administration. A trading station had been opened at Basrah by the East India
Company before the middle of the eighteenth century, and
shortly afterwards another station was opened at Baghdad.
Here from 1810 Consul Rich raised British prestige and
power to unprecedented heights, making the Residency second in importance only to the Serai, the seat of the Turkish
Governor. Before a third of the last century was gone British
surveyors were mapping Mesopotamia; Major General
Chesney led an expedition financed jointly by the British Government and the East India Company to survey the Euphrates, and two steamers from England arrived to navigate it.
So great had British power become that, notwithstanding
the prevailing insecurity, Captain Lynch was actually able
to start a regular river service between Basrah and Baghdad.

The second half of the nineteenth century witnessed the
further consolidation of Britain's power, and some two hundred thousand square miles more came under the shadow
of the Union Jack; British supremacy could no longer be
questioned, and certainly not opposed by another European
power. A prospectus issued by the promoters of a Euphrates
Valley railway recorded that "Basrah, from its matchless
situation, would with the slightest fostering care, become the
grand center of English" commerce. It was abundantly clear
that, while satisfied with the status quo, Britain would occupy the territory the minute another power threatened to
establish itself. How effectively the work had been done
became evident as soon as the World War broke out. The
day after Turkey's entrance into the war a British-Indian
force landed at Basrah and began to roll up Mesopotamia.
Britain's absolute control of the Persian Gulf and the Red
Sea was not endangered for a moment. The navy's oil sup-

plies at Abbadan were safe. All the petty sheikhdoms with whom exclusive treaties had been signed fell into line. They never made any trouble, nor could they. In the Arabian Peninsula, Ibn Saud quickly threw in his lot with the British and engaged in battle a sheikh suspected of supplying guns and camels to the Turks. More important, the Residency in Cairo accepted the offer of Sherif Hussein, ruler of the Holy Cities of Mecca and Medina and a descendant of the Prophet, to raise a revolt in the desert against the Turks. The Sherif did not like to fight with "infidel dogs" against a Moslem country; but being a realist, he knew who was the effective ruler of the Near East. Lawrence jumped into the fray. Before the armistice with Turkey was signed, the whole Near East from the Suez Canal to Anatolia and from Palestine to Basrah was under British occupation.

By 1919, then, the dream of ambitious British imperialists of an empire from Gibraltar to India had become a reality. Gibraltar guarding the entrance to the Mediterranean was in British hands; the Inland Sea itself was a British lake, with its numerous British-controlled naval stations; Egypt was more under British control than it had been at any time since 1882; Palestine, Syria, Mesopotamia, the Arabian Peninsula—all had come under British control or influence. As to the Gulf and Red Sea, British supremacy there had never been seriously challenged; now it was axiomatic. A vast new empire had been added to reinforce the old one—an empire extending over almost a million and a half square miles, containing a population of about fifteen millions, with vast resources only awaiting exploration and development.

One great question confronted the British masters: How were the new territories to be administered? Two schools of thought developed. Some old-fashioned imperialists were strongly in favor of outright annexation. They thought that the best thing to do would be to set up a number of British administrations along the colonial model, which would rule the territories as Trinidad or Fiji is ruled. That Britain, having won the war, had the right to form such an administration could not be questioned; still less could one question her power to do so.

On the other hand, a number of intellectuals and enthusiasts favored a more enlightened policy. They pointed out that, in essence, Britain's interest in the Near East was limited to guarding the area against encroachment by a powerful Western state which might menace the security of the Indian Empire. Could not this be accomplished, they asked, more cheaply, more humanely, perhaps even better by entering into special treaty relations with Arab governments which could be established to fill the vacuum left by the collapse of the Ottoman Empire? Instead of colonial annexation, they asked, would not declaration of a Monroe Doctrine, that the territories constitute a British sphere of influence, serve all basic British purposes? As in other spheres of influence, Britain would of course reserve for herself the right to supervise and control administration through her Resident and through English officials in the native governments; their foreign affairs would be in the hands of the British residents; their economies would be tied to London; and His Majesty's armed forces, though maintained for purely imperial purposes and not as an army of occupation, would always be there as final resort in case of emergency. But whatever the ultimate policy, the ability of His Majesty's Government to enforce it could not be doubted. Never before had London's domination over this part of the Outer Empire been as absolute as it was immediately after the war.

BRITAIN OVER CENTRAL ASIA

Britain's early attempts to establish contact with Persia did not augur well for the future. Anthony Jenkinson, appearing at the Court of the Shah in 1561 with a letter from Queen Elizabeth, was unceremoniously expelled from the capital; the arrival before the end of the century of Sir Robert and Sir Anthony Sherley, backed by the Earl of Essex, produced no permanent results. Even appointment in 1627 of Sir Dodmore Cotton as Britain's first Ambassador to the Shah of Shahs brought no improvement. Sir Dodmore was sent to cool his heels at Kazwin, where he died shortly afterwards. A later attempt to establish commercial relations was brought to naught by Catherine the Great of Russia, who thus opened a rivalry that was to persist to this century.

As in the case of Egypt, the British were awakened to the importance of Persia as India's first line of defense by Napoleon, who sent an envoy to the Shah to arrange for the passage of a French army across Persia, which would be joined by a Russian force on the plains of India. Alarmed, the government of India instructed its representatives at Oman to sign a treaty with Sayid Sultan, by which he undertook to deny the French access to his territory, to prohibit entrance of their vessels to his ports, and, on the other hand, to permit the British to construct a fort and "factory" at Bandar Abbas on the Gulf. An offensive and defensive alliance provided that "should any army of the French actuated by design and deceit attempt to settle with a view of establishing themselves on any of the islands of the shores of Persia, a conjoint force will be appointed by the high contracting parties" for their "extirpation."

Thus was Persia drawn into Britain's far-flung net. Once established, Britain's power grew continuously during the rest of the century. Before long Persia emerged as a bulwark against Russian aggression. Prosecuting with relentless determination their old ambition to gain an outlet to southern waters for the immense land-bound empire, the Tsars saw in Persia an ideal field for expansion. Not only would they reach the waters of the Gulf; no less important was it that occupation of Persia would bring them to the gates of India—a development the British were determined to forestall. A fierce struggle therefore raged throughout the last century between Britons and Russians, each one biting off two mouthfuls for every one devoured by the other. Russia strengthened her hold on the north; Britain solidified her position in the south. The struggle was terminated only in 1907 with the signature of agreement dividing Persia into two spheres of influence, England taking the southern part and Russia the northern portion.

No fundamental change was effected by this agreement and the rivalry continued with England gradually gaining the upper hand in Teheran. "What is happening to Persia?" cried a member of the Russian Duma. "In Persia we are being pushed out.... And what is it that is driving us out? It is England." In 1901 a British colonial, D'Arcy, obtained a concession to dig Persia for oil and founded the Anglo-Persian Oil Company, one of the most important petroleum concerns in the world, in which the British Government before long acquired a controlling share. British banks came to dominate Persian economic life; the government could make no move without first consulting the British Minister. When an American financial expert was engaged by the Persian government to reorganize its tangled finances, pressure from the British Legation was sufficient to secure his dismissal. Another area of more than three hundred thousand square miles with a population of about eight million had come under Britain's shadow.

The gains of more than a century of steady penetration were consolidated at the end of the last war. The moment was propitious for a solid advance: a large part of the country had been occupied by British troops; the collapse of Russia removed from the field the one great competitor; "Little Ahmed"—as the undergrown, overfed idiot sitting on the throne of the Shahs was called by foreign diplomats in Teheran—could easily be persuaded to give all that Lord Curzon, Britain's great Foreign Minister, wanted. And Lord Curzon was an ambitious man. Accordingly, the treaty of 1919, notwithstanding the noble article on Persian independence, virtually turned the country into a British colony. Natives were to retain ministerial portfolios; but ministries would receive British advisers "endowed with adequate powers," and their staffs of experts; a British military mission was to take charge of the army; Persia was to take a loan from Britain "for which adequate security shall be sought... in the revenues of the customs and other sources of income at the disposal of the Persian Government"—in other words, leaving all finances in British hands; fourth, the British were to build a system of communications adequate for their purposes and for which, presumably, the Persians were to pay; and, fifth, tariffs were to be revised by a special British mission. The British Board of Trade hurriedly dispatched a mission to shape Persia's economic form in the image pleasing to British eyes. What if the Persians protested against the treaty? Lord Curzon told Parliament that withdrawal "would be immoral, feeble, and disastrous."

Farther east in Asia the British again confronted the problem of checking Russian influence "in a quarter which from its proximity to our Indian possessions, could not fail, if it were once established, to act injuriously on our system of Indian alliances." No Napoleon was necessary to teach the British the importance of Afghanistan and Tibet for the defense of India. While an expedition from India to Tibet would meet with tremendous natural obstacles on its steep ascent, an expedition from Russia via Tibet would be much less difficult. Nearly all invasions into India had come through the Tibetan passes; and what could be done before, could be done again. As to Afghanistan, the problem was how to turn it from a spearhead threatening India into a sword directed against Russia.

The story of British expansion into these territories dates from the thirties of the last century, when an army was sent to Afghanistan to place on the throne an unpopular incompetent who promised to reign as London ordered. There had been some Russian intrigue in Kabul; it is doubtful, however, whether it was serious enough to warrant such an invasion. More likely, good imperialists that they were, the British were not averse to stretching a point in execution of the policy laid down by the board of directors of the East India Company that "no just and honourable accession of territory or revenue" should be neglected. A revolt against their protégé brought to an end British hopes of establishing a strong state under their control, to the great satisfaction of the Muscovites. But the latter had not reckoned with British pertinacity. Shere Ali, one of the ablest of Afghanistan's rulers during the century, was persuaded to accept a generous British subsidy; and so great had Britain's power become even in those high altitudes that Shere Ali asked the government of India to guarantee his frontiers against Russia and to acknowledge no other "friend in the whole of Afghanistan save the Amir and his descendants."

Amusingly enough, only a few years elapsed after signature of the treaty with Shere Ali, which had legalized British preponderance, before British troops were again on their way to Kabul for the second Afghan war (1878). The explanation is of course that, unable to strike at the Russians, who had resumed their advance and intrigue in Afghanistan, the British decided to hit at the Afghans, hoping that the former would see and beware. Shere Ali could not resist the British troops and his son Yakub was placed on the throne. The new Amir accepted in May, 1879, a treaty by which he relinquished certain districts to Britain; promised to accept the guidance of the Viceroy of India in the conduct of his foreign policy; and agreed to accept a British mission in Kabul. But the treaty was too good to last. Yakub showed himself incapable of maintaining a semblance of order, and in the following year a new Amir came to the throne who forced the British to evacuate the city of Kandahar.

Yet the years of intrigue cannot be said to have been spent in vain. Far from it. Before the last century came to a close the British had consolidated their control over Kabul. The native ruler, a pensioner of the government of India, had become a British agent; an Indian railway had been built to the Afghan frontier; Russia had acknowledged that "Afghanistan is entirely outside the sphere of Russian action"; many powerful chiefs had come to depend on subsidies from the government of India, and the Amir recognized the right of the British Viceroy to conduct all his foreign relations. Foreign dispatches to Kabul had to go via Delhi, where the replies were penned. Anxious as ever to gain a foothold, Russia attempted in 1902 to reopen the question of direct communication with Kabul. But the British had done their work thoroughly, and at a Durbar the assembled chiefs advised Amir Habibullah against it. The Amir rejected Russia's demand and advised that in the future all communication be made through the Viceroy "in accordance with the precedent established" by his father.

Conclusion of the Anglo-Russian agreement of 1907 and the subsequent years only strengthened Britain's position.

Russia not only acquiesced to Delhi's prerogative to conduct the Amir's foreign relations; it agreed not to send any
agents to Kabul and to refrain from subsidizing trade. In
the meanwhile, Amir Habibullah came to rely increasingly
on British support for maintaining his position. His subsidy
was paid regularly; Afghan trade with India increased; and
the Amir co-operated in maintaining peace on the frontier.
The tables were now turned, and before the war broke out,
it was the Russians who were appealing to London to restrain Afghanistan from embarking on acts of aggression.
The World War witnessed a further increase in British power
which enabled Britain to remove troops from the North
West Frontier for Europe; and the idea that the time had
arrived for converting the protectorate into part of the
Indian empire was not strange to many British circles.

No less decisive was England's victory in Tibet. Nominally under Chinese sovereignty, Tibet was actually ruled
by the Lamaist theocracy headed by the Dalai Lama and
the Panchan Lama. England did not want Tibet; she had
learned the fanatical nature of its people and the savage
jealousy of the Lamas against foreign influence; information carefully collected by British agents revealed that the
alleged immense natural resources of Tibet were a fable. But
the safety of India demanded that no rival power—meaning
Russia—be allowed to establish itself on "the roof of the
world."

Rivalry between England and Russia for supremacy of
Tibet raged throughout the second half of the nineteenth
century. Moscow used every means for extending its power;
more than once it appeared that this strategic territory
would come under its influence. Gradually, however, working in its own inimitable, silent manner, London began
to make its power felt. British influence at Peking was
brought into play, and there were always the vast resources
of India. By these means England succeeded in counteracting Russia's inherently superior strategic position and her
greater military powers for action in those mountain-locked
territories.

In the early years of this century, however, the Russians
converted with fat bribes a certain Lamaist priest named

Dorjieff, who persuaded the Dalai Lama to accept a treaty opening Tibet to their influence and trade. Russian ammunition arrived in Lhasa, and a series of raids upon Indian territory took place in 1903. Reluctant though they were to embark on so dangerous and profitless an adventure as the conquest of Tibet, the British accepted the challenge. After a winter such as the British troops had never experienced before, and after suffering immense losses, Lhasa was entered and the struggle which had extended over more than half a century came to an end.

The treaty signed by the National Assembly banished effectively, as one writer has said, "the Russian Bear from the Tibetan plateaus." The Assembly agreed to establish marts to facilitate trade with India; not to erect any customs barriers between the two countries; above all, there was the pledge that without the previous consent of Britain "no Tibetan property shall be sold, leased or mortgaged to any foreign power; no foreign power shall be permitted to concern itself with the administration of the government of Tibet or to send either official or non-official persons to Tibet or to construct roads, railways or telegraphs; and no land containing minerals or precious metals shall be mortgaged, exchanged, leased or sold to any foreign power."

The military expedition and the Convention with Russia (1907) put to rest all British worries about this exposed flank of the Empire. Further penetration could be effected best by quiet if persistent methods. And British influence grew rapidly. In 1910, when the wrath of the Chinese authorities forced the Lamas to seek shelter in India, British officials were able to install them again in Lhasa. The influence of the British Raj now became stronger than ever. British advice was sought on all matters affecting relations with Russia and China; the telegraph line to Lhasa erected by Younghusband was improved; British uniforms were adopted for the higher officers of the army, while British ammunition found its way to the uplands. A large part of Tibet's trade now made its tortuous way to the frontier of India.

The World War marked another milestone in the British advance. British troops again climbed the steep mountains, and the Dalai Lama, having learned his lesson, declared himself a stanch ally of Britain. He went so far as to offer a Tibetan expeditionary force for the European battlefields. The British did not favor the idea, as the troops might be more useful closer to home; and the Panchan Lama used all his religious influence to support the Allied cause.

Thus slowly, quietly but with an amazing pertinacity the British had constructed a wall around the Empire, which by 1919 had become larger and more solid than at any previous time. Hardly an important point for the security of the Empire and for facilitating British control of "the Sea"[2] but was either in British hands or had come under their influence. The Outer Empire supplied essential links in the chain of imperial communications stretching from London to Melbourne and Calcutta. And beyond India the British were entrenched not only in the crown colonies of Singapore and Hong Kong, but China and Siam as well were to a very large extent under London's influence. Only the rivalry of other European imperialisms saved these two countries from being absorbed by the Empire.

[2] Writes Commander Stephen King-Hall: "To an Englishman . . . there is not one Mediterranean sea—there is The Sea. I think of the sea as a medium . . . which both links and separates the units of the British Commonwealth of Nations. . . . It is the general principle of British foreign policy to create conditions which will permit of the control of the sea routes when The Empire is at war." "British Policy in the Mediterranean," *International Conciliation*, January, 1938, No. 336.

VII

THE EMPIRE OF FINANCE

THERE HAVE BEEN MANY political empires; and Britain is not the only imperial nation possessing large foreign investments. The unique feature about the British Empire is that, on the one hand, a whole imperial category has been based —not on military might, not even on political interest or the ties of race—but on financial power; while on the other hand finance has been used to bolster up and to reinforce the political structure. The French, for example, have many foreign investments and have a great empire; but the two have been kept apart. It remained for the British to show how foreign investments and political empire could be combined into a harmonious unity, and how each could be used to strengthen the other for the greater glory and benefit of the imperial power.

For the spheres of influence have by no means been the ultimate limit of the British Empire. Beyond the far-flung boundaries of the political empire, Britain constructed during the last century another imperial expanse held together by finance, which stretched over eleven states with a population of one hundred millions and an area of about six million square miles. During most of the past seventy-five years Britain's financial Empire included Sweden, Denmark, Norway, Portugal and its colonial possessions, Argentina, Bolivia, Brazil, Colombia, Paraguay, Finland, and Estonia (since independence). On the map these states are not colored red; they are independent in every way and have never been ruled by British officials. Yet any realistic analysis of the British Empire cannot overlook the fact that finance created between these states and Britain a very special relationship which has had far reaching implications in fields not strictly economic.

Great as has been the usefulness of finance in tying these states, in varying degrees, to Britain, greater still has been its utility in reinforcing the pillars holding together the political empire analyzed in preceding pages. Like a scaffolding of steel the financial structure has risen over and above the political empire, transferring strain from one place, preventing a weak construction from giving way in another. Indeed, it is doubtful whether the political structure, and especially the Outer Empire, would have been able to survive but for this reinforcement.

Obviously the financial empire was not constructed merely for reinforcing the other or for adding to Britain's prestige. Economic profit was its main motive; the other factors came as by-products, and helped increase the purely economic benefits. Britain recognized that coupling the financial and the political empires would not only react favorably on the latter, but would be of immense benefit to the former. And so it has been. The financial empire was strengthened through this connection; moreover, the profits from the purely political structure were greatly increased.

The financial empire has been of vital importance to Britain. It is safe to assert that without it the national standard of living would have had to be much lower. The proportion of income from foreign investments, interest on short-term investments and bankers' and brokers' commissions to the total national income, has been on the increase since the latter part of the nineteenth century. According to Professor Colin Clark, the index of national income increased from 100 in 1924 to 109.8 in 1930; during the same period, however, "net income from abroad" jumped from 100 to 139.5. Expenditure on social services would have been smaller but for this source of income; military and naval budgets would have had to be kept down; it is indeed doubtful whether Britain's social structure could have survived without the tribute from the political and financial empires.

THE BOND OF STERLING

The most obvious link connecting those vast areas with England has been the pound sterling. All the colonies, India, the Dominions, and all the other states enumerated above base their monetary unit upon the pound sterling of Great Britain, and their medium of exchange is subject to the fluctuations of Britain's currency. One might go so far as to state that, in effect, a common currency exists for all these countries, control of the value of which is in the hands of the British authorities.

Of course the relation is neither as simple nor as one-sided as the above statement would imply. First, the concept of Sterling Bloc is very loose. Britain cannot directly prevent, say, Sweden, from severing the connection should the latter's interests so warrant. Second, the Bloc is an effect—not a cause. Britain's currency would have no more been an international unit of value than that of France had not Britain had the strongest industrial and financial economy throughout the last century, when sterling became as reliable as gold. Third, while the connection of so many economies to sterling normally strengthens it, it must not be overlooked that a fatal weakening of one of the dependent economies reacts unfavorably upon Britain's currency. If Sweden has an unfavorable balance of trade, she can meet her obligations only by calling in her sterling reserve in London or by borrowing sterling. In either case, Britain's currency is called upon to meet a difficulty which originated in a foreign country.

Yet these facts cannot obscure the major truth that the existence of a common currency has given Britain a vast amount of economic power. Though not compelled by law or treaty to adjust the value of her currency to the fluctuations of the British pound sterling, Sweden has continually done so. When Britain devaluated her currency, not only the empire followed suit, but also the states included in the Sterling Bloc. Experience has shown, also, that the exchange rates of those currencies follows that of sterling, the value of which in turn, is determined by the economic and political policies of the British government.

The usefulness of a common medium of exchange is not difficult to see. Not only does Britain's monetary unit draw strength from the fact that so many economies revolve around it, giving the pound a position in world finance held by no other currency; the relationship has done much to encourage trade between the members of the financial empire and Great Britain. Traders in the Sterling Bloc find it much easier to enter into long term contracts with one another than with firms of countries outside the Bloc. Fluctuations in value of the currencies being synchronized with that of the pound sterling, certainty is assured and long-range planning is possible with a minimum of risks. It is one thing when a purchaser from a franc country has to enter into financial obligations in pounds which are to be met after a number of months or years, during which period the value of his own currency in terms of the pound may undergo violent changes, and perhaps double his obligations; it is a totally different thing when he knows that, come what may, the exchange value of the two will remain constant.

A galaxy of facts can be cited to show the far-reaching economic consequences flowing from the existence of the Sterling Bloc. Britain has had the largest re-export trade in the world (which amounted in 1913 to 110 million pounds or more than a fifth of her total exports; in 1937 re-exports amounted to more than 75 million pounds, or to a seventh of the total exports); and a very large part of that has been due to the fact that British merchants found it easier to contract in advance, say, for Australia's wool or Egypt's cotton than did French merchants, who had to worry about future exchange rates. And if London was able to retain its position as the financial center of the world in spite of extremely active competition, that again must be explained, to a certain extent at least, by the same cause. With its currency tied to sterling, Argentina, for example, found it safer to borrow in London than in New York, since it could rely upon the relationship between the two currencies remaining unchanged until the time of repayment. Again, the various members of the Bloc have had to maintain considerable gold or exchange reserves in London, which normally not only helped to strengthen Britain's financial structure, but enabled British banks to profit from the necessary payment transactions.

How important connection with the Sterling Bloc actually is, can be seen from the deliberations and resolutions of the Imperial Economic Conference held at Ottawa in 1932. Again and again every speaker from the Dominions brought up the question of stable currency as a supreme factor in economic policy. The head of the South African Delegation, Finance Minister N. C. Havenga, struck the note which every subsequent speaker repeated, when he said: "International commerce is carried on a small margin of profit. If, therefore, the proceeds of a transaction may be dissipated by a change in the rate of exchange before the due date of payment, commerce becomes speculation, and this tends further to restrict the value of transactions.... Instability of foreign exchange is therefore not necessarily an evil of lesser magnitude than instability of prices; it may in fact sap the roots of international commerce." "We need," repeated the Head of the Australian Delegation, the Rt. Hon. S. M. Bruce, "money that will enable a debt contracted in one year to be repaid by a comparable service when it falls due in another." The Conference adopted the following resolution:

The Conference recognizes the great importance to traders of stability of exchange rates over as wide an area as possible. The complete solution of this problem must await the restoration of conditions for the satisfactory working of an international standard as referred to below. In the meanwhile, and pending such a solution, this Conference has considered the possibility of achieving valuable results in two directions—first by creating an area of stability among countries regulating their currencies in relation to sterling; and secondly, by avoiding wide day-to-day fluctuations between sterling and gold.

Nor has the value of the Bloc been limited to the economic sphere. It is of course impossible to show that the accommodating attitude which Swedish diplomacy, or that of Denmark or of Argentina, has normally shown in questions involving British rights or interests was due to this or that particular factor. Influences of this kind cannot possibly be disentangled and weighed. The fact is, however, that British diplomacy has more than once been able to use the political weight of these countries, especially in times of stress. It is only logical that membership in such a financial family should create the psychological atmosphere necessary for close relations, and a feeling of common interest, which could be used whenever the need arose.

EMPIRE EQUALS CREDIT

"Empire is debt," H. N. Brailsford has written. True as far as it goes, this statement overlooks the fact that a far more fundamental relationship exists between Britain and the members of the financial empire. Debt alone cannot hold an empire together; on the contrary, it may be a very good reason for disintegration. Nations love their creditors no more than do individuals.

Far truer is it to say that empire equals credit; and not until the full implications of this statement are analyzed can one fully appreciate the role which finance has played in maintaining the unity of the British political empire and in consolidating the financial structure. It is not only that the countries of the Empire and a number of foreign countries owe British nationals vast sums of money; more important is that the debtor countries are poor and they constantly have to come back either for new loans or for renewal of old ones. Experience over many years before 1914 demonstrated to them that, if worthy thereof, the only place where they could always obtain new credit was London. It became eminently wise therefore, to maintain close and friendly relations with the financial capital of the world.

Possibly as much as thirty to thirty-five billion dollars of British capital has been invested in the world, income from which is still drawn by British nationals. The immensity of this sum will perhaps be best realized if it is recalled that American foreign investments in 1935, according to the rather optimistic calculations of the then Acting Secretary of Commerce Draper, amounted to a total of $12,600,000,000.

It is true that income from only part of the thirty to thirty-five billion dollars is transferred to England in any given year. According to the very conservative estimate of Sir Robert Kindersley, income from only £3,725,000,000 was transferred to the United Kingdom in 1930. Although in this study we shall follow Sir Robert's figures, it should, however, be borne in mind that they represent only about half of British investments, the other half being held by Englishmen residing abroad whose income is not transferred to the United Kingdom. Sir Robert estimates, for example, total British investments in Argentina at £360,000,000; a British economic Mission, however, placed the total between five and six hundred million pounds. The difference is even more glaring in the case of China, where, according to most reliable estimates yet made, British investments amounted in 1931 to $1,189,000,000, while Sir Robert allocated only £40,000,000. The difference is explained of course by the presence of a very large British community in China, whose income from the investments does not directly come to the United Kingdom.

Britain remained the first creditor nation of the world from the beginning of modern foreign investment practice until 1914. There is hardly a country which did not have to come to London, at one time or another, to ask for loans. A great part of the development work by federal and municipal bodies the world over—and many wars—was made possible by British capital; a large percentage of the world's railway lines, public utilities, mining developments as well as many other industrial and agricultural projects were carried out with capital from the same source.

If thus far we have not seen anything which might distinguish British foreign investments from, say, those of France, which during the last century was the next largest capital-exporting country, the fundamental difference will appear when the distribution of British investments is examined. Although Downing Street only rarely intervened directly with the banks in favor of one country or another, British bankers, supremely conscious of the national interests, which, as we shall see, usually harmonized with their own private interests, instinctively and without official directions channelized their capital exports into clearly defined streams, which generally were synonymous with the boundaries of the political and the financial empires.

First, a good deal more than half of the total foreign securities held in the United Kingdom in 1930—£2,158,000,-000 out of a total of £3,725,000,000—represented investments in the Empire; of the larger figure for British total investments regardless whether or not held in the United Kingdom, probably more than two-thirds went into the Empire. And the lion's share of the Empire investments went to the Dominions and India. The New Zealand Minister of Public Works and head of his country's delegation at the Ottawa Conference stated unhesitatingly, "The general development of New Zealand has been carried out mainly with British capital." He estimated that "the total indebtedness, both public and private, to Great Britain, would probably be not far short of £200,000,000" (Sir Robert Kindersley: £123,-000,000). In Canada, according to Prime Minister Bennett, 2.2 billion dollars of British capital had been invested; while Australia took close to £500,000,000, India and Ceylon £460,-000,000, and South Africa £225,000,000.

If most of the investments were made within the political empire, the majority of £1,567,000,000 placed in foreign countries, to use Sir Robert's extremely low estimate, were also unevenly distributed. Certain countries were favored over others; and the favored were those which stood on special political relationship with Britain or were at least members of the financial empire. In South America, Argentina, Brazil, and Uruguay were the recipients of the bulk of British investments; the influence of close economic or political relations on London's loan policy was even greater in the case of loans to European and Asiatic countries. Turkey, having become a British sphere of influence, was an early recipient of financial favors, for which of course she paid a good price; so was Portugal and its empire; so was Greece, for which an Independence Loan was floated in 1824-25.

The power resulting from control of the purse is too obvious to need detailed enumeration; and Britain early learned that the purse can be a mighty instrument not only for maintaining the integrity of the political and financial empires, but for keeping foreign states on good behavior. Governments throughout the world found during the last century, when capital for development was greatly in demand everywhere, that the shortest way to the financial market was frequently through Downing Street. If the British Government looked with more than ordinary benevolence upon any political activity of a fully independent state—in other words, if the activity was either inspired or approved by London— the necessary funds came forth. The approval of Downing Street became even more necessary when, as in the case of Greece, economic reasons alone could not justify further loans. Greece defaulted early and often, and stock exchange quotation had to be refused. That, however, did not prevent her from obtaining new loans. When political considerations overweighed economic ones, the British Treasury would guarantee either interest or amortization or both.

Even when Downing Street did not directly intervene in the affairs of a borrowing state, control of credit gave London immense power. Unlike American banks, which showed complete lack of scruples in arranging foreign issues, British banks were generally extremely careful and demanded all sorts of confidential information from governmental bodies prior to floating loans. Frequently they insisted that the debtor government engage itself either to accept British advice on matters likely to affect its financial position, or even to appoint British officials to its service. And to consolidate the net of influence and the system of information issuing from and coming into London, British banks early developed throughout the world a system of "correspondent" banks, which stood in very close financial relations with them and often contained British directors. Those correspondent banks gave London a back door to ministerial councils, especially as those banks were usually the strongest and most important in their respective countries. To increase further this influence, the City began toward the end of the century to spread out directly over the political and financial empires by means of branch banks. In 1904 Great Britain had 50 colonial banks with 2,279 branches, and by 1910 their number had increased to 72 and 5,449 branches respectively. By 1933 the number of banks had been reduced by a series of mergers to 46, but the number of branches had increased to 7,209.

There is no need to go beyond the last few years to see how finance was used as a hypodermic for keeping alive the political and economic empires. Since 1932 an embargo on foreign capital issues has been purposely used for strengthening the imperial structure as political or economic expediency dictated. New credit in London has been open only to members of the political empire and the countries of the Sterling Bloc needing London assets to minimize exchange fluctuations or to facilitate trade with Britain. The effects of this policy have been quick to make themselves felt. It is possible that close relations with Turkey would have been established without the influence of finance; but that sterling paved the way is beyond doubt. Having expanded beyond Russia's capacity to finance her agricultural and industrial schemes, Turkey recognized in the early thirties that only Britain could supply her needs, and political rapprochement followed. Since then British gold has flown steadily to Ankara. Loans to Greece, Rumania, and Poland have had similar political effects.

Greater possibly has been the effect of finance on the political empire, where it has been used to solidify the political connection and to give the British Treasury greater control in the finances of the borrowing territories. Colonies seeking loans under Treasury guarantee—and almost all such loans have had to be so guaranteed—have had to satisfy the Exchequer that ample provisions had been made for charging to the general revenue and assets of the territory the amount required to meet interest and sinking-fund payments —which, in effect, gave the Chancellor of the Exchequer almost complete control over the taxes and expenditures of the territory. He can claim with justice that, in virtue of this contract, he has the right to disapprove of certain expenditures, or to insist on the imposition of certain taxes, because otherwise services on the loan which he had guaranteed would be endangered.

Dependence on London for credit was one of the strongest ties binding the Dominions to Great Britain. Until 1914, when London's financial power was greatest, the Dominions were very careful not to antagonize too much the London authorities; and many a policy was defeated when Britain objected to it. Although, as we shall see, Britain's financial power seriously declined after the last war, enough has remained to influence Dominion policies. Thus when the New Zealand Minister of Finance came to London in the summer of 1939 for the purpose of raising a loan of £16,000,000 to redeem an earlier loan falling due on January 1, 1940, he found the money market inhospitable. The British government had long been dissatisfied with the economic and financial policy pursued by that Dominion, which, it was asserted, affected unfavorably British exporters. A government guarantee was accordingly refused, and the loan had to be raised on "onerous" terms. *The Times* commented editorially: "If future assistance is to be more easily forthcoming, and if New Zealand is to be able to arrange her London finances on a basis less burdensome to herself, then the Government of New Zealand must first prove its worthiness...."

Empire is credit; and Britain's enormous credit resources have helped not only to hold together the political empire, but to extend its boundaries by forging spheres of influence, and, beyond those, to hold a dozen states which, though politically independent, must look to London to survive economically. The power resulting from control of credit need not always be used; sufficient is the fact that it is there. Britain has learned in centuries of experience that too frequent use of the power leads to misuse which in turn produces resentment and eventual defeat. On the whole, Britain has not misused her power and has interfered but rarely in the internal affairs of states forming the financial empire. On the other hand, the situation is bound to change in war, when, indeed the full importance of this power comes to the surface. By virtue of her economic control Britain is then in a position to restrict the trade of her enemies; her banking net makes it possible to restrict if not deny credit to firms trading with the enemy, and the insurance structure which is used together with the banking net helps further in this direction. More decisive still, war inevitably sharpens political problems, and the influence resulting from this financial net is sometimes of immense value.

One needs only to examine statistics of Great Britain's imports and exports to see what investment abroad meant to her. For year after year imports have exceeded exports, and usually by huge margins. During the World War, to begin with recent years, the surplus of imports over exports was immense; but that was to be expected. Britain was fighting for life, and she was anxious to purchase goods wherever and in as great quantities as could be found. However, the situation did not change in the following years. Between 1922 and 1928, when the postwar prosperity reached its highest peak, the average unfavorable balance of trade was around £390,000,000 per year; in 1931, excess of imports over exports amounted to £408,000,000. The balance was somewhat less unfavorable during the following years; but in 1937 excess of imports over exports amounted to £443,000,000 (total imports £1,028,000,000; exports, £597,000,000), and in the following year the figure climbed to almost £450,-000,000 (imports, £920,500,000; exports, £471,000,000).

No other nation has imported so much goods per head of the population as Great Britain. The amount of retained imports (that is, after subtracting re-exports) increased from £14 8s per capita in 1913 (exports: £11 10s) to £25 17s in 1925 (exports: £17 3s). Even during the depression years, the figure did not fall below £13 9s (exports: £7 18s), and it climbed steadily upwards in the subsequent years. In 1937, when exports amounted to only £11 per capita, imports reached £20 3s. In other words, while every person in the United Kingdom produced for export in 1937 less than he did in 1913, the amount he imported for consumption increased by a third.

What do these figures mean? They mean that the world has become one huge workshop delivering goods, both agricultural and industrial, to England. Every day close to two hundred thousand tons of goods is brought by hundreds of ships to British ports, from there to be distributed to every city and village of the Kingdom. There is hardly an article produced or handled by man which is not brought to this world metropolis: immense stocks of raw materials; all sorts of manufactured goods; mountains of agricultural products from onions and peas to doughnut flour and steaks. Rugs from Iran, the art of the Orient, and precious stones from all over the world are shipped there. Of course, Britain ships in return all sorts of manufactured goods; but, as the above figures have shown, the value of her exports has been only slightly more than half of the total imports.

How has Britain been able to pay for these immense quantities of goods? The answer is that a very large part of the money came from interest and profits on the investments abroad, from the banking services connected with those investments, while another major part of her foreign resources came from shipping and the various imperial services. Until 1914, also, trade balances were not nearly as unfavorable as those which became a habit after the outbreak of the first World War. In 1913, Britain imported more than she exported; but exports covered a larger part of the former. Imports amounted to £769,000,000 and exports to £635,-000,000, leaving an unfavorable balance of no more than £145,000,000.

In that year, income from overseas investments alone, which amounted to £210,000,000, was sufficient to pay for all the surplus imports and to leave a good margin of foreign credit. In addition, shipping netted some £95,000,000, short interest and commissions, another £25,000,000; and we still have not mentioned remittances from British officials in the Empire and income from other sources which probably totaled £25,000,000 more.

Not only was Britain able to pay for the surplus imports, but income from the various services annually left large margins for reinvestment. Britain's international balance of payment showed in 1913 a surplus of £194,000,000—almost double the highest surpluses attained in any year since 1914. As a result, total foreign investments grew rapidly, which made possible the strengthening of imperial bonds. In 1850, Britain's foreign investments totaled less than £150,000,000; thirty years later, however, the figure had jumped to close to £900,000,000; by 1902 the figure had almost trebled, having reached the astronomic total of £2,500,000,000; and when war broke out in 1914, British investments abroad amounted to at least as much as they did in 1930.

Not only, then, was this financial strength sufficient to move mountains of goods to England; enough was left for strengthening constantly the golden threads which bound the vast political and financial empires to London. The World War and subsequent years, we shall see, dealt very serious blows to these empires and weakened then considerably, but still left Britain the greatest financial power in the world.

POLITICS AIDS FINANCE

Finance has no doubt been one of the strongest of imperial ties; on the other hand, existence of the political empire did much to strengthen the financial one and to increase vastly the profits of the latter. If, as was pointed out above, the political empire might not have survived in its present form without the financial reinforcement, it is certain that the financial structure would neither have grown to its immense dimensions nor would it have survived without the political empire. For unlike the United States, which lost heavily upon venturing into the field of foreign investment, British losses were insignificant until 1914, and have been comparatively small even since then.

We can no more than glance at the various financial benefits springing from political power. First of all, British trade has had a privileged position on all empire markets. As could be expected, the privileges have been greatest in the colonies, which took in 1937 about 13 per cent of all British exports. That about 3 per cent of the total world population—and economically among the most backward—took 13 per cent of Britain's exports was not the result of accident. And the net benefits of the colonial trade are greater than one would judge on the basis of these figures; far higher prices in such trade can usually be charged for goods not of first-rate quality. In India, too, British trade enjoyed an exceptional position, while the Dominions granted Britain tariff preference. In the spheres of influence, part of the influence was always directed to gaining trade concessions.

We will not spend time discussing all the benefits that have accrued from the employment of British officials in the governments of the Empire, although remittances from those officials helped Britain's balance of payments by millions of pounds annually; nor will we take up in detail the industrial concessions, benefits to shipping, monopoly on government orders which political control invariably meant—although the share of these and numerous other direct and indirect benefits in helping Britain build and maintain her financial supremacy was very considerable. Rather we will go directly to the major financial benefits in the field of investments. For by concentrating their investments on the areas politically under the control of London, British investors insured their capital in a most effective manner.

Take Egypt as a clear illustration of what political control meant in preserving investments. "The origin of the Egyptian Question" Lord Cromer admitted "was financial." Egypt's indebtedness to French, Belgian, and British bondholders grew very rapidly between 1865 and 1879, although only a fraction of the total debt of close to one hundred million pounds represented honest investment. It is estimated that the Egyptian Treasury received only $225,000,000 out of loans totaling $350,000,000; out of a loan of $160,000,000 made in 1873, only $55,000,000 came into the Treasury. That, however, did not matter. When Egypt became insolvent, England intervened, and took over control of the country, its finances and everything else—and European investors began to breathe easily. Once under the tutelage of Britain, Egypt could no longer default. Only independent countries could permit themselves such a luxury. Between 1884 and 1935 Egypt paid in interest on her public debt a total of $1,055,000,000; she had to use 17 per cent of her total exports in order to pay, but pay she did.

Since the third quarter of the last century Egypt has been a great producer of at least one important raw material—cotton. Every year saw the export of about one hundred twenty-five million dollars worth of cotton, not to mention many other raw materials. Year after year, Egypt lived under one of the lowest standards of living in the world (average per capita income for 1937, according to Sidky Pasha, was $60). So little did Egypt consume that she had between 1884 and 1934 a favorable balance of trade of at least $1,133,-545,000—and probably the balance of trade was much more favorable because her exports are much undervalued in this figure.

Every autumn saw a great wave of gold flowing "into the country to move the cotton crop," as one of the most reliable students of Egyptian economy has written. "The incoming wave of gold" swept "inland from the exporters to the ports to the merchants in the interior and thence to the farmers until it penetrated into the remotest parts of the country." With all this gold coming in, not to mention gold coming in in the form of invisible exports, Egypt should have been rich. But Egypt has not been rich; on the contrary, she has had to resort to additional borrowing almost every year during the last half century. For the gold did not stay long in Egypt; having come in the autumn, the following spring saw the wave returning "from the villages to the towns and thence out of the country in payment for the imports (a small fraction) and of interest on investments from abroad."

More than that: in spite of her large favorable balance of trade during the whole of the last half century, with the exception of the war years, "there was a deficit indicating that the favorable balance of trade was not sufficient to pay the interest due to Egypt's foreign creditors." Consequently, during the pre-war years Egypt went ever further into debt; and after 1915-19, when a net profit was earned, she paid for the deficit by unburdening herself of profits made during the war and by resorting again to borrowing. Instead of raising her standard of living, instead of offering better educational opportunities, instead of providing even remotely adequate social services for her people, Egypt paid and borrowed more in order to pay. But Germany, which was not "protected" by an imperial power, did not curtail any of the social services—and when it could borrow no more, default came very easily. That is how political power has helped the financial empire. The same has been true with regard to every other Empire country. Not a single one has defaulted. Both Australia and New Zealand have made immense sacrifices in order to meet interest and amortization charges falling due in London. At the Ottawa Economic Conference of 1932, the head of the New Zealand delegation reported that, "two years ago, the external debt charges of New Zealand absorbed one-sixth of the value of our exports; this year they are absorbing one-third of the exports. Owing to the fall in export prices about 80 per cent more exports must be sent abroad to pay interest on ... debts than were required in 1928." Other delegations reported similar situations. All the Empire countries, however, tightened their belts during the depression and did not default.

No less important, although normally Empire countries pay lower rates of interest than do countries in no way connected with Britain (a privilege which constitutes one of the most obvious benefits to the Dominions and other territories flowing from the imperial connection), in times of crisis, interest on Empire loans and profits on investments remain much more stable than those placed in foreign countries. Interest on Empire loans, to cite a recent example, changed only slightly between 1928 and 1937: in the former year, the average interest rate was 4.2 which remained unchanged until 1936, and only in the following year did the rate decline to 3.9 per cent as a result of heavy refunding; but interest on foreign loans declined from 5 per cent to 3.5 per cent. The proportion of the nominal value of foreign loans to Britain's total overseas loans decreased from 26 per cent in 1928 to 22.4 per cent in 1934, while income from such investments sank from 29.2 per cent of the total income to 19.7 per cent in 1934. A similar tendency has been observed with regard to investments in foreign corporations as compared with investments in Empire corporations. The former did not stand up nearly as well as the latter both with regard to interest and dividends.

THE EMPIRE AT THE
CROSSROADS

VIII

CHALLENGES TO THE EMPIRE

IN THE PREVIOUS PAGES we have briefly analyzed the structure of the British Empire and the main forces at work. We have seen that the Empire is larger but of a different nature than is commonly supposed. It is larger, because the spheres of influence and the countries of the financial empire have to be included; on the other hand, the territories which are under Great Britain's legal control constitute a small fraction of the total area of the Empire. We have observed, too, that the engineering principles underlying this imperial structure are unlike those of any other empire. In the overwhelmingly larger part, which has also been the most profitable economically—namely, in the Dominions, the spheres of influences, and the countries of the financial empire—Britain has relied for the maintenance of imperial unity, not on force, but on intangible loyalties and common interests. Even in India and the colonies, where force played a decisive role, relations were generally governed by less brutal factors.

As to the dynamics of the Empire, we have seen on the one side the forces operating to solidify the structure; and on the other, those at work to break it up. Racial, economic, and cultural factors operating in both directions were most clearly discernible in the Dominions. In India and the colonies nationalism was emerging as a centrifugal force, the more menacing to imperial unity since the British Empire had become far too large to be held together by brute force. By race and culture Britain had nothing in common with these parts; and everywhere the nationalist movements were beginning to receive impetus from the serious economic and social grievances. As to the last two categories in the imperial structure, their survival was dependent on such peculiar cultural, economic, and political conditions—since military might played a role in only two or three of the territories—that the slightest change in balance was bound to upset them greatly.

The system persisted well enough until 1914. Although the relationship between England and the overwhelming part of the overseas territories was even then much more vague than in all other imperial systems—a situation which in normal times produced such serious defects that most German statesmen including the Kaiser were convinced that the British Empire was no empire at all but an anachronism— events during 1914-18 demonstrated that, based largely on the consent of the governed, the Empire was able to attain a high degree of self-sacrificing co-operation in moments of danger. Far from suffering from lack of clearly defined principles governing interimperial relations, history showed that the British communities were able to work best in an atmosphere of political and legal fogginess. The Dominions then asseverated in a very effective manner their approval of the imperial connection. They joined the mother country in the greatest war in history, and made tremendous sacrifices for the sake of common victory. Even Indian nationalists rushed to the aid of England as did all the colonies, which contributed considerably to the Allied victory.

The war, however, was not to pass without leaving a very profound imprint on the Empire. The forces of disunity gained momentum everywhere, while those operating in the opposite direction, which until 1914 had been strong enough to maintain an effective counterbalance, were everywhere weakened. A profound reaction against the Empire and the whole culture which produced the gigantic world slaughter swept over the Dominions, where the centrifugal forces were immensely strengthened. The colonies began to show unprecedented signs of restlessness; India, more advanced than the Asiatic and African colonies, launched a mighty struggle to win complete home rule. Even greater was the effect of the war on the Near Eastern and other spheres of influence, being far more advanced than India and lacking the reactionary forces so powerful in the latter. Revolts spread from Portugal to Afghanistan; everywhere the foundations of the Empire trembled and threatened to collapse. On top of everything, the war blasted away the economic superstructure which had done so much to hold the Empire together. Britain emerged from the war impoverished and crippled, her foreign trade disappearing, her industry losing in competition with other industrialized countries, her investments vanishing. By 1930, the British Empire seemed to be on its deathbed, and its early demise was freely predicted.

REVOLUTIONS IN CULTURE

It is impossible to understand the menaces which the Empire has confronted since 1920 without an appreciation of the cultural revolution introduced by the last World War. To a very large extent, this revolution underlay and made possible the concrete changes in the imperial structure which took place between 1920 and 1935. Every part has been affected by the changed cultural currents, Great Britain no less than the Dominions, India as well as the more advanced colonies, and above all the spheres of influence, many of which succeeded in breaking away completely from the Empire.

The intellectual cornerstone of the imperial structure was laid many centuries ago. Cromwell shaped it into the form in which it would remain till the end of the World War. "We are a people," wrote he, "with the stamp of God upon us... whose appearance and whose providences are not to be outmatched by any story." This was the crux of the matter: there was that divine confidence in themselves and their mission (*Beruf,* to use Luther's word) that almost made imperialism inevitable. Statesman after statesman repeated Cromwell's words in countless different forms. By the time of Defoe it had already become a dogma which no one questioned; and it never entered the minds of, say, Gladstone or Queen Victoria to doubt that their race was superior to every other race and that the superiority was not accidental but was "entrusted"—a word actually used—with a definite purpose which carried with it certain obligations. Lord Cromer no less than Lord Cecil expressed it: Lord Curzon, really loving Persia, its culture and its people, considered all his life that its occupation by Great Britain would not only be for Persia's own good, but that it was Britain's moral obligation to occupy it. And Sir Arnold Wilson, who was chief of the British Administration in Iraq during the last years of the World War and immediately afterwards, recalls that at that time the words of Cromwell were "my innermost beliefs."

Corollary to the dogma of the "stamp of God upon us" went sublime confidence in the superiority of our Western civilization: that we alone, by the infinite wisdom and mercy of God, have produced a civilization not only superior to all others but eminently suitable for all peoples in all climates and one that ought to be imposed upon them. Those men, whether businessmen selling cotton goods or trinkets, missionaries tramping over desert and jungle to sell their God to the natives, explorers and engineers daring the elements to enlarge our knowledge of the earth and discover natural resources, officials going to administer savage, disease-ridden hinterlands from which many were never to return—all of them were missionaries of the same idea: that Western man and his products are supreme, and shall rule, convert and educate the others. This conviction gave them an all-conquering if smug self-confidence and that Herculean energy which laughs at the impossible and scoffs at the insurmountable. The Victorians knew the meaning of progress; they knew that every additional mile of railroad, every new factory, every additional yard of Manchester fabrics is progress. They did not question its existence; they saw it and created it. It was this spiritual imperialism that made the other possible. England could crush colonial revolts with blood and yet remain satisfied in its good faith because, like the inquisitor of the Middle Ages about to burn backsliders and heretics, it was punishing people for their own good, albeit they were too ignorant to realize it. It was, in fact, fulfilling the glorious work of God and carrying out His mission.

If the ignorant nabob was fully contented with his pile of money and required no further justification for the conquest of India, British publicists and philosophers who created public opinion, as well as ministers who formulated policy,

and parliamentarians—they needed a sufficient justification
for assuming control over foreign territories, in which the
amassment of wealth certainly did not figure very prominently. Their philosophy was based on the ideas indicated
above. It must be borne in mind that the diplomat, the
soldier, the parliamentarian of Great Britain no less than
the publicist, the philosopher, or the great mass of humanity
believed in the rationalization. They not only proclaimed it
for public consumption, but they wrote about it to their
wives and meditated upon it in the privacy of their diaries.
For this ideal they were willing to sacrifice their lives and
to make their homes in savage surroundings.

But the World War brought about an abrupt change in
this cultural atmosphere. When the air cleared of the smoke
and dust of battle, it was not long before observers noticed
new winds blowing over the Western world. The nineteenth
century had come to an end. In 1918 began a new century
which, though yet in its infancy, already promised to be
very much unlike its predecessor. For one thing, war left
the West very tired. The terrific strain of four years of war
gave an irresistible urge to "take things easy," to throw off
responsibilities, to enjoy life while it lasted and not to think
of the morrow which might never come. For another thing,
a strong reaction against our fathers, their ways, their ideas,
their moral codes which had led to the colossal massacre,
inundated the West. Among the things we rebelled against
most was this very thing called imperialism. Once a term to
be gloried in, it now had a decidedly unsavory odor. And
when the statesmen who had made the war gathered at
Versailles to make the peace and attempted to come to terms
with the spirit of the new times by replacing the now de-
tested term "colonies" with the brand-new "mandates," they
found to their great chagrin that the new word deceived no
one; and retreat was inevitable.

Lord Lloyd and others still talked in the flowing sentences
of the bygone century; but they were a small clique clearly
out of touch with the spirit of the times, and the noble lord
became known as "the last of the great Viceroys." A British
imperialist publication still wrote that the "imperial knap-
sack may be heavy, but it must be shouldered"; a former

high commissioner for Iraq, like the prophets of old, delivered impassioned pleas against the "utilitarianism" of British imperial policy, calling for a return to the bold, imaginative, glorious ways of his fathers. All these people, however, were voices crying in the desert, where sand dunes, not mountains, faintly echoed their words. Or there was no echo at all.

In the Dominions these new intellectual currents took a different form. Here the reaction was directed not so much against Western culture as against the Empire and Great Britain and their own conservative statesmen. The view that British "imperialism" was responsible for the gigantic massacre gained ground everywhere and gave birth to very powerful separatist movements. Demands that imperial ties be weakened were heard in all Dominions. The war cabinets rapidly followed each other out of office; the press reflected public opinion by writing in a "never again" strain. Pronouncedly anti-imperial labor parties came to power in the Antipodes Dominions. So determined were the Dominions to avoid being dragged into future British wars that, with unanimous voice, they set themselves to tear up the last legal ties binding them to the mother country.

It was on the dark races, however, that the war was to have the greatest effect. As was to be expected, not all colonial countries were influenced to the same extent by these ideas. Most Asiatic colonies and all African ones were too backward to know what was happening in the world. Yet even in the backwoods of Asia and the jungles of Africa new whispers made themselves heard, which spread farther afield as the years went by. And gradually these new ideas began to influence the ideas and deeds of the multitude, which became less amenable to imperialist rule. If the West was no longer fit for imperialist rule, the East ceased to be safe for it.

First of all, in the hot-house of war and fertilized by European propaganda, the nationalist plant grew more rapidly than anyone had expected. Nationalism, no longer confined to a small upper class, became a force to be reckoned with. Wilson's Fourteen Points had a mighty influence. Ibn Saud told Ameen Rihani in 1922 that to Wilson goes "the credit for awakening the small oppressed nations.

Wilson showed them the way to freedom and independence. He has infused, especially into the people of the East, a new spirit." Every patriot from Siam to Angora would have repeated the identical words. Secondly, by sidetracking Europe's whole industrial plant to produce armaments, the war gave a strong stimulus to industry in the overseas parts of the Empire. A new class of manufacturers sprang up, the economic interests of which were directly opposed to the policies fathered by the imperialist nation. Above all, the strain and stress of these years, when the world turned into a huge boiling caldron, produced a profound change in that most intangible of all things on earth, but nonetheless real for all of that, the *"Weltanschauung"*—which might be defined as the sum total of one's emotional and intellectual adjustment to the world around one.

How it happened may be difficult to explain, but it is a fact that, as war raged through Europe, the colonial world became conscious of itself. The next step, desire to shape its future with its own hands, to lead a life unhindered by foreign controls, was inevitable. The dark races also "found out" the Europeans; they ceased to respect the white man. This is the root of the matter. They no longer believed that "the stamp of God [is] upon us" any more than it is upon them. They saw Western nations fighting a war exceeding in its brutality and madness anything they had ever done; they seized upon books written by Westerners for Western consumption showing the rottenness of Western civilization and read them with the greatest avidity. At the same time they saw themselves constantly improving, gaining in education and wealth.

SUBVERSIVE NATIONALISM

"Our flag is our Color"—this became the slogan of rebellious Africa and Asia. "The Blacks have slept long. But beware! Those who have slept long and soundly...will not easily fall back to sleep again," exclaimed a black at a Congress of Colonial Peoples of Asia and Africa held in Brussels in 1927.

Far from accepting meekly British domination, as it had done until the end of the first World War, the Colonial

Empire suddenly sprang into consciousness early in the twenties and refused to settle down. From the Mediterranean to the Indian Ocean and the coasts of the American continent revolutionary nationalism made its appearance, and again and again challenged British rule. Hardly a year passed between 1920 and 1935 without its quota of rebellions; every colony and dependency was affected by these developments. Although in only a few instances were the revolutionary forces sufficiently strong to be a serious menace to the Empire, their mere existence indicated whither the wind was blowing; for the number of rebellions, and their seriousness, kept on increasing. A new threat to the Empire arose when colonial labor began to show discontent. It could not carry through a socialist revolution; but British administrators trembled when black laborers whispered among themselves the new slogan—"Time longer dan rope." They could not but wonder whether this part of the imperial structure, which had seemed so solid only a few years before, would also crumble under the impact of the new forces that were shattering the other parts.

In the Mediterranean, both Cyprus and Malta raised the banner of rebellion. The majority of the population of the former being Greek in descent and sentiment, public opinion veered strongly in favor of unification with the mother land. Economic stagnation gave point to the nationalist sentiment, which crystalized in 1931 in the form of a first-rate revolt. Malta, too, staged an uprising, which was suppressed only by the arrival of British battleships. Five major revolts took place in Palestine, each more serious than the previous one. In 1920, 1921, again in 1929, 1933, and 1936 the Arabs rose in rebellion and defied imperial troops. Thousands of people were killed; hundreds of houses were blown to splinters; effective government disappeared from large areas.

A strong nationalist movement in Iraq flared up as soon as the war ended and continued to be a source of trouble. Crisis followed crisis. The British authorities had to retreat from one position after another. Four or five treaties were negotiated with Iraq between 1922 and 1931, each giving greater concessions than the previous ones, till complete independence had to be granted.

Insurgent movements arose also in Africa, and nationalism became a force there, too. The movements were distinctly anti-white and anti-imperialist. Some took a religious form. The Watch Tower Movement used Biblical texts in a struggle against the whites. Its preachers organized strikes and pitched battles against white settlers and tax collectors. A commission which was sent to investigate one serious disturbance found "that the teachings and literature of the Watch Tower bring civil and spiritual authority...into contempt; that it is a dangerously subversive movement; and that it is an important predisposing course of the recent disturbances." The Israelite Movement, founded after the war by a native "inspired by God" to lead the Bantu against the whites, spread like wildfire and brought about a series of uprisings. Another commission reported that "there is a growth of race consciousness with its natural outcome of social and political aspirations among the natives.... These pseudo-religious movements usually begin as a revolt against white missionary domination, and later take on a more definitely anti-European attitude...."

Of far greater importance were the outright political organizations. The South African National Congress, modeled after the Indian prototype proclaimed its aim: "to encourage mutual understanding and to bring together into common action as one political people all tribes and claims ...and by means of combined effort and united political organization to defend their freedom, rights, and privileges." The Independent African National Congress, consisting of educated youth, became active in arousing the natives to realization of their social, economic, and political condition. Organizations like the Aborigines' Rights Protection Society in the Gold Coast sprang up, which for the first time in history dared to defend native land rights, and prevented transference of ownership to the British Crown. They put up a strong fight to defend civil right and to prevent enactment of tax laws falling heavily upon the poorest section of the population. Of course, despite these movements, African nationalism did not become a menace to the Empire, and the revolts were not such as to threaten its existence. But the spread of education awakened desire for wider political liberty, and the influence of the educated youth, though few in number, increased.

Ceylon, where British traders and administrators have been active for centuries, also became restless. Although nationalism did not progress there as far as in India, a movement aiming to give back "Ceylon to the Sinhalese" struck roots, and the white traders and the other foreign communities became restive. To come to terms with Sinhalese nationalism Britain decided to make concessions; but the formation of a series of pan-Sinhalese ministries showed whither the wind was blowing. The native press made itself the herald of an advanced nationalism, arousing the people against British exploitation, discrimination in government employment, lack of educational opportunities, etc.

Prestige of the white man declined in the Malay States, and there also a class of native intellectuals came into being. The natives began to feel that they could stand on their feet without foreign assistance. Faced with growing popular opposition, the British tried to rely more and more on the native princes: "to me the maintenance of the position, authority, and prestige of the Malay rulers is a cardinal point of policy," the Under-Secretary of State for the Colonies wrote after a visit. These tactics, however, only served to antagonize further the nationalists. Too weak to demand complete independence, they began to agitate for more local autonomy and greater social reforms than the British considered prudent to allow.

The rise of colonial labor was a threat to the established order potentially more serious even than colonial nationalism. Everywhere colored labor became bitterly anti-imperialist in theory and practice. Strikes took place with increasing frequency; labor riots were reported from nearly every colony; even attempts to form labor parties were not lacking. As Colonial Secretary Malcolm MacDonald admitted, "labor in the Colonies is become more articulate. Labor leaders are demanding for their followers the best conditions of work and wages that local industries can afford. The situation is sometimes delicate."

The demands of labor—wages, hours, better conditions of work—hit at the economic foundations of the imperialist system. Before long, moreover, the demands grew. Labor begins by demanding the right to strike and to organize, and then proceeds to use the organization as a weapon against political oppression. The British had learned in India that it was not the eloquent intellectuals who were the menace; it was only when these created a mass organization and aligned themselves with the trade unions that they became a serious threat. In Palestine, too, the movement launched by city intellectuals assumed threatening dimensions only when workers and peasants became active in the struggle.

Colonial labor was ignorant, superstitious, and unskilled. Illiteracy was a more serious handicap than one in the literate West can imagine. Labor leaders were primitive and many were corruptible. Groping in the darkness, colonial labor moved clumsily. It had not yet learned how to keep up a steady struggle for distant ends, and it could often be appeased by a few nice words. It was mercurial, moody, undisciplined. These weaknesses played into the hands of the whites, who knew how to exploit them to the utmost.

But objective reality did not permit colored labor to remain static. The miserable social conditions analyzed in a preceding chapter naturally resulted in rising tides of dissatisfaction. Not only did the new cultural influences make colonial labor—for the first time in history—conscious of the evils, but the expansion of industry, mining, and plantations brought together great masses of workers and gave labor unprecedented opportunities for concerted action. Incomplete figures indicate that after the war at least five million laborers became dependent on wages for livelihood. Explosions became inevitable.

The emotionalism and instability of colonial workers produced an amazing degree of solidarity and made possible strikes which perhaps would not have taken place had they stopped to calculate more coolly their chances for success. Strikes involving thousands of workers broke out because one worker was fired unjustly; and the low regard for human life characteristic of colonial society made them less afraid to embark on bitter struggles. The murder of a few troublemakers did not always spell the collapse of a strike. Far from being permanently terrorized by police brutality, such ex-

periences gave labor new conceptions of strength and served
to solidify its ranks.

Here is a typical call to war of colonial workers. It was
found posted up at a copper mine in Northern Rhodesia a
few weeks before the outbreak of a strike at the end of April,
1935, which cost many native lives:

Listen to this all you who live in the country, think well how
they treat us and to ask for a land. Do we live in good treatment, no; therefore let us ask one another and remember this
treatment. Because we wish on the day of 29th April, every person not to go to work, he who will go to work, and if we see
him it will be a serious case. Know how they cause us to suffer,
they cheat us for money, they arrest us for loafing, they perse-
cute us and put us in gaol for tax. What reason have we done?
Secondly do you not wish to hear these words, well listen, this
year of 1935, if they will not increase us more money stop paying tax, do think they can kill you, no. Let us encourage
surely you will see that God will be with us. See how we suffer
with the work and how we are continually reviled and beaten
underground. Many brothers of us die for 22s. 6d., is this money
that we should lose our lives for. He who cannot read should
tell his companion that on the 29th April not to go to work.
These words do not come from here, they come from the wisers
who are far away and enable to encourage us. That all. Hear
well if it is right let us do. We are all of the Nkana. Africans—
Men and Women.

A detailed account of labor movements in the colonies is
impossible here. Suffice it to mention that strikes appeared
even in sleepy Kidah and Johore (Unfederated Malay
States); picketing and even sit-down strikes invaded many
colonies. Militancy having been forced on them by the
authorities, strikers actually learned how to use force when
necessary—a totally new development. More important,
unions were organized which took root in nearly every dependency including Ceylon and the Malay States. A young
native of Nyasaland, Africa, with very great organizing
ability and political acumen, one Clemens Kadolie, organized
in 1919 the Industrial and Commercial Union (I. C. U.)
which in a few years grew to contain no less than 100,000
members, and became a political power of the first magnitude. The trade union of Gombia, known as Bathurst Trade

Union, carried on a number of bitter strikes, some of which were crushed by merciless police terror.

In the early thirties it became obvious that Britain confronted in the colonies a choice of two alternatives. She could continue along the path followed in the past and pile up new instruments of oppression, legal and mechanical. But coercion is financially costly, and oppression has to keep pace with the increasing discontent. Political and economic Bourbonism gives birth to terrorist movements, as in India and Palestine, not easy to crush. Underground labor organization had appeared already in some colonies, and their menace reached the floor of the House of Commons. On the other hand, the British government could attempt to stem the tide of revolt by providing constitutional means for expression of grievances and by making the necessary economic and political concessions. Never before had the colonial empire been in as turbulent a state, and its early disintegration was commonly predicted.

THE REVOLT OF INDIA

During the war of 1914-18 India had co-operated loyally with Britain. Not only was the peacetime Indian army of three hundred thousand placed for service overseas at the expense of the Indian government, but almost a million and a half more men were raised and sent to far-flung imperial fronts. India made a free-will offering of $500,000,000 towards the cost of the war; it accepted further obligations to the tune of many tens of millions; $375,000,000 was subscribed for war loans. Nationalist leaders toured the country to raise recruits; Mr. Gandhi himself formed volunteer ambulance corps.

But not many weeks elapsed after the Armistice before a hurricane of angry resentment broke out, which spread rapidly over the whole continent. British goods were boycotted; strikes were staged; days of national mourning were proclaimed and observed; above all, Gandhi launched a movement of passive resistance to, and non-co-operation with, the British authorities, for which the latter were completely unprepared. With mutinies they knew how to deal; but what is one to do with saints and passive demonstrators?

The Amritsar massacre was an indication of how close the British came to losing their normal self-control. General Dyer's order to fire into a meeting held in an enclosed area, when 379 were killed and 1,208 persons were wounded, was an act of sheer desperation—an expression of defeat. Even the police could not be isolated from the national movement: the Simon Commission admitted "that only the influence of the higher officers . . . prevented them from resigning in a body. This incident shows how near matters went to a complete dissolution of law and order." Within a few months India was stirred as never before in her long history; the whole continent with its half a million villages seethed with mass discontent. What had happened?

First, the war had had an even more profound effect upon India than upon the rest of the colonial world. Allied propaganda about fighting German militarism to make the world safe for democracy, liberty, and self-determination for oppressed nations did not pass without leaving a solid influence on the mass of the population. The inevitable economic dislocation, aggravated by the catastrophic fall in agricultural prices after the armistice, produced unemployment and starvation, the psychological effects of which were sharpened by a series of plagues which killed millions. The Amritsar massacre, the caliphate agitation among Moslems helped stir the already sorely grieved masses. Second, new men mainly of the middle classes had begun to influence the national movement; for them the lucrative jobs provided by the Montagu-Chelmsford Reforms for Indians of good birth meant nothing, and they despaired of compromises with Imperialism. Failure of the old nationalists to wrest significant concessions decided them to widen the base of the movement by associating the masses in the struggle, and to make it less exclusively political.

Triumph of this new movement was symbolized by the emergence of Mohandas K. Gandhi. Gandhi did not think in terms of jobs; he was interested in India, her culture, her people. He was not exclusively concerned with politics; the plight of the untouchables, the sufferings of the workers and ryots, the frightful communal divisions—these questions affected him and these he set out to solve; and the masses responded. They trusted Gandhi as they had not trusted any other leader before; his idealism stirred their imagination; his language of self-sacrifice and non-violence struck deep chords. His associates in the struggle were men like Pandit Motilal Nehru and his son Jawaharlal Nehru, Subhas Chandra Bose and others, whose thoughts moved along social lines. They went to the workers and the peasants preaching the connection between political liberation and economic and cultural reform. Although the National Congress retained its political character, an invisible bridge connected it with labor and peasant movements.

Indian labor suddenly gained consciousness and began putting forth demands. Close to 400 strikes took place in 1921, involving 600,000 workers and a loss of seven million working days. There were demands for shorter hours, better working conditions, higher wages. Labor learned to fight for itself—a lesson that was not to be forgotten. In 1928 almost thirty-two million working days were lost during strikes, and twelve million in the following year. An even greater menace to the existing order emerged with the peasant movement. It is fairly easy to cope with disturbances in cities; but what could the British authorities do against the peasantry spread over the whole vast continent? Millions of soldiers would be required for coping with such rebellions. When the peasantry responded to Gandhi's no-tax campaign the government was shaken to its foundation.

Eventually the British succeeded in breaking the back of India's first major revolt, though not without the help of Gandhi, who called off the campaign on the appearance of violence within his own ranks. But victories of this kind are always Pyrrhic; and it was obvious that a new battle would be fought. In reality, victory had been with the nationalists; for the masses had entered the struggle. And the eight years of truce which followed the first mass upsurge were far from peaceful. Terrorism was rampant; the Congress followed an obstructionist policy and gave very little rest to the British authorities.

Clearly a new India had emerged from the war—an India which the British did not know and could not understand. Communism made its appearance, not only among the intellectuals but even among workers. Government terror of the worst kind forced the movement underground, but it did not perish. Later the government moved against all workers' organizations, which served to increase popular bitterness. Imperial bonds were cracking rapidly.

Appointment of the all-British reactionary Simon Commission, whose report went to infinite lengths to emphasize India's woes while dismissing with contempt the new nationalism, hastened the day of the second major revolt. Again Gandhi issued a call for passive resistance and civil disobedience; and India responded wholeheartedly. In their tens of thousands peasants flocked to listen to Gandhi, Nehru, and other progressive leaders who toured the country; oaths of solidarity and non-violence were taken by millions. In the cities the Congress ruled without challenge. A boycott of British goods was effectively enforced by volunteers who would stand in front of non-co-operating shops. H. N. Brailsford, who was then in India, reported that "By the autumn of 1930 imports of cotton-piece goods had dropped between a third and a fourth of what they were in the same months of the previous year. Imports of cigarettes had fallen in value to a sixth of the old figure. Sixteen British-owned mills in Bombay had been closed down, and thirty-two thousand textile workers were idle." Peaceful strikes were staged almost every day; hartels, or days of national mourning, drew tens of thousands into the streets or completely off the streets, as the Congress ordered. For the first time women emerged from their centuries-old seclusion, and took part in the movement. They were among the strikers, among the demonstrators, and with the Congress volunteers threw themselves in front of passing vehicles carrying foreign goods. Gandhi's march to the sea to manufacture salt in defiance of the salt tax was a stroke of genius, dramatizing the movement and rallying millions to its support.

It is difficult to explain to those who have not been in the East the magnitude of the revolution that took place. More important than all the acts of defiance and rebellion was the new spirit that descended upon the masses of ryots. That pride of imperialists—the British policeman—ceased to be a demi-god and became a brutal oppressor whom tens of thousands were defying every day. Lowly peasants and workers ceased crouching before British officials and now looked them straight in the eyes. A new spirit of self-confidence descended upon the land. Caste barriers, untouchability, even religious antagonisms were melting. It is impossible to estimate the importance of Gandhi's campaign against opium, which resulted, according to C. F. Andrews, in a drop of consumption of nearly 25 per cent in six months.

The revolt was of course crushed. Not only was military might on the side of the British; more important was support to their cause rendered by India's own weaknesses. Misery, ignorance, lack of physical vigor, communal troubles, the reactionary princes—all these drove through Indian society like the four horsemen of the Apocalypse. Yet to reassert its authority Britain had to strain all its resources to the utmost, and had to resort to the worst kind of fascist tyranny. Hundreds of thousands of men and women—even children —were thrown into jail, where, according to English reports, "shocking" conditions prevailed. Lathi charges were almost daily occurrences, and the violence of the police grew with their desperation. Heads were smashed, limbs were paralyzed by the blows of the cavalry which used to charge suddenly upon perfectly peaceful groups. Not a trace of civil liberties remained: the policemen ceased even to carry numbers to escape being brought to book in courts of justice. In the villages they resorted to the diabolical tactics of introducing "criminal tribes" to purchase land and belongings of the peasants who refused to pay taxes; whippings and beatings were visited on thousands. Finally the government outlawed the Congress; all its leaders, including the Mahatma and Nehru, were sent to jail.

Lord Irwin in the Viceregal Palace knew that the Empire was at bay. For the first time since Clive's memorable victory, British authority was slipping; and no amount of violence would restore its vigor. Rather, violence hastened the day of doom; for when imperial rulers lose their "mystique," their day is gone. To crush the second revolt in a dozen years had been much more difficult than the first; what would be the results of the next effort? A "next" there was bound to be—unless constructive measures were

taken to forestall it. Could it be forestalled without under-
mining the whole imperial structure? Dark indeed was the
prospect during the early years of the last decade—infinitely
darker than at any previous time. India, the gold mine of
the Empire for so many centuries—was it to become the
Empire's graveyard?

FLIGHT OF THE DOMINIONS

The Dominions and England "are autonomous communities within the British Empire," wrote Lord Balfour in
1926, "equal in status, in no way subordinate one to another
in any respect of their domestic or external affairs, though
united by a common allegiance to the Crown, and freely
associated as members of the British Commonwealth of Nations." This typically British formula with its meticulous
emphasis, on the one side, on equality and freedom among
the self-governing Dominions and on unity through the
Crown and "free" association, on the other, was to solve
all the conflicts at work. Rabid nationalists of the Union
of South Africa and Eire were eager to parade at every turn
the untarnished nationhood of their countries? Of course
you are free and autonomous, said the British government.
New economic conditions demand that you conduct your
own foreign affairs? Of course you have the right to do so.
But the Empire must be preserved, asserted English imperialists, who were seconded, not without numerous qualifications, by the Britons of Australia, New Zealand, and of the
other Dominions. The Balfour formula satisfied this demand
as well.

Yet, laconic formulas could not camouflage the real forces
which operated between 1920 and 1935, not toward greater
unity and co-operation, but in the very opposite direction.
Although powers were granted to Dominion governments
of which no pre-war statesman dreamed, flight from unity assumed a constantly accelerating momentum; and the day
of the complete dissolution of the Dominion Empire—or,
at the very least, the loss of two or three of its most important members—seemed to be constantly approaching.

That slowly, quietly, without the fanfare of publicity and
emotional oratory new ties were being forged to replace the

old ones was not noticed in the universal applause which greeted each new step of the Dominions toward complete independence. Those new ties have been of a subtle character, as thin as spider webs and invisible in the powerful spotlight of political propaganda. Yet the fact remained that the main tendencies during this period were toward separation, independence, complete and undiluted equality, local control of all phases of national life, including those which had been reserved to the control of the Imperial Parliament.

Forces of separation had of course operated since the middle of the last century; but until after the World War the counterforces had been strong enough to preserve some equilibrium. Now the former became stronger than ever; the latter weaker. Before 1914 Britain had been able to point to concrete disadvantages which the Dominions would suffer from separation; and some years after the crisis had passed Sir John Simon gave the classic reply when questioned in Parliament about Dominion right to secession that one cannot question a "man's right to cut his own throat." Between 1920 and 1935, however, it was by no means obvious to Dominion statesmen that secession would mean cutting their own throats. Everywhere, including Australia and New Zealand, the forces of autonomy were gaining the upper hand, while her economic decline made Great Britain less able to put up a strong opposition. One of London's chief whips, its control of credit, shriveled rapidly as New York emerged as the financial center of the world. Between 1925 and 1930 America's export of capital was almost double that of England; and at last, after the onset of the world depression, Britain had to give way. The changed relationship between Great Britain and the Dominions received concrete expression in the form of the Statute of Westminster, which became law on December 11, 1931.

Time has somewhat attenuated the rigors of the change introduced by this law. "The Statute is not a revolutionary measure," wrote A. B. Keith in 1938. "It represents the outcome of a long process of development." In 1930, the chief actors felt differently. Few could see how the Empire could continue under the new legal arrangement: many saw in it the *coup de grace* to the whole imperial structure—for what is called "the might of the British Empire," whether economically or politically, is due to the connection with the Dominions far more than to the existence of the colonies. If the statute has not produced the radical results which many foresaw, that is only due to the sudden emergence of the fascist menace.

Nevertheless, the Statute brought forth concrete changes which gave the Dominion Empire a new aspect. All the changes, needless to add, were in the direction of greater independence; every year witnessed curtailments in the legal rights of the Parliament at Westminster, and in the power of the King. One Dominion after another made good its claim to complete independence of all British authority.

Shipping offers a good example of the effects of the Statute. Until 1931 only the British Parliament had the right to legislate on all matters pertaining to shipping other than that engaged in coastal trade of the Dominions. This meant that ships belonging to Dominion concerns had to submit to British laws, while the Dominions had to accord British ships engaged in trade along their coasts equal treatment with their own. Though Dominion shipping interests had for long protested against this situation, Britain, realizing the vast economic and political significance of shipping for preservation of imperial unity, refused to make concessions. But clamor for revision gained ground in all the Dominions during the postwar years; and Britain had to give way on this, one of the last vestiges of imperial control. In 1931 the Dominions obtained full jurisdiction over all shipping matters.

The controversy over shipping involved the far wider question of "repugnancy." The supremacy of the British Parliament had been an accepted principle since 1865, when the Colonial Laws Validity Act was passed providing that any law or provision enacted by a colonial parliament is null and void if "repugnant" to the law of England. The wide extent of this provision was later circumscribed, yet its effects in restricting the powers of the Dominion Parliament can be readily appreciated, and the Dominions had long since demanded removal of this brand of inferiority. In one mighty sweep this was now done. The great significance of this step became evident when the vehemently nationalist government in Eire used the new status of its Parliament to abolish agreements with England. This departure was pregnant with grave possibilities: Boer nationalists made attempts to use it, although on dubious legal grounds, for severing the last vestiges of connection with the Empire and with the British Crown.

Nor has the Crown escaped the devastating effects of the new tendencies. Once a very real power, the Crown degenerated to an influence and later became a symbol; now even its symbolic value for unity was seriously impaired. The ancient right of appeal to the King for redress against injustices of colonial courts was abolished in Canada and the Irish Free State, and in the other Dominions was allowed, or compelled, to lapse into abeyance. The Crown lost also its traditional prerogative of mercy. In the Dominions, the Governor General as representative of the King ceased to exercise personal discretion in applying this right. The last time when a Governor General exercised power of any sort was in 1925, when Lord Byng refused to grant a dissolution of Parliament demanded by a new Canadian cabinet. Since 1930 the King chooses his representative on the advice of the Dominion concerned, and he must act entirely as advised by the local government.

The changed position of the Governor General of course bespeaks the new independence from all British influence won by the Dominions. As late as 1926 the Imperial Conference still admitted the right of the British Government to advise Governors on constitutional changes and other questions involving empire-wide interests. The latter's power was to be expressed through his right to reserve bills for signification of the Royal pleasure. The British Government naturally used this power with extreme moderation; yet a backdoor for influence and in certain circumstances control was left open. Since 1930, however, it has become clearly established that the Governor General in no way represents the British Government and reservation of bills can take place only at the request of the Dominion Government.

More than that: the Dominions put forward the view that the King's decision on reserved bills must be guided not by the advice of the government at London, but by the Dominion authorities. As usual, Eire and the Union carried matters farther than other Dominions and officially abolished the right to reserve parliamentary measures.

One of the most important bonds was snapped with the enactment of new nationality legislation. Under the old imperial law, the British Parliament had the right to determine what persons should be regarded as British subjects; and no distinction was drawn between residents of one part of the Commonwealth or another. Surely, if empire meant anything at all it certainly meant common nationality. But the very fundamental implications of this doctrine made the anti-imperialists the more determined to abrogate it at the first opportunity, which came with enactment of the Statute of Westminster. In 1935 the Dail refused to recognize the existence of a common nationality, or even dual nationality as a British subject and as an Irish citizen. The new law knows only of Irish citizens and non-citizens, making no provisions for members of the British Commonwealth. The Boer nationalists have been clamoring for similar legislation in the Union.

How utterly devoid of meaning the imperial connection tended to become is illustrated best by the controversy over the creation of an Imperial Tribunal for adjustment of differences between the various governments of the Commonwealth. Clearly there was a need for a tribunal to arbitrate in disputes between members of the Commonwealth, instead of leaving matters to *ad hoc* negotiations; and exponents of the imperial idea did not cease demanding its creation to give visible expression of the special relationship existing between the members of the Commonwealth. Yet the mere fact that pro-Empire circles favored the proposal sufficed for Eire and the Union nationalists to oppose it violently, and they succeeded in preventing its establishment. The controversy revealed, better than any other event, how agreement had become impossible among the so-called "component parts of the Empire" even on a matter of crucial importance.

CONTRACTING SHADOWS

Never since the phrase "sphere of influence" emerged to plague European diplomacy was Britain's sphere—the Outer Empire—so large and so completely under control as in 1919. Every territory which radical imperialists of the previous century had coveted and which had seemed beyond reach, now lay at her feet. But before the magnificent structure could be consolidated revolutionary cataclysms began to rock it, and one part after another collapsed about the heads of the ambitious builders. Caught unprepared, the British stood witless, too paralyzed to act. They blustered, they threatened; Lord Curzon and Lloyd George, the Foreign Minister and the Premier, thundered about the might of the British Empire. But they did nothing. They surrendered and retreated, not in very good order. One retreat followed another; at no time did they stop long enough to dig in.

Many factors contributed to this debacle. There was, first, the dawning force of Asiatic nationalism. Everywhere, as we have seen, the war stimulated a cultural revolution; but nowhere as powerfully as in the "spheres of influence," which were culturally more advanced than India and the colonies. Some of these territories—Turkey, Egypt, Persia—had developed during long contact with Western culture an intelligentsia which took its ideas about liberty, independence, self-determination from the French Revolution; in other areas, British imperialism had not had the chance to strike deep roots. Second, the reaction in England against imperialism was given impetus by the clamor of the conservative press for financial retrenchment. In their opinion Mesopotamia, Turkey and all the rest were not worth the money that was being spent to hold them down. Lord Curzon could haughtily scorn the agitation to scuttle out "bag and baggage"; eventually, however, the government had to bend before the storm and to execute a retreat along the whole line. Third, the united front of the Allied Powers did not survive the war. Old jealousies and rivalries came to the surface almost the moment hostilities ceased. France was suspicious of Britain, the latter suspected France, and lesser allies played one against the other as suited their interests.

At that very moment, finally, the Bolsheviks who had come to power in Russia turned to the East to attack the mighty Empire from the rear. One of their first acts after seizing power was to issue a "Proclamation to the Oppressed Peoples of the East," inviting them to throw off the yoke of imperialism. Echoes of the Soviets spread as far as Iraq, Egypt, and Siam; but it was in the buffer states between Russia and the British Empire that Soviet influence helped overthrow completely Britain's settlement. Soviet aid helped the Ataturk to rebuild nationalist Turkey; Soviet support became a powerful factor with the new regimes in Persia and Afghanistan; and Moscow was instrumental in bringing these three together in an alliance frankly directed against "European Imperialism." Let us see how these forces worked themselves out.

Egypt had not made serious trouble before 1914; now she wasted no time before rejecting the protectorate forced on her during the war. Zaghlul Pasha, eloquent leader of the young nationalism, informed the British High Commissioner on the second day after the armistice of his intention to proceed to London to demand of the British Government nothing less than complete independence and the evacuation of British troops. Monster petitions empowering Zaghlul to speak for Egypt obtained about half a million signatures before the police could confiscate them. Anti-British demonstrations broke out when London refused to take seriously the new spirit spreading over Egypt. The hand of the British military descended heavily. Egypt, however, showed itself able to rise to the situation. Deportation of Zaghlul and three colleagues to Malta produced more demonstrations which soon developed into a rebellion of no mean proportions. Dozens of people were killed; hundreds were imprisoned. Students ceased to attend classes; lawyers absented themselves from courts; government officials stayed home, leaving the British officials to carry on the administration. For the first time, natives could not be found to form a ministry!

Confronted with so much opposition, Britain decided to compromise. Zaghlul was released and invited to London to negotiate a treaty which would acknowledge Egypt's independence—within limits. Egypt had become too important economically and strategically to be relinquished at the asking. But Zaghlul thought the British minimum demands far too high, and negotiations broke down. Riots in Egypt. British troops had to patrol the streets of Cairo and of other cities. Communications had to be guarded. Another attempt at negotiations in 1921 ended with no more success. Again riots. Englishmen were killed by Egyptians; many more Egyptians were killed by British troops; there was martial law and the usual clashes, trials, and prison sentences.

Suspecting now that the new nationalism might be more than a passing whim, Britain issued in 1922 a "Declaration of Independence" announcing that "The British Protectorate is terminated, and Egypt is declared to be a sovereign State." However, a) the security of imperial communications in Egypt; b) the defense of Egypt against foreign aggression or interference; c) the protection of minorities and of foreign interests; and d) the Sudan—all were "absolutely reserved to the discretion of His Majesty's Government until such a time as . . . by free discussion and friendly accommodation on both sides" agreement shall be reached. Surely, the British thought, the pleasant words of the first part of the formula would suffice for the naïve Oriental politicians. Egypt was not impressed. It saw that the "absolute reservation" of every vital point made independence meaningless. Violence continued. An election showed whether the Wafd —Zaghlul and his fanatic friends—or the accommodating moderate politicians expressed best the will of the country. Anti-British feeling rose to boiling pitch; the police found itself unable to cope with the rising tide of political murders, which culminated with the assassination of Sir Lee Stark, Governor General of the Sudan and Sirdar of the Egyptian army.

Britain then hit hard, and Egypt was muzzled. Not for long. Though a "strong man"—the redoubtable Lord Lloyd —now came to the Residency, Egypt showed clearly that it would not settle down to the status assigned to it. Government crises followed in monotonous rhythm; waves of popular discontent swept over Egypt periodically; troops and men-of-war had to be dispatched constantly. Subsequent attempts at negotiations ended without results. Britain granted more real independence at every successive attempt at negotiations; but Egyptian demands also grew. By 1935 the situation had become thoroughly unsatisfactory. British troops were of course still in the country and British officials in government offices; yet the number of the latter was decreasing constantly and real authority and influence was rapidly slipping from their hands. Egypt looked on them as alien usurpers, and refused to be ordered around. And it was perfectly obvious that Egypt was only biding her time—waiting for the Empire to get entangled in a dangerous crisis, when it would strike again and strike hard.

Equally disastrous were postwar developments in the other parts of the Outer Empire. Britain's firm control over Portugal's economic life and over her African colonies prevented the anti-British reaction that swept over the country immediately after the armistice from achieving full expression. Yet even there the movement away from the British orbit could not be checked; and it attained unprecedented force when Dr. Salazar made himself local dictator. As Minister of Finance and still more after seizing the Premiership in 1932, Salazar followed a consistently anti-British policy. German, French, and American capital was introduced; Britain's commercial hold over the country was deliberately weakened; he reorganized the army to drive out the last vestiges of British influence, which until 1920 had been especially strong in the general staff. Many of the highest officers, known for their pro-British views, were replaced by fascists; and for the first time in centuries, Portugal objected to the sending of a British military mission to strengthen relations between the two countries; and when the British persisted, the Mission was isolated in Lisbon. Although still tied to Britain by treaty, Salazar consistently followed an anti-British policy in his foreign relations. He set out to create a "Peninsula Alliance" with Spain for the purpose of "expelling foreign interests." At first Salazar hoped to place the Peninsula bloc under the tutelage of Italy; later, the upswing in Nazi power convinced him that Germany might be the better protector. To symbolize the revolt against Britain Salazar went to the extent of refusing to receive the admiral of a British fleet which he could not prevent from steaming into Portuguese waters on a "friendly" mission.

More disastrous were the developments in Turkey, Greece, and Persia, where by the end of the third decade nothing remained of Britain's traditional influence and power. A nationalist revolution such as the East had never seen before swept over Turkey. Determined to reconstruct a modern state from the ashes of the polyglot Ottoman Empire, the young nationalists, led by Mustafa Kemal—the Ataturk, Father of Turks, as he later became known—set themselves to expel all the obstructing foreign influences, the most important of which, they recognized, was Britain. Bands of patriots were organized which, against all odds, swooped down upon the British-supported Greek invaders, and in a series of spectacular victories drove them together with the British out of the country. Britain supported the Caliph-Sultan, who had become its tool, and he was deprived of power and finally expelled; Britain had tried to perpetuate its domination by inflicting the Sèvres Treaty, which the nationalist government flatly rejected. Aided by Moscow, with whom Mustafa Kemal established close relations as early as 1921, which, to the great chagrin of London, he was to maintain for the rest of the decade, the Turks could afford to disregard British protests, threats, and financial influence. At the Lausanne Conference Lord Curzon threatened and banged the table; but the shrewd Turkish representative played a game of patience, and in the end Britain was compelled to sign a treaty such as Turkey wanted.

How far from the days before 1914, when the British Ambassador in Constantinople practically ruled the Ottoman Empire! For the first time in centuries, Turkey, not Britain, determined what kind of a treaty was to regulate relations between the two. Indeed, seeing in the British their greatest foe, the nationalists came to co-operate with all the enemies of Britain, and especially with the Soviets, whose spearhead in the Mediterranean they became. Moscow sponsored an alliance between Turkey, Persia, and Afghanistan specifically directed against Western—that is,

British—imperialism; the Turks refused to accept Britain's Mosul settlement; they played havoc with British financial and commercial interests, the value of which almost reached zero during those years.

Identical were developments in Persia, another old and important member of the Outer Empire. It, too, revolted against British domination and proceeded to assert its independence. Hardly had the ink dried on the Anglo-Persian treaty of 1919 than the Soviet Government expressed its readiness to sign a treaty with Persia "on the principle of free accord and mutual respect of peoples." As a token of sincerity it relinquished all Tsarist concessions. The Soviet-Persian Alliance established a precedent of vast importance. For the first time in decades an Asiatic country was given a non-imperialist treaty. In the following year, the Soviet fleet bombed Denikin and the British out of Enzeli. Faced with these difficulties, the British decided on the "master stroke" of—as one foreign diplomat reported to his government—installing new men in Teheran who would accept their tutelage. The "master stroke" consisted of marching an army into the capital under the command of Colonel Riza Khan, an officer in the British Rifles, who was to be Britain's front man.

Unfortunately for London, its representatives in Teheran completely misjudged the caliber of their protégé. Instead of meekly submitting to dictation, Riza signed the Soviet-Persian treaty five days after his coup, which made him master of the country. He then began using the Soviets against the British. The British advisers who had come to execute the 1919 treaty had to depart quickly; British forces had to evacuate the country; and in 1925 Lord Balfour announced that "the Anglo-Persian Agreement was now history—indeed obsolete history." Persia assumed the offensive and remained on the offensive till after 1930. British concessions were annulled; the British banks were subjected to stringent and vexatious control; even the concession of the Anglo-Persian Oil company was revoked.

The British did not fare much better even in Greece. Premier Venizelos, the pro-Allied statesman who drove George I out of the country to bring Greece into the war, was driven out of power and the pro-German King returned on a wave of anti-British feeling which followed the disastrous campaign in Turkey. The situation improved somewhat when, probably not without British machinations, the King had to leave for exile again. London's influence increased during the following years; yet not a single British Minister after 1922 was to have as much influence as had the Ministers before the war. British capital was never again to play its former preponderant role; nor did the Athenian Foreign Office become a branch of London's.

British power and influence touched bottom with the coming to power of John Metaxas in April, 1936—the same Metaxas who during the world war had been the spearhead of German intrigue—who now embarked on an effective alliance with the Nazis. A trade agreement was signed with the Reich, which all but made Greece a German colony. Imports from Germany increased from 10 per cent of the total imports in 1930 to about 33 per cent in 1937; exports underwent a similar expansion. Germany became between 1936 and 1939 the cornerstone of Grecian economy: up to 1931 Britain supplied most of Greece's coal requirements; but in 1938 Britain sent only 158,000 tons as against 606,000 sent by Germany. Similarly with machinery: Britain exported 282 tons, while the Reich sent 6,500. The value of the latter's exports increased to $40,000,000 as against Britain's total of $17,000,000.

Nor was Central Asia to remain immune from these mighty anti-British movements. In March 1919 Britain's old ally in Afghanistan, Amir Habibullah, was assassinated and his son Amanullah came to power. Soviet agents had been active in Afghanistan, the people had been incited, and stories of British oppression in India had gained wide circulation. Amanullah did not wait to let the British know of his policies. Before April was over the frontier was in turmoil and a series of "incidents" took place. Leaflets detailing British cruelties were distributed, which ended with "cursed be the English tyrants"; and Amanullah issued a *firman* which, after enumerating British outrages, continued "I am prevented by international law from interfering with the internal policy of the British Government [in India] . . . ; but from the point of view of Islam and mankind, I dislike their laws, and, in my view, Indians, in rising and creating disturbances, are right." Declaration of a *jehad* against the British Raj brought tribes streaming to the frontiers of India. The British threatened, pointing out that they had just defeated "the greatest military power in the world," but hostilities could not be prevented.

The war was brief. Fearing the effects of the *jehad* on Moslem opinion throughout the world, London preferred submission to prosecution of a costly war to set up a new regime. The peace treaty, signed in August, marked the end of British influence in Afghanistan. The Amir scornfully rejected a British subsidy and Britain was compelled to relinquish "the arrangement under which the late Habibullah Khan, agreed to follow the advice of the Government of Great Britain in matters affecting the external relations of Afghanistan." The new treaty, officially noted the British representative, "contains nothing that interferes with the complete liberty of Afghanistan in external or internal matters." British intrigue in Kabul failed to overthrow the troublesome Amir. Supported by Moscow, he maintained his independent attitude for many a year and lived to introduce many reforms, social, cultural and political.

Moscow's influence also reached out to Lhasa, where the Young Tibetan Party started agitation against the pro-British theocracy. England's generous financial and military aid—for which India had to pay—was not sufficient to reestablish its authority over "the roof of the world" through the Dalai Lama. Matters took a turn for the worse with the death of the Dalai Lama and the exile of the Panchan Lama, who fled to China. The Young Tibetan Party, now the predominant power, followed a consistent policy of keeping the British as far away as possible.

Thus had the anti-British reaction swept from Portugal to Tibet, and every part of the Outer Empire was in ruins by the middle of the last decade.

VANISHING INVESTMENTS

The menace of these revolutionary forces in every part of the Empire was vastly enhanced by the disintegration of the economic superstructure—or foundation, if you prefer. Not since the early days of the industrial revolution in the eighteenth century was Britain's economic and financial structure in such hopeless confusion. Exports declined to catastrophic lows; factories closed and did not reopen; unemployment increased; taxation devoured an ever larger share of the national income; the national debt swept upwards; income from shipping and banking transactions fell; foreign investments showed an amazing ability to vanish into nothingness.

The World War left Britain crippled economically even more than politically. All energy and resourcefulness seemed to have left British veins. Not only could Britain not retain her pre-war position in world industry, trade, and finance; in nearly every crucial field she lost ground, the decline being both relative and absolute. Taking 1913 as 100 for industrial production, we find that Japan had climbed to 297 by 1929 and the United States to 170; England with an index figure of 99, was actually below the 1913 level. Pig iron production declined from 10.3 million tons in 1913 to 3.6 millions in 1932, while her share in world production fell from 18 per cent during the period 1901-10 to 7.9 per cent between 1924-29. Consumption of cotton sank from 8.7 million quintals in 1913 to five million in 1932, or from 20 per cent of world consumption to less than 12 per cent. The production of coal, a staple British industry, declined from 287 million tons in 1913 to 207 million twenty years later; production of steel sank from 7.7 million tons to 5.2 million in 1932. Unemployment became chronic, the number of jobless almost doubling between 1923 and 1930, when one out of every five insured workers was unemployed. Symbolic of England's economic degeneration was the decline of the birth rate from 24.2 per thousand of the population in 1913 (when 1.1 million children were born), to only 15.3 twenty years later (when births totaled about seven hundred thousand).

Yet the years which saw these declines in production were years of world prosperity; the situation became catastrophic during the following years of depression. The number of unemployed increased by a million, reaching in many key industries 40 per cent of all insured workers. Shipbuilding, one of Britain's traditional industries, declined disastrously: 1.2 million tons of shipping were built in 1913; less than 200,000 tons during the two years 1932-33. Figures of capital investment tell eloquently the story of Britain's industrial decline. While close to £42,000,000 was invested in basic industries—iron and steel, metal working, mechanical engineering, coal-mining—during the ten year period 1904-13, only £27,000,000 went for these basic industries during the ten years 1924-33. On the other hand, while breweries received £6,000,000 during the first period and hotels, theaters, and so on, obtained £7,200,000, the amount of investment in these luxury enterprises increased to £15,-000,000 and £20,500,000 respectively during the second period. How tragic the situation became is seen more clearly if we look at the last five years of the second period, when £11,500,000 was invested in breweries, £8,200,000 in theaters, hotels, and such, and only £6,400,000 in all the basic industries. Indeed, hundreds of factories were actually scrapped during these years.

The decline in production was naturally reflected in trade figures. Export of coal decreased from more than 73,000,000 tons in 1913 to 39,000,000 in 1932; export of pig iron fell from more than 1,100,000 tons to about 200,000 tons. The most catastrophic fall was in export of cotton goods, which declined to about a quarter of the 1913 amount and to about a third in value. Total exports declined by more than half, falling from £800,000,000 in 1924 to an average of £380,000,000 between 1931-33. How far behind British industry had fallen is brought out by the catastrophic decline in exports of manufactures which sank from £620,-000,000 in 1924 to £282,000,000 in 1933.

But imports did not show a similar decline. Between 1922 and 1928 Great Britain had an average annual excess of imports over exports of £331,000,000; in 1931 the unfavorable balance of trade reached the gigantic figure of £408,-000,000. Until 1930, however, income from overseas investment, commissions, and similar services were sufficient to compensate for this unfavorable trade balance, and even to leave a net surplus for new foreign investing. In 1929 these services netted the gigantic total of £484,000,000, which left a net surplus of £103,000,000 after reducing £381,000,000 for excess imports. But an extremely dangerous situation developed with the onset of the world depression in 1930, when the net surplus fell to £28,000,000, and the situation became catastrophic in the following year, when the net surplus gave way to a net deficit of no less than £104,000,000. While the balance of trade became more unfavorable than in any year since 1920, leaving Britain in 1931 with a deficit of £408,000,000, income from the services—the role of which in the total economy had dangerously swelled—declined from £484,000,000 in 1929 to £304,000,000. In the following year income from services declined further to £260,000,000 leaving Britain with a net deficit of £51,000,000.

No less serious was the fact that Britain had come to depend more and more upon the Empire to absorb its falling exports. The percentage of exports to the Empire rose from 37 before the war to 42 in 1928 to almost 44 in 1931; but British imports from the Empire increased only from 25 per cent of total imports in 1914 to 27 per cent in 1928 to 28.7 in 1931. In other words, while the trade of England was becoming less widely distributed and increasingly dependent upon the concessions which could be extracted from Empire countries, the trade of the latter was becoming more widely distributed and less dependent upon the British market.

No less significant was it that while Britain was laboring under the signs of decline, the United States was making continuous economic inroads into the Empire. Imports of United States products into the Empire increased from 22 per cent of total imports in 1913 to 26 per cent in 1929. In that year America completely dominated the Canadian market: 68 per cent of Canada's imports came from its southern neighbor while only 15 per cent came from the United Kingdom. While Britain's share in India's private imports fell from 65 to 40 per cent, that of the United States advanced from 3 to 7 per cent. The same phenomenon repeated itself in South Africa, where Britain's share declined 57 to 44 per cent while that of the United States doubled, advancing from 9 per cent of total imports to 18 per cent; even in "98 per cent British" Australia, the share of the United Kingdom in total imports fell from 52 to 40 per cent, while America's share jumped from 14 to 25 per cent.

More serious even was America's rivalry for world financial supremacy. Britain had strained every resource to maintain its position as world banker: home industry had been seriously neglected to make possible flotation of overseas loans; yet New York was constantly gaining ground. Between 1920 and 1930 America's annual foreign investments amounted to $877,000,000; all that Britain could accomplish was a total of £115,000,000, or about two-thirds of the American figure. At the same time, America's gold holdings in central banks rose from less than two billion dollars in 1913 to almost $4,700,000,000 in 1931, while Britain's gold holdings declined by about 20 per cent, falling to slightly more than $600,-000,000 in 1931.

It did not take long for the political implications of these developments to appear on the surface. At the Imperial Conference of 1926 the Dominions actually began to question Britain's economic stability. "Not until the present year," wrote a well-informed British politician, "did it enter their heads to raise so intimate a question as the economic stability of Great Britain herself." Prime Minister Baldwin pleaded that Britain had lent the Dominions £850,000,000 and that "From no other source could such large sums have been provided on such favorable terms." But the Dominions were not interested in the past; their chief concern was where they would be able to get funds in the future. "If during the next few years," Australian Prime Minister S. M. Bruce said in 1926, "British surplus capital is insufficient for a lending policy on the same scale as in the past; let this fact be freely and frankly admitted." The colonies were not yet free to resort to the New York capital market, and since Britain could not provide the necessary funds urgent works of development were everywhere neglected; but the self-governing Dominions had no mind to retard their progress by waiting for the aging mother country, and they began to look to New York for salvation.

As to the effects on the financial empire, they can be described only by the word disastrous. Finance had been the bond tying the centers of the financial empire to London;

now the bond gave way, and they made a rush for New York. Argentina, one of the oldest members of the British financial empire, was now among the first to transfer allegiance. American capital there had been insignificant before the war; but between 1920-31, American investments jumped from seventy-five million gold pesos to more than eight hundred millions, while British investments remained practically stationary. All of Argentina's national, provincial, and municipal foreign financing between 1914-28 was done in the New York market. Greece, another traditional British preserve, was invaded, American loans totaling close to $60,000,000 while Britain could advance no more than £18,000,000. Colombia had been financed almost exclusively by London before the war; but the last British loan was made in 1920, and from 1913 to 1929 about $260,000,000 of American capital streamed into that country. According to one authority, United States investment in South America increased from $173,000,000 in 1913 to $2,294,000,000 in 1929, while British investment barely increased, advancing from $3,836,-000,000 to $4,486,000,000 in the latter year.

Britain had been compelled to lag in the bitter race though she had strained every resource; and onset of the world depression brought matters to a tragic conclusion. We have seen that London continued making overseas loans at a rate of £115,000,000 per year; but the net credit balance between 1925-30 had been only £62,500,000—in other words, the strain of keeping up with New York was so great that a net yearly deficit of £52,500,000 was incurred. The situation was even worse if the figures of the London *Economist* are accepted, for according to this authoritative journal the net deficit on capital accounts averaged £85,000,000 between 1922-28. In 1928 balance of trade and other forms of income left Britain with a surplus of only £28,000,000; yet circumstances compelled her to make overseas investments totaling £109,000,-000, leaving her with a net capital deficit of £81,000,000. In the following year the situation took another turn for the worse. For the first time in many years the balance of trade showed a deficit of £105,000,000; yet to stay in the race with American finance, foreign investments of £46,000,000 had to be made, which left Britain with a net capital deficit of £151,-000,000.

Onset of the world depression played havoc with British investments. Britain had staked her economic life on the prosperity of other countries; now with world trade in abeyance, one country after another defaulted and industrial concerns went into receivership, while bans were clamped down on the export of capital. Even the Dominions found it increasingly difficult to meet their London obligations. At the Ottawa Conference the representatives of both Australia and New Zealand spoke in mournful terms of the Herculean efforts they had made to keep up debt services; and they more than hinted that default could not be prevented for long. Exact statistics of British financial losses during 1930-33 are not available; but Lord Mancroft's estimate, in a speech at the House of Lords, that two to three billion pounds had been lost by British nationals, although undoubtedly an exaggeration, gives an idea of the immensity of the loss. Income from overseas investments declined during 1931 and 1932 by more than a third as compared with the previous six years, falling from £250,000,000 to about £160,000,000. Disaster was bound to come.

It did. Britain had to acknowledge bankruptcy. Gold payment was suspended on September 20, 1931, and the pound began a march downward in comparison with the American dollar. It was an open acknowledgment that the British technical and financial machine had disintegrated under the strain of American competition; that Britain could no longer maintain her leading position. No longer could Britain provide a financial bond for tying together the far-flung empire. The financial collapse came at the moment when political bonds as well were snapping and disappearing. There was of course an interaction between the two forces; the financial collapse could not but further the political disintegration, while the political decline would make economic recovery more difficult. Not only would the empire countries rush to tie their currency to that of America which had proved more stable; protective tariff walls would rise higher, while the Statute of Westminster served as a visible indication that the Dominion Empire was disappearing.

IX

MENACES FROM THE OUTSIDE

THAT THE EMPIRE was on its deathbed became a truism during the early years of the past decade. The British made their peace with what appeared to be the inevitable, and were busy congratulating one another on the beauty of the imperial sunset. The economic problem, of a certainty, they attacked with courage and intelligence. The Soviet menace evoked a few efforts to recapture some of their prestige in the former areas of the Outer Empire. But if their success in the first sphere was notable, the results in the second were indifferent and the British themselves had to acknowledge that their moves were rearguard actions to prevent the retreat along the whole line from turning into a stampede.

It was due largely to development of the internal weaknesses that the fascist menace emerged between 1931-35 to threaten the existence of the Empire from the outside. Like carrion crows waiting to swoop down on the dead and the dying, militarist states in every part of the world began watching the Empire's disintegration. Japan in the Far East, Italy in the Mediterranean and the Near East, Germany in Europe with ambitions as wide as the world began to shout from the housetops that it was only a question of time before the decadent Empire would disintegrate and they would inherit what Britain could no longer hold together. To hasten the inevitable *Der Tag*, tremendous rearmament and vast propaganda campaigns were launched to convince the various peoples involved of the wisdom of hitching their wagons to the rising fascist stars.

That their overexuberant optimism provoked reactions very different from what they expected will become apparent in the following chapter. Far from weakening the Empire, their extravagant bluster and threats did more to mold it together than anything Britain could have done. Here, however, it is important to notice that the foreign menaces, insignificant at the beginning of the decade, grew steadily during the subsequent years, till they came to constitute a more serious threat to the British Empire than Germany had been in 1914. If the first adventures of the new robber states were undertaken with Britain's permission or at least tacit toleration, it was not long before they began feeling sufficiently strong not only to dispense with British good will, but even to blackmail the Empire into impotence.

The fact that the sun does not set upon the British Empire, once a proud boast, became its greatest weakness. By the end of 1938 there was not a single territory marked red which was not menaced by the fascist powers—except the Dominion of Canada which was protected by American, not British, guns. Humbly British spokesmen had to admit that the erstwhile "mistress of the seas" could no longer protect her far-flung possessions; and the self-governing Dominions were advised to assume responsibility for their own territorial defense. Even India was informed that "Britain could no longer ensure that her coasts would be immune from invasion unless" she "herself were able to render substantial help."

To see how far the mighty had fallen one needs only to compare Britain's position in 1913 with that at the end of 1938. Before the first World War no part of the Empire was threatened by direct or indirect aggression. No state dared to question Britain's domination of the seas. A two-power naval standard was accepted as an axiom. In the Far East Japan was the Empire's watchdog, no one dreaming that a day would come when Japan would menace British interests in China, not to speak of those in India and Australia. In Europe, a careful balance of power assured British influence everywhere. No conference, no important peace treaty, no territorial deal could be consummated without London's approval. The Lion needed only to roar for nations to tremble into submission; and Albion's prerogative to sit in judgment on nations and peoples was rarely questioned.

Symbolic of the new reality was the Vienna Conference at

the end of 1938, when the Foreign Ministers of Italy and Germany decided what part of Czechoslovakia should be given to Hungary, while British diplomatic observers waited patiently in anterooms to hear the verdict. The two-power naval standard had become a half-forgotten memory; the British army and air fleet were the laughingstock of the fascist capitals. Contemptuously Hitler's own newspaper, the *Völkischer Beobachter,* wrote in the summer of 1939 when Englishmen were being humiliated by Japanese soldiers: "East Asia, where for a hundred years the British flag was the sole law, laughs today at threats from the British Lion— the Lion that stands with one paw in the Baltic, with a second in the Black Sea, a third at the West Wall, and a fourth at Gibraltar and therefore can only wag its tail in the Far East. Such a grotesque animal is not likely to arouse fear!"

STORMS IN ASIA

Japan's invasion of Manchuria was to have vastly greater repercussions than could have been anticipated in 1931. By defying with impunity civilized world opinion, the League of Nations, the Nine-Power Treaty, and the Briand-Kellogg Pact, the Japanese militarists forced a breach in the floodgates against aggression which was to prove exceedingly dangerous to the British Empire. That they acted with plan and logic is undeniable. Every fact pointed against British interference. British financial interests in Manchuria were insignificant compared with those at stake in Japan; the steady disintegration of the Empire and the terrible economic crisis then raging presented the British government with more pressing problems than the raids in a Chinese province; and economic rivalry with the United States during the previous decade precluded co-operation between the only two powers who could check them. The Japanese repeatedly assured the world that no change in the status quo in China was contemplated by them; and knowledge of Japan's inherent weaknesses did not lessen Western faith in the value of its promises. Who could foresee that a day would come when the absurd militarists would be able to threaten the British Empire in the Far East?

But after Manchuria came North China; after North China

came Shanghai; then came the turn of South China—and by the first part of 1939 every British possession in the Far East was menaced. Japan was not weakened by the military adventures. Assuming control over the government, the military imperialists reorganized the whole industrial and economic structure for war purposes; and an imperialism more virile than any known in the West came into being. Intoxicated by easy victories, the imperialists constantly expanded their territorial ambitions, the ultimate end of which they no longer needed to disguise. They could now afford to announce openly their intention of driving the white man out of the whole of Asia, which was to be united under the aegis and control of the Empire of the Rising Sun.

Great Britain being the European power with the largest stake in Asia, Japan's chief efforts naturally came to be directed against her. A furious anti-British propaganda drive was carefully organized. An organization called Taiei Doshi-Kai, or Allied Comrades in the Policy Towards England, counting the support of powerful economic and political bodies, was set up to propagate hatred against Britain, the Public Enemy Number One, which was "rarely referred to in print except as 'crafty England.'" Admiral Nobumasu Suetsugu, one of Japan's most distinguished naval officers, declared before assuming the Ministry of Home Affairs that England is "the root of all evil" in the Far East and must therefore "be extirpated." Meetings under the banners "Break off relations with England" and "Redistribute Britain's Colonies," became popular; responsibility for China's heroic resistance was consistently traced to British machinations. And the Japanese carried their propaganda to the Asiatic continent. In China, dozens of carefully prepared anti-British demonstrations were staged: the anti-British gospel was carried to Siam, Tibet, the Malay States, even to India.

Not satisfied with this, the Japanese set themselves to humiliate the British before the whole of Asia and to undermine the prestige of the white man. British traders were driven out from conquered territories; British ships were bombed and British seamen were killed. When the Japanese military authorities excluded foreign shipping from Foochow, Swatow, and Wenchow, the British protested that "The right of British vessels, including warships, to proceed to and remain in any place in Chinese waters...remains unaffected"; yet the order was not revoked and Britain had to bow to it. The brutal campaign culminated in the blockade of the Tientsin concession in June 1939, because the British authorities refused to surrender without sufficient evidence four Chinese accused of a political murder. Britons were humiliated and slapped in the face; English women were forced to undress before Japanese soldiers; the British residents faced starvation. Offers for a rational solution were rejected by Japanese militarists. The Tientsin "incident" assumed wider proportion when Japanese newspapers launched a campaign for the unilateral abolition of all concessions, which, in the words of the paper *Hochi* point "like daggers at Japan's holy enterprise of building up a new order in East Asia." Japanese spokesmen actually had the temerity to demand that "the British authorities co-operate with the Japanese in the construction of a 'new order' in the East." But the British surrender was inevitable, and in the beginning of September, the Chinese prisoners were handed over to the Japanese authorities.

Meanwhile, Japan had conquered vast territories and had taken up strategic positions from which to menace directly British possessions. A drive was launched in May 1939 to place Shanghai, the center of British and Western trade and finance in China, under Japanese control. Aiming to convert the entire Yangtse Valley into a domain as private as Manchuria, the Japanese demanded nothing less than that Britain and France withdraw their troops from the concession. Shanghai, however, faded into insignificance compared with the more direct threats to British imperial safety represented by the occupation of Hainan, which, situated strategically between Hong Kong, Siam, and Singapore, is in a position to threaten Britain's whole defense system in the Far East. The Spratly Islands, located only 640 miles from Singapore, were occupied by Japan. Operating from those reefy islands, a submarine fleet could make shipping between Singapore, British Sarawak, the Philippine Islands, and Hong Kong well nigh impossible. Yet even this occupation hardly provoked more than a mild protest. Of what account were seven strategic islands at a time of full retreat along the whole front? Japanese militarists were certain that no fleet would be sent to drive them out, and they were right.

Moves against Hong Kong became a logical inevitability after this. But rather than run the risk of war by placing Britain in the predicament of fighting for Hong Kong or retreating to Singapore in the full glare of daylight, the Japanese preferred to follow the old policy of gradual nibbling, which offered as great rewards as a direct attack, at much smaller risks. The security of Hong Kong was made dependent upon Japan's mercies. All Chinese territory surrounding the crown colony was occupied, which brought Japanese soldiers to the Empire's back gate, enabling them to quarantine Hong Kong at a moment's notice. Communications with the interior of China, Tibet, and India through the overland route was severed; a British air service between Hong Kong and Chungking, seat of the Chinese Government, had to be suspended, thus further lessening British influence. Hardly two weeks had elapsed after the Japanese occupation of the Chinese mainland when, in self-protection, the British authorities were compelled to demolish bridges connecting the crown colony with China, and its isolation became complete.

The Rising Sun then began to cast its rays over territories much wider afield. The Japanese began to show an interest in Mongolia and Tibet. The latter is not only valuable for its high quality wool and musk, but control of Lhasa would give the militarists a religious trump card in their drive for Asiatic consolidation.

Another field marked for occupation was Siam. Until a few years ago under British influence, Siam became a center of Japanese activity. Japanese trade increased rapidly during the past few years, to a large extent at the expense of the British; Japanese cotton goods replaced Manchester products in whole districts of the country; a great number of trade missions were sent; and new consular connections were established; the number of Japanese in Siam multiplied many times. And more threatening than all the commercial and political expansion is the project of the Kra Canal across Sawi Bay which the Japanese are anxious to build. Should they succeed in this effort, the value of the Singapore fortifications would disappear overnight, and a front door to India would be opened. With control of Hainan in their hands, the Japanese fleet would be completely unassailable in Chinese waters, and once having entered the canal it would be almost within a stone's throw from Colombo, Calcutta, and Rangoon. It was significant that Commander Ohno, Japan's recent naval attaché at Bangkok, stated that "There is a considerable number of protagonists in Siam of an Asiatic League, with Japan as its leader."

Military success in China and especially Britain's retreat from one position after another made ambitious Japanese imperialists look even further afield. No less than Hitler and Mussolini they became convinced that the sun was setting over the British Empire; and, *mirabile dictu,* that the setting would begin in the East. Count Carlo Sforza, who knows the Far East well, reported the emergence of an entirely "new idea"—a "repulsion and . . . contempt . . . for those Europeans who were so feared and respected during a century" and especially for "the British, who, when confronted by the ruins of Shanghai did not find anything else to say than: 'Do not touch the British banks on the Bund.'" Seeing nothing but retreat—which they interpreted to mean weakness and cowardice—it was inevitable that the Japanese militarists should begin casting a greedy eye on India, Australia, New Zealand, and their territorial possessions. They began to devote considerable efforts to strengthening cultural relations with India, and pro-Japanese societies were subsidized. And an examination of the press in the Antipodes Dominions during the years 1938-9 will show how seriously responsible leaders and well-informed observers began to view the Japanese threat. "We are now realizing that the Far East becomes to us the Near North," wrote Frank Milner, one of New Zealand's best informed political commentators, early in 1939. "Our complacency is being rudely disturbed as we learn more and more of the policy and the activities of the naval expansionist school of Japan . . . What counts . . . is not the mileage between Yokohama and Sydney but between Palau and New Guinea."

Britain could blame nobody but her own statesmen for the

emergence of this menace to the Empire's existence. Japan could have been stopped very easily in 1931-32; but in the spring of 1939 a totally unprecedented situation confronted Britain, and Prime Minister Chamberlain has had to acknowledge the Empire's impotency in the waters where it was once supreme. "It makes my blood boil to hear and read some of the things which have been happening there," he told Parliament in connection with the Tientsin affair; but, "We must remember what are the limits of what we can do at this particular time to help our people there. At the present moment we have not in the Far East a fleet superior to that of the Japanese." Far from becoming weaker as a result of her military adventures, Japan had constantly gained in strength. Never before were the Empire's Far Eastern skies as overcast as they were during the last part of 1938 and the early months of the following year.

ITALY AMONG THE MENACES

Who would have predicted even ten years ago that a day would come when Italy—a second-rate European power and most of the time one of Britain's satellites—would defy the Empire and dare to menace its most important life line? Yet this is precisely what happened in the autumn of 1935, when Mussolini invaded Abyssinia and by threatening war blackmailed Britain into inactivity. Since then, fascist Italy has been a dagger at the heart of the Empire.

As was to be expected, success of the first effort only whetted Mussolini's appetite for empire, which soon assumed Gargantuan dimensions. The first part of the program was to consist of converting the Mediterranean into an Italian lake, and the surrounding territories into Italian colonies. Italy must be freed from "the eternal weight of Malta, Suez and Gibraltar." Gabriele d'Annunzio wrote: "Malta is no longer an island but an infection which requires to be cured. If cure is impossible, Malta will have to be sunk in the depths of the sea like a gargantuan monster." Suez will cease to be an "eternal weight" only when Egypt, the Sudan, and Palestine are converted into Italian colonies. Nor can Italy feel secure as long as the second gate of the Inland Sea, Gibraltar, is in British hands. After these objectives are attained, there will be no difficulty in rounding out the Empire with control over the Greek harbors and the Mediterranean's third gate at the Dardanelles.

It would be a mistake, however, to suppose that Italian ambitions stop with the Mediterranean and the lands on its eastern shores. "We affirm our skepticism," a fascist dignitary has written in a very interesting book, *Italy and Her African Policies,* "and repeat that there is a hard law of Nature that he who has, keeps, and. he who has not, has to take by force." Control of the Near East would obviously be incomplete without bolstering the new Roman Empire in the Red Sea, the Persian Gulf, and the Indian Ocean. "Mussolini has made his the dream of Crispi—seeking the key to the Mediterranean in the Red Sea," Il Duce's organ, *Il Popolo d'Italia,* wrote in 1938. Nor has the African Empire assumed its final borders. On the contrary, Abyssinia was to be a mere beginning—valuable not for itself but as a base from which to advance to the more fertile lowlands over which flies the Union Jack. And beyond all this, though not too far removed not to come within the range of the farseeing fascist eye, lies India and its tremendous wealth.

Ambitions of a maniac? Perhaps; but the maniac proceeded very methodically and went amazingly far in a short space of time to translate them into reality. A campaign was launched to win the sympathy and support of the Arabic world. A net of schools was woven by Mussolini's agents from one end of the Near East to the other, the pupils of which were taught that the Italian dictator is the savior of the world; the numerous Italian hospitals became centers of anti-British propaganda. Italian agents learned to make use of both the mails and the air. The Arabic news announcer at Bari made it a practice to recite stories of British atrocities in Palestine, Trans-Jordan, Hadramaut, and elsewhere, while waxing eloquent over the "traditional friendship of Moslem Italy" for the Arabs. To eradicate the bitter memories of their terror in Libya, the Italians began to send to thousands of Arab households two Arabic journals from Libya telling of the new fascist policy toward Islam. A typical issue of the *Illustrated Libya* contained an article about the opening of a school for Moslem learning. "The opening of the school," the writer announced, "shows that the policy of the Fascist Government is not only to respect the religion of its Moslem citizens, but to provide for them every means for scholarship. And this policy is followed by the Fascist government not only in Libya but in all its colonial possessions." Other articles dealt with The Flourishing Cities of Libya Under Fascism, Italy and the Education of Libyan Women, Mussolini's Rome, Italy and Islam, and the like.

Signor Mussolini's trip to Libya in March 1937 was only an outward expression of the "uninterrupted friendship" Italy had shown to the Arabs. Arab journalists from the whole Near East were taken to witness the Duce's triumphant procession; newspapers were paid for publishing photographs of the glorious event; Italian consulates in Near Eastern cities invited Moslem notables to hear that "the four hundred million Moslems in the world appreciate Mussolini's friendship to Islam and thank him for the benefits he showered upon them." The climax of the demonstration came with the presentation of the "Sword of Islam" to the Duce, who, styling himself "Defender of Islam," proclaimed: "Fascist Italy intends to assure to her Muslim population in Libya, peace, justice, prosperity and respect for the laws of the Prophet. Further, she wishes to show her sympathy for Islam and for Muslims throughout the world." And an official document issued on that occasion contained the following illuminating words, after a detailed reference to the unrest in all Moslem countries under the tutelage of Britain and France: "We state without fear of contradiction that no power has a more strongly sympathetic policy towards these Islamic States and their legitimate aspirations [to throw off the yoke of British and French imperialism] than has Italy." This proclamation constituted a direct challenge to Britain, the greatest Moslem power in the world.

Mussolini was, however, too realistic to rely exclusively on propaganda. A large military machine was constructed to reinforce it. Italy's capacity to produce armaments was vastly increased; a navy specifically adapted for service in the narrow Inland Sea with the world's largest submarine fleet, was built; the airfleet was expanded till it was without rival in the Near East. To menace Egypt and the Suez Canal, Libya was converted into a vast military camp and roads were constructed to the Egyptian border. Extremely important was the fortification of the Italian islands in the Mediterranean and especially the islands of Pantalleria, which, lying about seventy miles south of Sicily, divides the Mediterranean in two and dominates its most important shipping lanes.

To neutralize Britain's control of Gibraltar, Mussolini hit upon the master stroke of installing in Madrid his protégé, General Franco, who could be relied upon to take orders from Rome. Tens of thousands of Italian troops were sent to occupy Spain and to battle for Franco; the highly strategic Spanish islands in the Mediterranean and Atlantic came under the domination of Rome. Above all, it was over the body of the Spanish Republic that the Axis with Germany came into being, and was forged to become a mighty anti-British weapon.

With its African empire towering above the Red Sea and the Indian Ocean, Italy became ready to challenge Britain's traditional supremacy in those waters and to drive another wedge in British imperial communications. Aside from the mechanized Italian army and about one hundred thousand native troops, an air force was concentrated in Abyssinia which was certainly larger than any found in the vicinity. An excellent submarine base was constructed at the ten-mile mouth of Annesley Bay; the ports of Massaua and Assab in the Red Sea and Magadiscio in the Indian Ocean were dredged for the use of naval units, and the whole region was fortified with long range guns. Britain of course maintained its own defenses in this highly strategic area, notably the fortified island of Perim; but it became clear before the end of 1938 that if Britain was still in a position to keep Italian ships out of the Red Sea, Italian submarines and airplanes operating from the newly constructed bases could do an enormous amount of damage to English shipping in the narrow waterway and in the Indian Ocean as well.

No doubt the spring of 1938 witnessed a turning of the tide in the Inland Sea in favor of Britain. Military defenses were everywhere seriously taken in hand; and for the first time Britain began to take measures to counteract Italian propaganda. Entrance of Greece and Turkey on the side of the democracies introduced changes which the Axis had not foreseen. It became evident also that the fascist propaganda among the Near Eastern peoples had overreached its mark. The Arabs, far from throwing in their lot with their new "protector," became mortally afraid and began to solidify relations with Great Britain. Italian broadcasting stations still told the Maltese that their island is part of *Italia altra confino* and the pro-Italian propaganda was still subsidized. But an election for the local Council of Government gave the pro-British Constitutional and Labor parties seven seats, while the Italian Nationalists won no more than three.

Yet there could be no escape from the fact that in case of conflict Mussolini would have remained master of the Inland Sea for many months, when it would have had to be closed to all Allied shipping. The solid work which the Duce had accomplished during the previous few years could not be undone in a few months. The Italian legions operating from Libya, Eritrea, and Abyssinia would have been able to dislodge the British from more than one position in the Near East. British diplomacy had succeeded only too well in creating a menace far more serious than any which Britain had confronted since the days when the Inland Sea had become an important route in imperial communications and the adjoining territories integral parts of the Empire.

THE MENACE OF GERMANY

Not till after Munich did the Third Reich assume the dignity of chief menace to the British empire. The reaction to Britain's capitulation was instantaneous, and made itself felt in one continent after another. British prestige went down so rapidly that one found it difficult to measure the extent of the decline from day to day; German influence and power rose correspondingly. Munich echoed throughout the Balkan countries, which had long been tied to England; its reactions were felt in Turkey and the Near East generally; indeed Africa and Asia, including India and China, did not escape the reverberations.

Munich of course was an effect, not a cause. Since coming to power in January 1933, the Nazis had been arming at breakneck speed. The Reichswehr had been transformed from an army of one hundred thousand professional soldiers to a conscripted army with more than a million men; officers' training schools had sprung up like mushrooms after a rain; a careful propaganda campaign had revived the military tradition of the whole nation. More than fifteen billion dollars had been spent on the military machine. An air force second to none had been constructed which counted at least four thousand planes; more important, reorganization of industry gave the Reich a potential production greater than the combined output of any two other nations. The country became one gigantic training field, with officers everywhere in command.

The totalitarian reorganization of society enabled the Nazi rulers to utilize every national resource for military ends. Foreign trade was made subservient to military requirement; every factory and shop was conscripted and placed within the scheme; all human power was mobilized. The doctrine of "total mobilization" meant that not a million or ten million men were in the fighting service, but every man, woman, and child. The nation was taught to accept a standard of living much lower than it had known for many years. "Guns or butter?" asked Hermann Goering; and there was no doubt about the answer. Guns, more guns, and ever more guns. Never before had the world seen a human society so keyed up to the sole end of acquisition of military power.

The British had been warned. "Step by Step" Winston Churchill had exposed the extent of German rearmament; a hundred other men told a similar story in the press and in Parliament. It is inconceivable that the British Government did not know what every reader of newspapers imbibed with his breakfast coffee. The Nazis made no secret of their ambitions. The years 1937-38 witnessed the evolution of doctrines about *"Lebensraum"* (living space), *"Grossraumwirtschaft,"* aiming to create a system of economies in second-rate states which would supply raw materials and agricultural products to the dominating economy of the Big Power, and *"Verbundwirtschaft,"* or compound economy, by which all states from the North Sea to the Indian Ocean were to tie their economic lives to that of the mighty Reich.

All these doctrines and ambitions aimed directly at the

empires of "the rich but decadent" democracies; yet the British government remained undisturbed. It continued along its leisurely pace; its efforts at rearmament usually remained in the blueprint stage. Not even formation of the Axis shocked the British rulers out of their complacency. They forgot—or never read—Hitler's words in *Mein Kampf:* "Germany will either be a world power or it will be nothing." He outlined a vision of a mighty German empire comprising two hundred fifty million people, dominating not only Europe but occupying the stage of history as the "highest master race which in a distant future may be called upon to solve the problems for which it might need the resources of the entire globe."

With infinite care and minute attention to detail the Nazis had been at work since 1934 to realize their imperial ambition. A complicated net of propaganda offices were stretched over the Balkans, the Near East, Africa, and India. Newspapers were subsidized; political groups friendly to the Reich were heavily supported; everywhere organizations of Germanic inhabitants were overhauled and tightened to act as spearheads of the Nazi penetration. Much attention was devoted to organizing political parties opposed to the existing regimes which would be under the Reich's influence. In Hungary, the Arrow Cross and other fascist organizations were aided; Rumania had its Iron Guard, and other Balkan countries had their corresponding organizations. The leader of the Iron Guard appealed once to Berlin for funds on the ground that "solidarity of interests ... binds us in an indestructible manner"; and Berlin gave its support. The avowed aim of all these parties was to expel British and French influence from their countries, which in the future were to be tied to the Nazi chariot.

German influence increased everywhere. German support was invaluable to the Greek dictator, who was not unwilling to pay for it. The Rumanian government was compelled to extend all sorts of privileges to the German minority, and a series of commercial agreements all but gave the Reich complete control of the country's economic life. Both Bulgaria and Yugoslavia came to be dominated by German influence and economy. Vastly greater even became German influence in Hungary. Here the government could no longer ap-

point a professor without Berlin's interference; the best possible recommendation for a high government post was one
from Herr Erdmannsdorf, Hitler's minister. German pressure
precipitated more than one cabinet crisis; and Berlin was able
to force a pro-Nazi foreign minister upon the country.

Commerce, which lends itself to statistical analysis, reveals
best the role the Greater Reich came to play in the Balkans.
Almost 50 per cent of the total foreign trade of the various
Balkan countries was in the hands of the Reich during 1938.
The Reich's share in Bulgaria's export trade grew from 25
per cent in 1930 to 48 per cent during the first eight months
of 1938, when it supplied 49 per cent of that country's imports. Hungary sold 11 per cent of its total exports to the
Reich in 1933; five years later, it is estimated, the proportion
was about 40 per cent. Preliminary figures for 1938 indicate
that the Greater Reich controlled almost half of Rumania's
foreign trade. Yet even these figures do not reveal the full
importance of the German trade. Of more significance was
the fact that Germany bought most of their agricultural exports of the Balkan countries, making them dependent on
the Reich's market. And these years witnessed an almost
steady decline in trade with Britain and France, which only
a few years before held in their hands all the strings of Balkan
economic life.

Having attained a preponderant position in the Balkans
the Nazis next invaded the Near East, the Lion's own lair.
Realizing that the Near East offered an ideal field from which
to harass the British Empire, the Nazis began at the end of
1936 to devote a good deal of attention to that part of the
world. Numerous agents visited the Arab countries and a
great deal of precious foreign currency was sent to subsidize
anti-British movements. In Palestine they subsidized the
Grand Mufti of Jerusalem in his guerrilla war against the
British and the Zionists. Not only was money sent, but also
arms, munitions, and, perhaps, military instructors. The
powerful official broadcasting station in Berlin began sending out daily propaganda in Arabic; hundreds of pamphlets
designed to appeal to every shade of opinion were circulated.
It is the known fact, the semi-official *Great Britain and the
East* wrote in the Spring of 1939, "that a certain Power has

for some time been busy in trying to create difficulties in Iraq for the British. How else can be explained the pamphlets that were circulated in Baghdad on the day after King Ghazi's death, attributing that death to the machinations of the British?"

German efforts came to be as multifarious as they were thorough. German economic missions went out to Afghanistan to negotiate trade agreements and special concessions; parties of German engineers followed to prospect for minerals and oil. In Teheran there began a steep upswing in both German trade and influence. Instead of Czechs and Swiss being employed to build railroads, bridges and factories, an increasing number of Germans began to arrive. In Iraq, Syria, Palestine, and Egypt, native newspapers began publishing news from the D. N. B., the official German news agency; the legations and consulates began to exercise an influence on newspapers through control of all German advertising and by means of direct subsidies; German Orientalists arrived, who proceeded to make themselves popular in native clubs and in political parties; prominent members of native youth organizations were given free trips to the Reich; supernationalistic youth organizations like the Syrian National Youth League and the Green Shirts in Egypt came more and more under Nazi influence, while anti-Jewish parties were subsidized.

Nazi propaganda reached as far as the Union of South Africa and India. In the former, German agents and even diplomatic representatives co-operated with anti-British and anti-Jewish organizations. The German inhabitants of the Southwest African territory were regimented; and it is not impossible that they were prepared for a *putsch*. Reliable reports indicated that Berlin intended to use there the technique perfected in Czechoslovakia and Austria. In India, the most extreme anti-British groups seem to have received both moral and financial aid from Berlin. That numerous anti-British publications were subsidized cannot be doubted; and the "cultural" propaganda assumed important dimensions.

Serious threats to the Empire individually, Japan, Italy, and Germany became a menace of immense potentialities once they joined in the Berlin-Rome Axis and the anti-

Comintern Pact Triangle which was directed far more against the British Empire than against Soviet Russia. Essentially both groupings were for the purpose of blackmail; however, there could be no telling when they would develop into full-fledged war instruments. The "technique of rhythm," by which one partner of the triumvirate grabbed territory in one part of the world while the others made threatening, warlike gestures in the other parts to prevent the democracies from concentrating their forces anywhere, proved exceedingly costly to Great Britain. This co-operation enabled Japan to stage one anti-British demarche after another; Germany expanded her frontiers to the south and the east; Italy was able to occupy Albania, and the world was kept in a state of "nerves." Yet neither grouping would have come into existence but for British foreign policy since 1931.

WANTED: PEACE

How is one to explain British foreign policy during the past eight or nine years? How is one to account for the failure to foresee the ultimate consequences of allowing aggression to go unpunished, and of cultivating potential enemies until they became strong enough to challenge the Empire's security? It is true that the power of the Empire had declined seriously by 1931 and Britain was disarmed. However, the original aggressors were very weak and it would have taken very little to bring them to book, especially as in the case of Japan and Italy, Britain could have had the co-operation of the whole world, including the United States. Why, then, did Britain give them the opportunity to encroach on the outskirts of the Empire and to swallow independent states till they became sufficiently strong to attack the Empire itself? Why were they permitted to consolidate their gains?

Not until the present war ends and the archives are opened will it be possible to answer these questions satisfactorily. At present, all that one can do is to give a tentative reply based on the known facts and on those official statements which appear to be most in harmony with the known trend of British policy. And the few facts already established place much less guilt on the British Government than many had supposed.

Two explanations have already become popular. First, some observers have informed the world that Chamberlain, Lord Halifax, and a group christened "the Cliveden clique"— fascists at heart—were consistently willing to sacrifice the Empire for the sake of universal reaction and to advance their own class interests. The British rulers, according to this theory, were loath to check the actual fascist aggressors because they hoped until the last moment to form a quadrangle of their own—which would include Germany, Italy and Japan—for establishing a fascist-tory dictatorship in Europe, Africa, and Asia and, ultimately, for attacking the Soviet Union.

Another theory, which originated in Nazi circles, claims that, faced with the gradual dissolution of the Empire, Britain purposely created enemies who by menacing the Empire from the outside would strengthen the imperial connections. This theory is a *post hoc* creation, produced after Downing Street had wearied of the endless efforts at appeasement which did not appease; after the Nazis were compelled to recognize that their threats and propaganda, far from weakening the Empire, as they had expected, actually did more to strengthen it than anything Britain could have done. And this theory overlooks that the British could not desire war, because they are inevitably bound to lose even from a victorious war far more than they can possibly gain.

Years of observation from front-row seats have convinced me that motives totally different from those commonly attributed to them swayed British statesmen. I am convinced, in brief, that a sincere and deep rooted hatred of war and fear of the ultimate consequences to Western civilization— and the Empire—of a world-wide slaughter were far more powerful factors in shaping British policy than any love for Hitler and Mussolini, or even for the system which they represent. A close analysis of British foreign policy since 1920 will bear out this conclusion. So strong was the reaction in Britain against all the policies and ideas and practices which had led to the colossal massacre of 1914-18 that the quest for peace was, on the whole, the mainspring of policy.

That British diplomacy between 1920 and 1938 was not the best fitted to attain permanent peace is obvious. There were errors of commission and many more errors of omission; even crimes against the ideals of peace and justice were not lacking. One might, for example, incriminate their pro-German efforts immediately after the war as an expression of the old and dangerous policy of "balance of power." Floods of Nazi propaganda have made the world forget just how many concessions were made during the twenties. The history of the postwar years is one long story of concessions to Germany; and Great Britain was prepared to make even greater concessions. We know now that world peace would have been served better had France had her way with Germany and had the letter and spirit of Versailles been implemented. But the fallacy of the British policy is obvious only in the light of the wisdom which comes after the event. One needs only to recall that it was Britain's policy towards the defeated enemy, not France's, that won the applause of every progressive the world over.

It should not be forgotten that "appeasement" was not born in 1931, nor has it been directed exclusively towards the fascist and militarist powers. British policy had been all along in favor of appeasement to Hungary; nor was it British diplomacy that made impossible a Hapsburgian restoration. The minor Balkan States were the chief culprits in both matters; and it was they—not Britain—that defeated the customs union between Austria and Germany before Hitler came to power. Britain's guilt lay in her all too easy submission to the forces which thwarted a fundamental reconstruction policy in that part of the world.

It is true—and this is the most serious accusation that can be made—that Downing Street did not fully support the League of Nations, which alone could have assured permanent international security, and its attitude toward efforts at world disarmament were lukewarm. Certainly, no British government used its power and influence to carry through any of the fundamental disarmament schemes which were discussed at international conferences called for that purpose. Fatal vacillations, indecision, and aversion to long-range constructive policies characterized the official British attitude towards the League and disarmament.

Again, however, as one studies the relevant documents, it is difficult to avoid the conclusion that Britain's crime consisted not so much of sabotaging the efforts of progressive forces the world over to build a better international society as of cowardly fear to champion a bold policy to entrench collective security as the first principle of international life. In the face of uncertainty, and confronted with the endless currents and cross-currents of continental diplomacy, British cabinets followed a policy of hesitation, of wait-and-see. An anti-League and antidisarmament move by one power evoked a countermove by London; and the noble efforts for peace were drowned not in a sea of Machiavellian diplomacy but in a swamp of petty jealousies and intrigues. Indeed, the very strength of the craving for peace helped to bring the war. When urged in 1935 to adopt a firm policy toward Italy, British statesmen retorted with the question, "Are you certain that Mussolini would not fight?" No one could be certain; and Britain retreated.

Let it not be forgotten that so profound was the quest for peace in postwar Britain that the definition of imperial "vital interests," to defend and protect which major force was to be used, underwent an amazing liberalization simply to avoid use of force. Seeing that even the barest minimum of the "vital interests" which any good imperialist of the last century would have tolerated could be secured under the changed sociological conditions only by ruthless application of bayonets, British colonial administrators were ordered by London to scale down the implications of that hoary phrase in order to avoid resort to bayonets. It is absurd to say, for example, that Britain could not have held Iraq or even Persia and ruled them in the traditional imperialist manner. She had the money to do that; she certainly had enough bayonets to keep the lid down on those and other countries. What she did not have was the will to use the bayonets—because the British people, more than the people of any other country, had developed a conscience and were tired of bayonets and mass murder.

Only if the influence of this cultural change is taken into consideration can the events of the past few years be understood. Neither the Laborite Prime Minister MacDonald nor either of his two successors can be suspected of following a policy aiming to restore the old and dangerous balance of power by allowing the fascist states to become stronger through aggression. Nor is there sufficient evidence for the oft-repeated accusation that appeasement represented an effort on the part of the British Tories to support the foreign policies of Hitler and Mussolini so that they would be able to retain power and crush all progressive forces at home. That British governments have not considered it their duty to intervene in Germany, Italy, and Japan to upset the existing regimes was of course obvious. It should be remembered, however, that neither did any British government intervene in Soviet Russia after 1920.

Did Downing Street believe that appeasement would secure "peace in our time"? Did it not see—as did hundreds of observers and dozens of members of Parliament—that appeasement, far from assuring peace, made war the more inevitable, since it strengthened the aggressors? The answer is that it probably did see—and believed against belief. As Peter F. Drucker wrote (in *The End of Economic Man*):

The small boy who has smashed the jar while stealing the jam knows that he will be discovered and punished; but he prays, hopes, and believes against belief that he will escape. During the last few years the British Government has been doing the same thing. It knows that there is no lasting peace with the dictators; but it believes against belief, hopes against hope, that it can be found. Both the boy and the British Government hope for a miracle. . . . The British Government . . . asks fate for . . . unlikely miracles; it hopes for a revolution in Germany, an economic smash-up, or a Russo-German war. Both make themselves believe in a miracle because the alternative is too terrible to face. Both turn to the miracle because they are in despair.

Stanley Baldwin, Neville Chamberlain, and Viscount Halifax have reflected the common dread of the alternative that is "too terrible to face." "The very foundations of our . . . Western civilization cannot withstand a second explosion," Baldwin said; and Chamberlain told a Birmingham audience: "I do not believe there is anyone who will question my sincerity when I say there is hardly anything I wouldn't sacrifice for peace." This thought runs through all his utterances; there is no reason for questioning his sincerity. In his Chatham House speech as late as the end of June 1939 Lord Halifax did not fail to make clear that the door to negotiation of disputed points would be kept open to the last minute; and he offered colonial appeasement even as he uttered a grave warning to potential disturbers of peace.

The fact is that the British public sympathized with the policies of its rulers. It dreaded war more than anything else and it instinctively comprehended Mr. Chamberlain's desperate efforts on behalf of the common ideal. Munich, sad as it was, was applauded by the vast majority of the English people; for peace without honor seemed better than an honorable war. And not only the British public, but the common people of the whole Empire reacted powerfully to the desperate efforts of Downing Street on behalf of world peace.

Under any circumstances, all criticism on the score of failing to foresee the future is irrelevant. It leaves out a fundamental characteristic of the British mentality, and therefore of British policy. Whether for good or for bad, "muddling through," not clear and logical policies for decades in advance, has been the traditional method of the British Government. During the few years preceding the outbreak of war the one aim of Downing Street was to preserve peace for as long as possible. This much it accomplished, even if the aggressor states had to be bribed in the process. Nor can one deny that in the past the "muddling through" policy had been far from disastrous. The British constantly confronted difficulties which they had not foreseen and which might have been avoided had they shaped long-range and logical policies. Downing Street committed many more errors during the nineteenth century than is generally recognized. Yet this muddle-headedness enabled British statesmen to overcome the difficulties for which they were responsible in the first place, and to construct the world's greatest imperial structure.

Another factor which is usually overlooked is that, of necessity, Great Britain cannot have the freedom of action which lesser powers possess. Before adopting any policy, Downing Street must think not only of its effects on Britain and the reactions of the people in the United Kingdom, but of its effects on the Empire as a whole with its far-flung interests and what the people of Melbourne, Quebec, Calcutta, Cairo, Nairobi, and a hundred other places will think. Even the reactions of Ankara, Teheran, Kabul, and Baghdad have to be considered. So vast are the Empire's interests that a policy which would serve one part might be detrimental to another, and a balance has constantly to be struck. Hence the compromises, half-measures, and hesitations which have characterized British foreign policy since 1920. It is not impossible even that London's failure to co-operate with the United States in checking Japanese aggression in 1931 was due largely to the protests of Australia and New Zealand against any step which might antagonize Japan. Devoted though these Dominions were to the ideal of collective security, they feared that desperation might drive the Japanese to risk war, the brunt of which they would have had to bear.

More than that: not until after Hitler's occupation of Czechoslovakia could Downing Street feel a measure of confidence that it would have the support of the Empire in case of war. More even than the people of England, those of the Dominions were opposed to war; and it is doubtful in the extreme whether they would have joined the mother country had war broken out even at the time of Munich. Downing Street knew that to secure the co-operation of the vast Empire it would have to exhaust first every conceivable method for avoiding resort to arms: it had to convince five hundred million people in every part of the globe of its readiness to sacrifice selfish interests, the purity of its motives, and the sincerity of its pronouncements in favor of peace. Appeasement, so disastrous from one point of view, went however a long way toward bringing about this conviction. In the beginning of July 1939, Premier Menzies announced that "Australia takes her stand" side by side with Britain "because we believe Britain throughout has acted with honor, judgment, and long-suffering care and patience."

TOWARD THE ABYSS

Whatever the explanation of Britain's foreign policy, the effects became tragically obvious when, in complete disregard of solemn pledges and with a contempt of the "decadent Empire" such as no ruler of a state had dared to show since the end of the eighteenth century, Hitler invaded Czechoslovakia in March 1939, divided it, and annexed the parts to the Reich. No longer did Hitler appear in the guise of a patriot striving to remove an "injustice"; now he appeared frankly as the leader of the imperialist crusade that was to make the Reich master of the world. His victorious entrance into Prague announced that the era of "Lebensraum" had begun.

The future of the British Empire appeared darker during the first few months of 1939 than it had at any time since the days of Napoleon. Collapse and annihilation at the hands of the fascist aggressors, who stood armed to the teeth and poised to swoop down to claim their booty, was closer than was generally realized. The great danger was that, still praying for "peace in our time," Prime Minister Chamberlain might persuade his government to make another effort at appeasement, if only for personal reasons. The policies on which he had staked his political reputation were in the balance; and personal motives affect premiers as much as ordinary mortals. Another appeasement might have spared the fascist states the test of war. Not only would the states of the Outer Empire have smashed their newly reinforced bonds with Great Britain, even the more integral parts of the Empire would probably have set out, in sheer self-defense, to search for alliances to give them the security Britain could no longer deliver.

As the summer months wore on, however, it became obvious that there would be no appeasement. Czechoslovakia had stirred the British public to its depth; and no less profound was the effect on the peoples of the Empire. Everywhere it was recognized that appeasement had become, for the first time since the rise of the fascist menace, far more dangerous to the security and continued existence of the Empire than even war.

The German and other fascist rulers, of course, remained blind to the importance of the change; and therein lay the danger. They interpreted Britain's sincere craving for peace as impotence, and they did not know of the fundamental changes that the last few years had wrought in the imperial structure. Busy staging their theatrical coups, they failed to notice that the British Empire in 1939 was a totally different empire from the one which Mussolini had defied with impunity in 1935; they did not see that it had not only mastered the forces of disintegration, but had become again a living, functioning organism. To these revolutionary changes within the Empire we must now turn our attention.

X

IMPERIAL RECONSTRUCTION

ODDLY ENOUGH, THE emergence of the fascist menace was not to be an unmitigated evil to the Empire; and Britain owes a greater debt to Hitler and Mussolini than is at first apparent.

The foundations of the Empire were disintegrating—and not even slowly, we have seen—during the twenties; yet Downing Street remained either too complacent or too paralyzed to bestir itself. The colonies were shamefully neglected and were stagnant; one imperial bond after another was smashed by the Dominions; in India affairs had come to a dangerous impasse; efforts to check the disintegration of the Outer Empire, primarily to counteract the influence of Moscow, lacked both imagination and boldness. Only the prospect of financial bankruptcy in 1931 produced a series of brilliant efforts. Worse, the war seemed to have broken the moral stamina of the British rulers, who came perilously close to impotence. Problems were neglected; to avoid decisions and actions became a virtue; to postpone unpleasant matters, a policy. And these traits were aggravated by an absurd faith that the Empire was the best of all possible worlds and an optimism hardly justifiable by objective reality.

A series of rude blows from the outside were necessary to convince the British that the power of their Empire was rapidly becoming a thing of the past. Mussolini's contemptuous disregard of British threats in 1935 and Hitler's political and cultural challenges brought to the notice of the whole world—and eventually also of the smug British—that the Empire had become cancerous, its vitals eaten away by rival selfishnesses. The Nazi challenge especially was serious, for brute force was accompanied by the language of culture and humanitarianism. The Nazis gave wide publicity to the horrible social and economic conditions existing in the colonies and India; their question to world opinion—Britain, what have you done with your Empire?—had to be answered.

These attacks had two effects. First, rise of the threat of fascist aggression forced all parts to draw together in an effort at self-defense. Finding their security now menaced, the Dominions became a good deal less averse to strengthening imperial bonds. Members of the pre-1920 Outer Empire also made a rush to get under Britain's wings. But for Mussolini and Hitler, Britain would never have succeeded in staging the spectacular comebacks she has made in all the spheres of influence. It is significant that the number of colonial revolts decreased greatly after Mussolini's invasion of Abyssinia in 1936. Expansion of fascist imperialism convinced the colonies that Britain was definitely the lesser evil.

Second, the British began to devote much thought to the problems created since 1920 and some were attacked with almost un-British thoroughness. A marked increase in imperial consciousness became evident. The press began to carry much more information about the Empire; specialized publications on imperial problems began to show a much more intelligent appreciation of facts. Symbolic of the new interest were numerous volumes on the Empire issued by the Royal Institute of International Affairs, and the special study devoted to *The Colonial Problem*. Although many British publications still suffered from an exasperating complacency, the old optimism became tempered by a measure of doubt; and even the Colonial Secretary admitted that "there is no room for complacency; far from it."

Colonial administration was subjected to much devastating criticism in articles, lectures, books, numerous commission reports, and on the floor of the House of Commons, where Labor and Liberal spokesmen began to show unusual interest in colonial problems. No one could write a more devastating book on Britain's colonial record than one which Parliament produced every year during the debate on the

Colonial Estimates. Both the British government and numerous private organizations threw themselves into the work of consolidating relations with the Dominions, the states of the outer and the financial empires. Finance, trade, industry, propaganda, social connections—all were vigorously used. The British Society, of which Lord Lloyd is chairman, did much and useful propaganda work in Portugal, the Balkan countries, Turkey, Greece, Egypt, and other lands; the Royal Empire Society and the Royal Institute of International Affairs became very active in the Dominions. Efforts more serious than all previous were made to placate India and to devise a satisfactory solution for her problems.

Those efforts facilitated attacks on all the problems and produced tremendous results, coming as they did at a time when the overseas parts were also compelled to show a greater and more kindly interest in the Empire. Not only were tendencies toward disintegration placed under control, but ties with almost every part of the Empire were visibly strengthened. By the spring of 1939 the Empire was in a far better position to confront the foreign menaces than it had been at any time since 1920.

ECONOMIC RECOVERY

That the economic problem should have been attacked first is not surprising. For years British statesmen refused to take a realistic attitude toward the worsening economic situation, hoping to muddle through. But with bankruptcy staring them in the face during 1931 they attacked the problems with both courage and wisdom. A National government assumed office in September 1931, and a series of measures were launched which were to revolutionize British economic and financial life within a few years.

The national government based its solution on very simple ideas. We have seen that one of the weaknesses of British economy was its increasing dependence on a small part of the world for its lifeblood. Very well, said the authorities, let us convert this weakness into a source of strength. Instead of dissipating our industrial and financial energies over the whole globe, we will concentrate on that part which is allied to us by political and financial ties; and we will co-operate with that part to evolve a more stable economic order. Second, we will start cultivating our own garden. Since the World War we have neglected our own industries and our agriculture. To those we must now devote our attention and our financial resources.

Simple ideas these; but they spelled a revolution in the economic life of Britain and the Empire. Their application required as much financial virtuosity as it did courage. To clear the field, laws were enacted to preserve national capital and to protect industry and agriculture. The Abnormal Importations Act empowering the Board of Trade to impose duties up to 100 per cent *ad valorem* on manufactured articles imported in abnormal quantities was passed; in December 1931, horticultural products were protected by a similar measure. In February 1932, these temporary measures were replaced by a general Import Duties Act, imposing a minimum customs duty of 10 per cent on luxuries and on articles likely to be manufactured in substantial quantities at home. Two drastic financial measures were taken which followed logically from this policy. The United States having monopolized to a large extent the world gold supply, Britain decided to leave the gold standard; and an embargo was imposed on export of capital for foreign investment.

Britain's century-old policy of free trade was thus swept into the limbo of history; and the government began to create a new economic galaxy to revolve around the United Kingdom. The whole basis of British economic life was revolutionized at the Imperial Economic Conference which met at Ottawa, Canada, in August 1932. In seven agreements signed with all the Dominions except Eire, and including India and Southern Rhodesia, Britain agreed to give preference to imperial agricultural products in exchange for similar preference for United Kingdom manufactures. Britain agreed a) to exempt Empire goods, with certain exceptions, from the new tariff; b) not to reduce the 10 per cent duty without first obtaining Empire consent; c) to increase duties on certain agricultural articles and raw materials coming from non-imperial sources. In return, the Dominions agreed to grant preferences to British manufactures ranging from 5 to 50 per cent; to abolish certain import restrictions;

and to establish a "scientific tariff" by refusing protection to industries which could not reasonably survive in the Dominions, and British industrialists were to be given an opportunity to comment on tariff laws affecting them.

Obviously, however, Britain could not restrict her economic activity to the political empire. Both political and economic reasons made it vital to strengthen economic relations also with the states forming the outer and financial empires. On the other hand, fearing that the Ottawa agreements would rob them of the British market for agricultural products, those states, too, now became extremely eager to enter on special economic relations with Britain. Between April, 1933, and January, 1936, special trade agreements were signed with about a dozen and a half states.

Fairly representative is the agreement with Denmark. Britain guaranteed to accept from Denmark certain percentages of her imports of various agricultural products coming from non-imperial countries. In return Denmark agreed to admit free of duty a wide range of British goods; to reduce duties on certain other manufactures, including cotton goods; not to increase duties on a very wide range of articles coming from Britain, and finally, to purchase from the United Kingdom all her salt, jute, et cetera, and 80 per cent of her coal imports.

While making these efforts to cultivate trade with a definite group of states, Britain took another step to tie them to herself financially by re-creating the "Sterling Bloc" which would accept the British currency, instead of gold, as its standard of monetary value. As R. Palme Dutt put it, "Since America held all the trumps in the battle of gold, British policy went 'no trumps.' " In May, 1932, *The Times* of London editorialized on the need for a financial policy which, starting with the political empire, would lead to "the formation of an economic unit far beyond the bounds of the political empire"; and R. Palme Dutt quotes the following interesting statement from a Memorandum on Monetary Policy (1933) issued by the Federation of British Industries:

Our immediate effort should be directed to building up a British system based primarily on the Empire, and secondly on such other countries as desire to come into some system related to sterling, in the hope that this may provide a reasonable measure of stability and prosperity for Great Britain and the Empire and in due course form the nucleus of a new world financial system.

By every means at her disposal, then, Britain would couple the economic with the political empire, using each to reinforce the other.

Accordingly, the embargo on foreign capital issues was lifted in favor of countries on special political or economic relations with Britain. Loans would be made to states requiring London assets to remain in the Sterling Bloc, or for purchasing British goods. And to tie the Dominions more strongly to her economy, Britain began to develop central Dominion banks which would co-operate effectively with the Bank of England acting as their central bank. The Commonwealth Bank of Australia, founded in 1911, assumed the functions of a central bank with legislation enacted in 1932 which provided, *inter alia,* for holding of British sterling as reserve. Establishment of central banks in Canada, New Zealand, and India in 1934-5 was hailed by the London *Economist* as the "main Empire banking event of the year," since it marked "a definite move forward in the history of the Empire." The charter of the New Zealand bank provided for reserves in pounds sterling, while the Indian central bank was to hold its reserve either in gold or sterling.

A host of statistics bear out the success of these policies. Britain not only forged new links and reinforced the old ones binding the political empire to her, but the financial empire "far beyond" the political one assumed flesh and blood and became a living, functioning organism. Trade with the Empire assumed an increasing importance to Britain. While the Empire supplied about 30 per cent of her total imports between 1925 and 1929 and about 29 per cent during the subsequent three years, the percentage increased steadily during the following years, and reached 40 per cent in 1938. Exports to the Empire increased from 43 per cent of her total exports in 1931 to 48 per cent in 1935 and 49.9 in 1938. The Empire, in other words, came to absorb half of Britain's total exports, and to supply about two-fifths of her imports. The change is even more noticeable if the absolute figures are examined: British exports to the Empire increased from £165,000,000 out of a total of £365,000,000 in 1932 to £252,-000,000 out of total exports of £522,000,000 in 1937. Imports from the Empire jumped from £248,000,000 out of a total of £702,000,000 to £405,000,000 out of total imports of £1,028,-000,000, in 1937.

Trade connections were strengthened also with the Sterling Bloc. Imports from the twelve countries forming the financial empire amounted to 32 per cent of Britain's foreign trade in 1929; the percentage increased to 34.7 in 1937. Even more marked was the growth in exports to this Bloc, which took 38 per cent of Britain's total foreign exports during 1929-31, more than 42 per cent in 1937, and 44.4 per cent in the following year.

True, Britain did not as a result of these policies regain the value of her 1929 exports; but she did re-attain her percentage in the total world trade as of 1929 and recaptured ground lost during 1930-31. Total British exports fell from £729,000,000 in 1929 to £471,000,000 in 1938; as far as one can tell, however, world indices moved in almost the same proportion as did the British. It will be observed that a redistribution of British trade had taken place; a larger share of her exports went to, and a larger share of her imports came from, the Empire and from the Sterling Bloc.

No less momentous were the financial results of the new policy. Here, too, there was a redistribution in concentration. A far greater share of Britain's capital export began to stream to the political and the financial empires. In 1928, no less than 42 per cent of new capital issues in London were destined for foreign countries; in 1936 foreign issues amounted to a bare 10 per cent, nine-tenths of the new issues being destined for the Empire. Indeed, it became almost impossible for a country not on special political relations with Britain to float a loan in London; and nearly all foreign issues were for the financial empire. The result of the new policy has been that, while the total of British loans to foreign countries decreased from £364,000,000 in 1928 to £336,000,000 in 1937, loans to Empire countries increased from £1,036,000,000 in the former year to close to £1,100,000,000 in 1937.

Investment in private companies followed a similar course.

British capital shied away from companies operating in foreign countries, while showing greater interest in imperial industrial and mining concerns. In 1930 the Empire absorbed £2,158,000,000 of British capital and £1,567,000,000 was invested in the rest of the world; by 1936, however, Empire investments had fallen to only £1,981,000,000, while investments in foreign countries had declined to £1,257,000,000. Although complete figures are lacking, it is safe to say that a similar redistribution took place within the field of foreign investments, the amount of British capital invested in the states of the financial and outer empire having decreased less than in countries in no way related to the imperial structure. Above all, the years following the inauguration of the new policy witnessed a significant increase in the total overseas investment—a development the importance of which cannot be overemphasized.

That the new policy has been extremely successful both politically and financially cannot be doubted. Knowledge that their financial needs receive priority privileges in London has done much during the past few years to bind the Dominions and the members of the financial empire to the British political chariot. Both the Australian and the New Zealand governments expressed gratitude for the new imperial consciousness visible in London. Argentina's very important economic concessions to Britain, as compared with the treatment meted out to American investors, must be traced to the knowledge that in the future her financial needs would find a sympathetic ear in London.

No less was the value of the new trade policy to the Dominions. Ottawa transferred about £100,000,000 in purchases per year from foreign to British countries. In 1929 British imports from the Empire exceeded exports by £11,000,000, while the favorable trade balance of foreign countries amounted to £370,000,000; in 1938 however, the favorable balance of trade of the Empire countries had jumped to £125,000,000, while that of foreign countries had decreased to £263,000,000—a solid profit from the imperial connection amounting to about £114,000,000 a year, a gain which the Dominions learned to value and to appreciate.

One needs only to examine the situation in any part of

the Empire to see how these policies worked out. Take
Canada, which had traveled economically furthest from the
mother country. Between 1914 and 1932 New York satisfied
all of Canada's financial needs, while no new issues were
floated in London. Only about 15 per cent of the loans made
during this period in New York were for refunding purposes; the remainder represented new capital investment.
Financially, Canada had become a colony of the United
States, and the political affiliations drifted not far behind the
financial ones. But in 1933 an abrupt change took place.
For the first time in 19 years a loan of $75,000,000 was
floated in London, while no new issues were made in New
York. Since then, London became again, as during the last
century, Canada's financial center.

Britain had little reason to regret the new policies and
the reorganization effected at Ottawa. As Prime Minister
Chamberlain said: "Whatever difficulties have arisen over
the interpretation of the Ottawa Agreements ... they began
a new consciousness of the mutual sympathy which has
shown itself over and over again in conversations and conferences with Dominion ministers. I can truly say I cannot
remember any period when the harmony between the governments of the Dominions and ourselves in all matters of
common interest—financial, political, diplomatic and trade—
has been so complete as in the four years elapsed since
Ottawa." And Sir Thomas Inskip, Dominions Secretary, declared in July, 1939, that the Ottawa Agreements "now represent the keystone of the economic system of the Empire.
They had been an undoubted stimulus to United Kingdom
trade and also to Dominion trade. If the agreements have
not solved every problem ... we in this country have nothing
but gratitude for the advantages ensued as a result" of them.

These policies also greatly stimulated Britain's economic
recovery. Capital investment in the home market zoomed
up; production of agriculture and industry increased. From
1932 to 1938 new capital issues for the domestic market
amounted to four and sometimes eight times the issues for
overseas purposes. There was an almost steady increase in
the amount of land under plow; more important, industrial
production increased by more than 38 per cent between

1930 and 1937. The increase was greatest in the iron and steel industry—and evidence seems to show that armament played only a minor role even in this field—where production was 67 per cent higher than in 1930, in the non-ferrous metals industries, in engineering and in shipbuilding. More pig iron was produced in 1937 than in any year since 1918, and production of steel reached 13 million tons, as compared with 7.6 million in 1913. Unemployment decreased by more than a million, falling in December 1937 to 1.6 millions, while the percentage of jobless fell to 12, as compared to 21.6 in the same month in 1932.

One can point to the decline in the textile industry, in Britain's traditional shipbuilding industry, and other industries inherited from the nineteenth century. What is usually overlooked, however, is that numerous new industries came to the forefront after 1932, the growth of which were stimulated greatly by the new financial policies. During the past few years, for example, in Lancashire alone upwards of two hundred cotton factories were converted to other industrial production. The new factories, employing thousands of former textile workers, began to produce food stuff, footwear, scientific instruments, clothing, leather goods, and so on. In this connection it is interesting to note that while the volume of production for overseas markets fell by about a quarter during the ten-year period 1929-1938, production for the home market—which had always been far more important than the foreign market—increased by nearly 50 per cent. Even shipping recovered from the very serious decline which began in 1920. England's standard of living advanced almost continuously, and a tremendous amount of social service work was done—far more, in housing, for example, than in the United States.

REFORM IN THE COLONIES

Much useful work to better social and economic conditions in the colonies was done during the three or four years preceding outbreak of the war. No doubt the amount actually accomplished fades into insignificance when compared with the tremendous needs; important, however, is that the policy of *laissez faire* came to an end, and for the first time colonial administrators began to take a serious interest in problems of education, health, child welfare, nutrition, agriculture, and others of this nature. A great number of valuable studies on all phases of colonial society were executed, which laid the foundation for even greater progress in the future.

That the new policy was due largely to the Nazi cultural challenge is undeniable. It is not only that the wretched social conditions provided a fertile field for Nazi anti-British propaganda; more significant was the Nazi appeal to world conscience. German publications did much to call attention to "the wretched, joyless existence" led by tens of millions in the British colonies; and they pointed to the "many great successes" achieved by Germany before 1914 in the fields of public health, agriculture, and so forth. For Britain to point to the infinitely greater civil liberties prevailing in British colonies than the Germans ever allowed would have been useless; the new challenge had to be met on its own grounds. Britain's answer was not slow in coming.

A good beginning was made to deal with agricultural, land-settlement, and nutrition problems. Schemes to check soil erosion were launched for the first time in Tanganyika, Kenya, Ceylon, and other dependencies, while soil experts were sent for advanced study to the United States. There was a considerable amount of excellent specialized studies, which saved tens of millions of dollars for fruit growers in Palestine, the West Indies, and in some of the African possessions. Especially important, since colonial diets are seriously deficient in milk ingredients, were the investigations on pasture improvements in Mauritius, Tanganyika, Falkland Islands, and others. Forestry departments were set up in an increasing number of dependencies and schemes of afforestation were started to correct malpractices of earlier days and to check soil erosion.

Above all, colonial malnutrition, the plantation system, and overspecialization in the production of crops for export—evils developed during the decades when agriculture was considered beyond the sphere of government—came in for much serious attention. "The view is now accepted," wrote the Colonial Secretary in his report for 1938, "that small holders . . . ought to produce a larger proportion of their own food . . . that low prices for export crops are much less severely felt when growers have a considerable portion of their food supplies available from their own holdings. Coupled with this is the growing appreciation of the importance of the composition of native dietaries for the well-being of the population. The work of the Colonial Nutrition Committee has directed attention to the need for the improvement of tropical food crops and for a varied diet." Solution of these problems required large capital outlays and far-reaching cultural changes, and could not be effected in a day. But a beginning was made, and but for the outbreak of war in 1939 more would no doubt have been done. More than $3,000,000 was provided for creating new small holdings in Jamaica by breaking up large estates; two hundred families from Barbados, which is owned by planters, "are being settled in St. Lucia. Settlement schemes are also in progress in other territories," reported the Colonial Secretary.

Increased attention was given to public health and social welfare. Some dependencies began to distribute milk or a free midday meal to school children; increased efforts were made to stamp out malaria and a good deal of drainage work was done; venereal and embryonic diseases as well as tuberculosis, which are extremely widespread in all the colonies, began to receive special attention. Some colonies sent special health officers to England to study these diseases; the British Empire Relief Association began to help in coping with leprosy. More important was the inauguration of disease prevention work by means of propaganda through cinemas, lectures, and colorful posters. A staff organized in Nigeria to deal with the terrible problem of sleeping sickness demonstrated what concentrated health work could accomplish in a backward territory. The country was divided into areas and groups of trained African staff under European medical officers entered one area after another to give full treatment and to explain how the disease can be prevented. Re-surveys indicated "that in the main sleeping sickness belt the general infection rate is now only a quarter to an eighth of what it was in former years." Too poor to import large staffs of European nurses and health workers, colonial administrations began to give better training to an increasing number of natives, and many schools for nurses, medical orderlies, midwives, and sanitation workers were opened between 1936 and 1939.

"In all regions of the Colonial Empire there is evidence of an increasing demand for education facilities of all types," wrote the Colonial Secretary in 1938. He did not exaggerate. Continued inattention to this matter would have certainly produced dangerous dissatisfaction, and the British were not a moment too soon in providing greater educational facilities. Appropriations increased everywhere slowly but steadily; new schools were opened; everywhere an expansion in school attendance greater than in any previous similar period took place. Educational departments were formed in such colonies as Aden and Somaliland, which had not had any; above all, a beginning was made to change the quality and type of instruction.

The disastrous results of purely literary education having been brought home to the British, the policy was laid down by the newly formed Advisory Committee on Colonial Education to make the training much more local in character, to give the children a greater interest in their own problems and a profounder view of their native culture. "There is a clear need for more effective patronage of African art by governments and missions," wrote Arthur Mayhew, Joint Secretary of the Committee. Colonial governments began to recognize that the school offers the best medium for carrying through social, agricultural, and hygienic reforms. The Advisory Committee issued a memorandum to colonial administrations suggesting methods for "making the school a real community center, influencing the adults quite as much as the adolescent, a place to which young men and women can come to discuss their problems and new methods for cultivation or marketing...a place where the older people can find out more about the new ideas which the younger generation are absorbing and can contribute their own wisdom and experience." Without doubt, this new trend in education was among the most important happenings in the colonial world.

The measures taken after 1935 to provide instruction in engineering, agriculture, commerce, and other useful arts were in conformity with this new policy. Administrations also began to devote increased attention to girls' education. Quite a few general and specialized girls' schools were opened in the African and Asiatic colonies, where such subjects as hygiene, domestic science, and agriculture received special emphasis. Widespread criticism and dissatisfaction compelled the British to provide facilities for the entry of colonial peoples into the more advanced fields of knowledge. Only the barest beginning had been made in all these fields when the war broke out; but even the little which had been done was sufficient to encourage the colonial peoples and to enlist new support for the Empire.

The change in policy toward labor did not come a moment too soon; nor was it as thorough as it should have been. Colonial regimes still remained far too antilabor; not all the laws which had been enacted at the demand of London were being enforced. But a break with the past was made: local administrations and especially London, which is invariably more progressive, began to provide more civilized labor standards. Labor departments were established in thirteen colonies during the two years 1937-38; in others labor offices were organized; legislation empowering the governor to fix a minimum wage for any occupation when he was satisfied that the existing wage "is unreasonably low" was enacted in twenty-nine dependencies. Nearly every colony now passed child-labor laws, industrial hygiene regulations, and workmen's compensation ordinances. The movement against penal sanctions in masters and servants regulations was gaining ground, and they have been abolished in more than a dozen dependencies. Kenya, the Rhodesias, and other East African dependencies still felt, however, that the future of civilization in territories settled by a large number of white plantation owners depends on retention of those medieval laws. Necessity also brought about a change in the official attitude toward trade unions, legislation for the registration of which was enacted in twenty-six colonies. The Colonial Secretary wrote:

It should be realized that the prohibition of trades unions or the subjection of them to disabilities which used to be imposed by the Common Law in England, but which are now altogether obsolete, is almost certain to encourage the formation of illegal organizations which may easily develop into "secret societies" and extend their operation into the political field. A policy of restriction in this respect may therefore give direct encouragement to the formation of extremist associations.

Unfortunately, enforcement everywhere lagged far behind the enactment of laws. Most colonial governments seemed to feel that they could wash their hands of the matter once fairly decent laws had been placed on the statute books. All sorts of excuses were made for the failure to appoint a sufficient staff to enforce the laws.

Inevitably, the unsettled state of the world prevented similar progress in the political field. Britain felt that the time was not propitious for political experiments; and even the colonies somewhat sympathized with this point of view. However, it is obvious that decisive steps toward greater self-rule will have to be taken as soon as the international situation returns to normal. The future direction was clearly indicated by Sir Andrew Coldicott, the new Governor of Ceylon, who opposed the demand of the European Association and other foreign bodies for communal representation. "My reason for opposition," Sir Andrew wrote in a masterly memorandum, "is that any concession to the principle of communal representation would perpetuate sectionalism and preclude the emergence of true political parties. . . . The success of democracy in Ceylon depends . . . on the discipline and drive which party loyalties can alone infuse into democracy."

These reforms did much to appease the colonial peoples, and made them less ready to accept fascist aid for creating trouble for Britain. The latter became to them the lesser evil. And recognizing that much more would have to be done in the future if disaster was to be avoided, London undertook significant reforms in the Colonial Office and in the various services. Advisory committees on health, education, nutrition, agriculture, and so on, were appointed to lay down policy for the whole colonial empire. Dominated by professional men, social workers, and laymen, these committees brought a more progressive point of view into the musty official atmosphere of the Colonial Office. Equally important were the steps taken to organize the colonial service along professional lines and to give prospective officers more specialized technical training. The decision to give financial aid to agricultural and other technical appointees for spending one or two years in graduate study was wholly to the good, since, above everything else, the colonies need technical experts.

There is, obviously, no telling how fundamental these reforms would have been, whether they would have assumed the momentum necessary for the colonies to catch up with the West in a measurable space of time, and whether they would have for long prevented renewal of rebellion. Certain it is that many colonial leaders began to look forward to a better era in the future; but the war broke out before the new policies could be carried very far. Now, totally new forces are accumulating in the colonies, and it seems highly improbable that Britain will be able to begin at the end of the war where she left off in September, 1939. However, we are getting too far ahead, and we must retrace our steps to see what happened in the rest of the Empire during the years 1935-1939.

APPEASEMENT IN INDIA

Solution of the Indian problem proved more difficult in many ways than any of the others which confronted Britain in the early days of the decade. Some of those complicating elements were the creation of the British imperialists; many more had been made acute by them; the importance of others they exaggerated. All this was true; yet, whatever the cause, those complicating elements were there, and from this reality there could be no escape, as became evident during the Round Table Conferences held in London in 1930-32 when Gandhi's pretensions to speak in the name of all India were bitterly resented by the princes, Moslems, and other groups. As if to prove that India was not a unified nation, communal riots became more frequent during subsequent years than ever before; and the Indian delegates at the Conference were unable to reach agreement among themselves on any vital question. Perhaps this—to divide and rule—was Britain's intention: if so, it certainly did not lack native allies, and not only among the leaders.

Five years were necessary for evolving a solution least unsatisfactory to the many interests involved; and when this solution appeared, in the form of the Government of India Act, 1935, it of course failed to satisfy anybody. The Congress demanded that a native constituent assembly should write the new constitution; it opposed the favoritism shown to princes and minorities; it feared the reactionary influence of the princes in the federal government; above all, it refused to countenance the great powers left to the Governor General and the governors of the provinces. It saw in the innumerable safeguards infinite opportunities for British imperialism to play a deadly game. No less dissatisfied were, however, the minorities and the princes, who feared that too much power had been conceded to the Congress. Moslem opposition became widespread and there was an increase in communal riots.

Broadly, the act outlined (in 430 pages) federal and state systems of government, with the great innovation that the whole of India—the states and tribal areas as well as the British provinces—was included in the federal structure. The federal government was to consist of the King, represented by the Governor General; a bicameral legislature of a Council of State and a Federal Assembly, and an executive —composed of Indians—responsible to the legislature. Representation in the federal legislature was weighted heavily in favor of the states and the minority communities—to assure a solid bloc of votes for protecting British interests, nationalists said; to protect the lives and interests of the minorities and princes, the British argued. The powers of the responsible government were widened as compared with the scheme of 1919, though still far too circumscribed to satisfy the nationalists. The Governor General was to remain the final authority on all questions affecting a) relations with foreign states; b) the peace and tranquillity of India or any part thereof; c) the financial stability and credit of the federation; d) interests of the minorities; e) the legitimate interests of members of the Public Services; f) discrimination against British or Burmese interests, and actions which would subject goods from the United Kingdom to discriminatory treatment; g) the rights and dignity of the states and their rulers; h) the defense and security of the realm. The power of the Ministry and the Legislative bodies was circumscribed particularly in the spheres of defense and finance.

Similar was the division affected in the provincial governments. About thirty million people were given the right to vote for the Provincial Legislative Assemblies (only slightly more than 15.5 millions voted in 1937); and six provinces obtained upper houses, the members of which were elected by less than ninety thousand voters. The British governor of each province was to appoint a ministry from the party most able to secure a majority in the legislature, which would carry on normal executive functions, although special fields were reserved to the discretion of the governor. Were the ministry to resign office on account of a disagreement, the burden of administration would evolve upon the governor until a new ministry could be formed.

Notwithstanding its hundreds of clauses and subclauses the act was purposely left vague enough to make successful operation dependent on the good will of the parties concerned. The Congress naturally feared the worst, pointing to the innumerable loopholes for endless interference on the part of the British in every branch of administration. Obviously almost anything could be interpreted to fall under such "reservations" as "financial stability" or "peace and tranquillity." Radical nationalists therefore threatened to boycott the whole scheme; and it was only after the elections of 1937, which gave the Congress a majority in eight of the eleven States that it changed its tactics. The election itself showed that the British were genuinely anxious to evolve a new *modus vivendi*. They did not manipulate votes against the Congress, and official statements constantly emphasized that a new era had begun in Anglo-Indian relations.

Again and again during 1937-38 the British proved their anxiety to come to terms with the nationalists—if only to remove the ground from beneath the fascist propaganda. The growing tension in Europe and Asia forced Britain to make concessions to win India's support in case of war; and for the first time since 1918, India knew the meaning of orderly administration. Both the Governor General and the provincial governors co-operated loyally with the Congress ministries; important legislation aiming to ameliorate somewhat the lot of ryots and industrial workers was enacted and in every case received the sanction of the governors. Even legislation about the wisdom of which the British were skeptical, such as the prohibition of intoxicating liquor, was approved when passed by the legislatures. Members of the Civil Service learned to take orders from the men whom they had once persecuted and imprisoned.

There is no better example of the changed British policy than the new attitude to the princes. Recognizing that in an international crisis support of the Congress would be far more important than any aid which the princes might be able to give, the British authorities, in the early months of 1939, ceased to champion, at least temporarily, princely reaction against the progressive Congress forces. The Viceroy's intervention in support of Gandhi saved a very critical situation when the latter embarked on a fast-unto-death to obtain greater civil liberties from the ruler of Rajkut; and at the last meeting of the Chamber of Princes, held at New Delhi in March, 1939, the princes were compelled to listen to a long indictment of their rule and a clear warning that they must introduce reforms if they wished to keep their thrones. "Never had the Paramount Power spoken more plainly," commented an American observer. The warning was reinforced shortly afterwards by *The Times* of London which declared editorially at the end of July: "Those Princes who imagine that . . . they are bound for all time to be sheltered by the protection of the Paramount Power are deceiving themselves and ignoring the facts of British political evolution. . . . Public opinion in Great Britain is little disposed to support absolutism against popular government. This public opinion is not likely to support the Princes in declining to enter a Federation which ultimately aims at bringing India into equality with other units of the British Commonwealth; nor . . . can public opinion logically favor the Princes in maintaining indefinitely their existing positions of absolute authority." Those were strong words for the organ of a Conservative government, and the Indian nationalist press did not miss their significance. The editorial was widely reprinted, and the comments showed appreciation of Britain's new role.

The Round Table Conferences and the India Act were no doubt excellent sedatives and they enabled Britain to quiet the nationalists at an extremely critical period. But for the concessions, the nationalists would no doubt have launched another civil disobedience campaign between 1935 and 1938, which would certainly have been exceedingly costly to Britain and might have resulted in her expulsion. The fascist powers would have seized the opportunity while England's hands were tied in India to extract concessions, political and territorial, in other parts of the world. The new policy went far enough to forestall a rebellion, the Congress Nationalists having recognized the possibilities for introducing reforms and for expanding their influence among the masses. Thus far, then, the new policy was a success, and it harmonized with the efforts at reconstruction that were being made in other parts of the Empire.

Unfortunately it did not go further than that. India ceased to be an immediate menace; her problems, however, had not been solved, and there could be no telling when she would flare up again. Developments in Europe and the Far East also served to weaken the groups favoring complete immediate independence, and Japan's activities in China discredited the pro-Japanese cliques. But there was bound to be an increase in the demand for immediate Dominion status as soon as Britain became involved in war. Power increased the influence of the Congress among the ryots, which naturally did not make the nationalist leaders more moderate. True, Gandhi, more far-sighted than some of his colleagues, promised not to embarrass Britain with a rebellion in case she became involved in a war; but the election of Subhas C. Bose to the presidency of the Congress showed that the young radical elements were gaining in strength. The fact is that conservatism, fear of the unknown, and selfishness prevented Britain from attacking the Indian dilemma in as vigorous a manner as characterized the attacks on the other problems.

NEW DOMINION BONDS

One need only read the reports of the Imperial Conferences in 1930 and 1937 to realize how far the Dominion empire had traveled between these two periods. Separation and autonomy held the center of the stage at the earlier date; an entirely new note became perceptible in 1937. No longer were the Dominion representatives interested exclusively in winning additional powers; there was now a great deal of discussion about co-operation, and new centripetal forces were at work. The spirit animating this conference cannot be better expressed than in the words of the Canadian premier:

We are endeavoring to prove the enduring possibility of establishing peace and sharing the gains of progress among peoples situated in every continent, held together not by centralized control or reliance upon force, but by similarity of political institutions and political ideals, by common interests and common loyalties.

And Prime Minister Lyons of Australia added:

I feel that I speak for all sections of the Australian people when I say that we come to the Imperial Conference as willing partners in a great enterprise, the success of which will depend upon the spirit of co-operation, based upon mutual interest.

That much of the new attitude was due to the emergence of the fascist menaces and the disappearance of collective international security is obvious; and a perusal of the topics which received most discussion bears this out. Although voicing general support of the League of Nations and disarmament, all the delegates felt that questions of rearmament were of far greater importance. Not only was the state of the defenses of each Dominion reviewed in detail; measures for more effective co-operation were considered, and foreign relations came in for much analysis. As the other parts of the Empire, the Dominions now looked more kindly upon the imperial connection, seeing in it their sole protection against the new and mighty imperialisms.

Yet lack of security was not the only cause of the new

attitude. At this conference the effects of the new British policies and attitude toward the Empire became perceptible; and for this new attitude, too, as was pointed out above, the fascist menace was indirectly and to some extent at least responsible. After legal ties had snapped and economic bonds had weakened, which had led many observers to believe that the days of the Commonwealth were numbered, the British set themselves to develop new bonds of co-operation which, being of value not only to themselves but to all the Dominions, would give the Commonwealth a new lease on life. The renewed imperial consciousness set them exploring new services which imperial unity might render, and bonds which would give groups in the Dominions—and the larger the group the better—vested interests in the preservation of the Empire. And in this they succeeded to an amazing extent. Not only was the defection of the Dominions checked, the trend turned in the opposite direction; and in contrast to the situation prevailing a few years before, it became almost certain by the beginning of 1939 that war with Britain would mean war with most of the Dominions.

"*Mere* law," the very wise and old Lord Balfour wrote a few weeks before his death for a projected work on the British Empire, "is the weakest of all bonds." British statesmen, with centuries of experience in ruling behind them, acted instinctively on this maxim, especially as "*mere* law" was no longer a unifying bond. The years 1932-39 therefore witnessed the formation of a host of voluntary associations which aimed to make the intelligentsia of England and the Dominions Empire-conscious. Pro-Empire propaganda, previously conspicuous by its complete absence, was used extensively: inter-Dominion conferences were sponsored; the Royal Institute of International Affairs in England and the sister institutes in the Dominions held discussions on Empire problems; the radio, newspapers, magazines, lecturers, even tourist travel—all were utilized in the forging of the new cultural bonds. This policy reached its culmination with the visit of the King and Queen to Canada in the summer of 1939. A more effective way for bringing Canada back to the imperial fold could hardly have been devised. The few days' presence of their majesties did more to popularize the imperial connection among the whole Canadian population than a hundred laws could possibly have done.

Among the most interesting forms of Imperial co-operation are scientific, economic, and research bureaus which, supported with funds contributed by the various Dominions, render valuable services to all. There is, first, the Imperial Institute of Entomology, which acts as the clearing house of information concerning entomological research, classifies insects of economic importance sent from the various parts of the Empire, and executes upon request special investigations which individually governments could not afford. Second, the Imperial Mycological Institute collects and disseminates information on applied mycology and plant pathology, and studies fungi of economic importance at the request of Empire governments. Dominion and colonial mycological officers hold conferences, when the Director or the Imperial Institute submits a report reviewing past accomplishments. Third, the Bureau of Hygiene and Tropical Diseases, which issues two monthly publications to disseminate information and replies to direct inquiries on problems of tropical disease. Fourth, the Imperial Forestry Institute at Oxford not only carries on research and maintains an information department for the use of Empire governments, but provides advanced training to forestry officers from all over the Empire. In addition there is a Standing Committee on Empire Forestry, and periodic conferences of the heads of Dominion and Colonial Forestry Departments are arranged. Fifth, useful work is done by the Imperial Institute in connection with the determination of the quality and uses of Empire raw materials. Questions are constantly referred to it by all Empire governments, which have derived considerable benefit from its high quality work. It maintains exhibition galleries for the display of Empire products, enabling tens of thousands of visitors to learn about the Empire and its resources. Sixth, important research on the uses of new timbers is carried on by The Empire Timbers Committee, which also renders assistance in finding markets for timbers proved by the laboratory to be of novel usefulness. Seventh, the Imperial Shipping Committee carries out surveys of maritime transport facilities on imperial trade routes and studies how to improve facilities to stimulate imperial trade. An important part of its work is to investigate complaints from sources finding existing facilities inadequate for their inter-Empire commerce.

Eighth, a position of special importance is held by the Imperial Economic Committee. Organized in 1925 to increase Imperial trade, the Committee is now composed of two representatives from each of the Dominions, one each from Southern Rhodesia and Burma and two members from the colonial empire. It carries out investigations into the methods of preparing for market and the marketing of Empire foodstuffs in the United Kingdom; it studies how to improve methods of marketing of imperial products in non-Empire countries; surveys of the production of certain articles in the Empire are issued and the Committee is prepared to execute detailed studies on any economic question presented by any Empire government. The Economic Committee and the former Empire Marketing Board have carried out extremely important studies on very many agricultural products which have been of the utmost value to both producers and consumers. The former have been shown what type of articles and what quantity is used, while the latter have found in compact form information on the Empire's production capacity. A mass of invaluable information is buried in the reports of these agencies; and if full advantage has not yet been taken of those detailed studies, that is only because of the laissez-faire policy followed by imperial governments. Should a change in high economic policy come about, governments will find at their disposal reliable guides for future action. These reports will be of special importance during wartime, when detailed information of available resources and production capacity is of utmost importance.

This enumeration of some of the more important imperial agencies will give the reader a conception of the new type of co-operation that was evolved. These agencies are by no means the only ones. There is, for example, the Imperial War Graves Commission which supervises war graves of Empire soldiers throughout the world; there are numerous and important agencies for co-operation in scientific, industrial, and medical research. In a very real way, those com-

mittees and agencies are all-Empire enterprises, each part
sharing the expense and, in varying degrees, all parts of the
Empire derive concrete benefit. Very few Empire governments could afford to maintain similar organizations by
themselves. That they helped to promote imperial unity cannot be doubted. Many are of the opinion that the Commonwealth's future depends on the creation and extension of
similar agencies.

In a system like the British Commonwealth of Nations
developments such as the Imperial Press Conference, the
Empire Parliamentary Conference, meetings of Royal Institutes, and periodic gatherings of similar public-opinion-
creating bodies assume special significance. They make for
greater understanding of the problems of the various parts
so far separated in space, and create a feeling of unity. Criticism at an Imperial Press Conference some years ago served
to stimulate newspapers to devote much more space to news
of special Empire significance. Reuter, the great British
news-gathering agency supplying news to all Empire papers,
the Official Wireless of the British and other governments,
as well as the British Broadcasting Corporation no doubt
contributed a great deal to the strengthening of imperial
bonds, and these services were rapidly extended until outbreak of the war. Serious studies were executed on how to
assure more effective all-Empire radio services, and newspapers—only recently the heralds of separation—began to co-
operate effectively by carrying more Empire news than ever
before.

Another interesting manifestation is the congresses of the
Chambers of Commerce of the British Empire. At the last
congress, which met in July, 1939, and was attended by
about three hundred delegates, every phase of imperial relations from education to civil aviation and from defense to
trade was discussed. A representative from Australia put forward the suggestion that to increase intellectual co-operation
among the Commonwealth of Nations postage on printed
matter be reduced; a resolution "welcoming plans for car-
riage of all first class mail by air" was passed; a number of
civil aviation questions were debated, as well as trade policies and problems in connection with Imperial Preference.

A resolution was carried urging that every opportunity be taken to broaden the basis of historical and geographical teaching so that children should appreciate "that they are citizens of a united Commonwealth." In New Zealand, a speaker reported, "the children were taught to regard England as the Homeland. It was the ambition of every New Zealand schoolboy to take a trip Home"; a delegate from Capetown reported that to further imperial consciousness among children an annual visit of South African boys to England had been arranged. Members of Dominion parliaments met at London in informal sessions each July, and plans were made for holding official plenary sessions every three years. *A Journal of the Parliaments of the Empire,* containing the debates in the various parliaments on questions of Empire-wide importance, began to appear.

The far-reaching effects of these new forms of co-operation and consultation can be best illustrated perhaps with the developments in shipping legislation. We have seen that with the enactment of the Statute of Westminster each of the Dominions obtained the right to legislate for its own shipping. It was widely feared, not unjustly, that each Dominion would rush to make use of the new powers and confusion would ensue. Instead, an agreement was reached between the Dominions and Great Britain, which provides that no part of the Commonwealth shall deny to ships registered in another part the same treatment as is given to its own ships; that a central registry for all ships of the Commonwealth be maintained in England. Identical conditions of registry as a British ship were laid down for all vessels, whether belonging to a United Kingdom or Dominion concern; and agreement was reached on common standards for officer certificates and on other matters. As a result, the chaos expected to develop from repeal of the British Merchant Shipping Act did not take place; United Kingdom shipping was not driven out of the Dominions, as had been feared. On the contrary, removal of the element of compulsion made the Dominions more willing to co-operate in matters of shipping.

Defense provided a field for much effective co-operation. Each of the Dominions had become full master of its own defense forces; yet atomization did not come about, and the various defense systems remained connected in a very effective manner, as became evident after outbreak of the war. A great deal of uniformity was attained through use of identical methods of organization, types of equipment and establishment, and training manuals issued by the Admiralty, War Office, and Air Ministry in the United Kingdom. Of considerable importance for maintaining effective unity was the direct correspondence between military establishments in Britain and the defense ministries of the Dominions. The Dominion Staff Colleges sent students to the Imperial Defence College; Australia and New Zealand appointed Liaison Officers in England, and officers from the United Kingdom were constantly sent on leave to serve with the Dominion defense forces. The importance of these forms of co-operation cannot be overestimated; not only did they make for unity of establishment, but, which is more important, a common point of view was created, as well as a certain amount of *esprit de corps*. So effective were the results of these activities that anti-imperialists in Canada began to point with alarm to the fact that fifteen high-ranking Canadian officers had attended the Imperial Defence College during the ten years since its establishment in 1927.

Co-operation was also secured through the Committee on Imperial Defence. At first glance the value of this Committee, on which no Dominions are represented and which lacks all executive authority even in the United Kingdom, would appear to be not very great; and no doubt such a body would not have been of much importance among another people. The British, however, with their instinct for team work made it a very potent instrument, primarily by using it to exert indirect influence on the Dominions' general staffs. The personal contacts established through liaison officers were used fully, if unofficially, by the Committee to exert a definite influence. The work of the Committee was supplemented by the Imperial Defence College, which was attended by officers from all the Dominions except Ireland. Not only were the higher aspects of imperial strategy studied, but plans were elaborated "for the co-operation of forces in different parts of the world in the face of common emergencies." Again, then, loss of direct power did not spell disaster. The British learned to use indirect influence, and to use it very effectively.

A new tendency emerged during 1934-35 which contained immense possibilities for the creation of new bonds of unity for surpassing in strength the old legal ties. The policy, in brief, was to create economic concerns of Empire-wide value, and to associate the Dominions both in the benefits and responsibilities of the imperial structure.

Imperial preference, undoubtedly the most important single expression of this system, was discussed in a previous section; here a few words should be said about the trend to associate the Dominions in governing the Colonial Empire, once Britain's private preserve. At the last Imperial Conference (1937) the Colonial Secretary discussed the machinery which had been established in the Dominions for the recruitment of personnel for the various colonial services, and he expressed the hope that the number of Dominion applicants for appointment would continue to grow. For the first time the Dominions were taken in as full-fledged partners in a great enterprise, and they were thus given a concrete stake in the preservation of the Empire.

Very important was the scheme for speeding up mail service between all parts of the Empire by carrying all first class mail by airplane without an extra charge, which was brought before the British Parliament at the end of 1934. The governments acted quickly, having perceived the immense benefits of the scheme both to themselves and to private individuals. Communications between outlying parts were vastly improved; inter-imperial trade received a new stimulus; and—a fact of great importance—air transportation concerns in the various parts of the Empire benefited, as they were associated in the scheme with the (British) Imperial Airways. Contributions from each of the participating governments helped finance it. Its phenomenal development during the years 1937-39, far exceeding all expectations, showed the value of this link. "All-up" became a vital part in imperial life and trade.

Another step in the development of this type of co-operation came with the establishment of Imperial Cable and

Wireless, Ltd. The object was to unify and improve cable and wireless services for the Empire, and to reduce rates. The various governments of the Empire led by Britain entered into agreements with the new concern, which undertook to establish a unified system for transmitting messages by cable or wireless at reduced rates, while the governments agreed to accept certain financial burdens. Each of the Dominions and India thus obtained an interest vested in the maintenance of the system, which proved of great benefit to private individuals and rendered important services to the various governments. Announcement in July, 1939, of a scheme to improve imperial air transportation by establishing one large concern dominated by the governments of the Empire represented a further step in creating Empire-wide public utilities. It was proposed that the new company be managed by a board of about fifteen members representing the United Kingdom, the Dominions, India, and the colonies if necessary.

THE NEW OUTER EMPIRE

Nowhere did the upswing of the fascist menace have greater political effects than on the states of the Outer Empire, which had been lost so rapidly and so completely after the World War. Strategically situated and possessing great economic potentialities, yet unable to defend themselves against the new imperialisms, the vast majority of Britain's former "spheres of influence" flocked again to Albion's standard. Before 1938 had ended there was a wall around the areas colored red on British maps. And the new wall was more solid than that which had existed before 1920.

Return of the "spheres of influence" was preceded and made possible by a real change of policy on the part of Britain. Necessity forced her to recognize that the cultural changes everywhere had been too real for easy dismissal; and unable to make any headway by dint of force, she decided to become a "good neighbor." Calm stock-taking showed that the new nationalism of her former satellites need not be a menace to the Empire. On the contrary, it could be turned into one of the main pillars of the imperial structure. Determined more than ever, and prepared more than ever, to maintain their independence against foreign aggression, would they not make valuable allies against potential aggressors? Would not their efforts at economic reconstruction offer greater possibilities for financial investment and trade? And so when the wrath on the one side and the bluster on the other had passed, it was seen that both had too many interests in common; that friendly relations would not only be to mutual advantage, but that it was really necessary for the security and existence of either. Yet no change in British policy however great could have produced the spectacular results which took place between 1935 and 1939 had the fascist imperialisms not emerged to threaten the security of the world.

Under the changed conditions, of course, Britain could no longer impose treaties like that imposed on Persia in 1919. One-sided bargains, where the profit is entirely on the side of might and the weaker carries the whole burden, became impossible. To profit either economically or politically, concrete value had to be given in return. There were pessimists who contended that relinquishment of the right to control contained serious dangers for the future. Some pointed to a grim time when the erstwhile spheres of influence would reject outright even the circumscribed British influence left under the new dispensation; others were troubled with nightmares of European powers invading the field left vacant by Britain. Most British statesmen, however, thought that the new relationship would be more durable and firmer than the one which had existed before 1920 just because it was more fair and was based on common interest rather than on might.

Anglo-Iraqi relations are in an unsatisfactory state. The Iraqis are more suspicious at the present time than perhaps they have ever been at the integrity of British motives.... Almost everywhere ... there is to be found evidence of anti-British sentiment.... The Iraqis ... must not be allowed to drift into the arms of Great Britain's enemies, which spread widely and eagerly in the Middle East.... Is it not possible to satisfy at once Iraqi amour propre and Iraqi interests? We believe that it is possible. There must be a fresh definition ... of what are really essential British interests.

This comment from the issue of February 21, 1930, of the *Near East and India,* generally considered as the unofficial organ of the Colonial Office, expresses well the problem that confronted Britain at the turn of the decade not only in Iraq but in all the territories of the Outer Empire and the solution that was devised. Accordingly, the "imperialistic" mandate was put aside and in June 1930, a treaty was signed granting Iraq complete independence. Two years later an Iraqi delegate assumed a seat at the League of Nations as representative of an independent state.

The treaty was a momentous document, marking the beginning of a new era in relations between East and West. For the first time in modern history, a western Empire relinquished its "rights" over an Eastern people. Although Iraq agreed to "full and frank consultation on all matters of foreign policy" and to other obligations, Britain's concessions were far greater. She relinquished the right to control; her Air Force had to move from Baghdad into the desert; British officials in the service of the Iraqi government henceforth had to take orders from the native government; the high commissioner ceased to function, and an ambassador took his place.

Britain scrupulously observed the agreement; yet far from spelling the end of British prestige and influence, both actually increased under the new conditions. Native newspapers ceased to appear with headlines "Go to war, Oh Arabs," or "London, your hour has come." England having become an ally, the Iraqis were very eager to co-operate to the utmost, knowing that their independence would not be worth the paper on which the 1930 treaty was written if one of the totalitarian states emerged victorious from a war with Britain. Italian and German propaganda, which would have found a wide echo among the highly emotional populace had it come during the twenties, had very little effect— or an effect the reverse of that anticipated by the fascist powers. Instead of persuading the people to make trouble for Britain, all except the few paid propagandists became convinced of the reality of the fascist menace; and the authorities, both military and civil, began to co-operate with Britain more than ever.

With Ibn Saud and the Gulf Emirates the new policy was no less of a success. A number of concessions were made to the Wahabi war lord. Britain relinquished the right to control his foreign relations and the British Legation at Jeddah could no longer liberate slaves seeking sanctuary within its compass. Again, however, far from using his greater powers to the detriment of his ally, Ibn Saud constantly rejected in no uncertain manner all advances from the totalitarian powers. He knew that Britain had become the best guarantor of the independence of his kingdom and he showed every inclination to co-operate, especially during the years 1937-39, when the fascist powers became actively interested in fomenting disturbances in the Near East. He did not even make trouble during the disturbances in Palestine; his attitude was correct in the extreme—which earned him not a little animosity among Palestinian Arab zealots.

Arthur Henderson, Labor Secretary for Foreign Affairs, defined in 1929 the new policy toward Egypt as "the establishment of firm and lasting friendship ... by the removal of those sources of suspicion which in the past have been the cause of so much damage." However, the Italo-Abyssinian war and the consequent tension in the Mediterranean were necessary before this policy could be implemented. Both Britain and Egypt were prepared to make concessions now that a common menace appeared at the gates, and the treaty of 1937 was signed in record time. Egyptian independence was made real, and the British have since been careful not to violate it. They relinquished all sorts of privileges, including the Capitulations; and although both Italy and Germany spared neither labor nor money, Egypt refused to listen to the siren song of totalitarian propagandists. Egypt was henceforth to be master of her own house. The Residency—symbol of British power—was abolished, and an ambassador replaced the high commissioner. Yet relinquishment of the symbols of power, did not put an end to the power itself. Never since 1882 was Britain as popular as she became after signature of the treaty. Britain then became their "mighty and dear ally," with whom they were only too glad to co-operate in the protection of their country. They spent large sums of money on modernizing the army;

they built roads and barracks; and Egypt became far more useful for the protection of the Suez Canal than it had been at any time since 1882.

Extremely gratifying to the Arabs was the change in Britain's policy toward pan-Arabism. Until 1937 Britain would have nothing to do with it. Fearing lest unification of the Arab states would spell the end of her influence in the Near East, she was not averse even to cultivating minor jealousies to keep them apart. This policy, too, was changed. Britain became active in promoting Arab unity, thus identifying herself with the extreme nationalists. The Arabs recognized the reality of the change when Ibn Saud concluded treaties of good neighborliness in the winter of 1936-37 with Iraq and Egypt, largely through the good offices of Britain. The nationalists were not ungrateful. "Why should we not co-operate with Britain to the limit if our own interests are identical with hers?" wrote a nationalist paper at the end of 1938.

The weaning of Turkey, Persia, and Afghanistan away from their Soviet godmother presented a more difficult problem. Hostility to Britain had been deep-rooted there, and all these states had profited exceedingly from the Soviet alliance. Nevertheless, the change of policy was as effective there as in all other "spheres of influence," and before long Britain emerged victorious. Sir Percy Lorraine, as polished and gentle a diplomat as was ever produced by the Foreign Office, was sent to Teheran with the not easy task of making the Persians forget the past by convincing them that Britain had adopted entirely different policies. He acquitted himself brilliantly, and his successors carried on the good work.

By 1935 it became obvious that Teheran was not blind to the value of closer co-operation with Britain. There was an upswing in the influence of the British Minister, and a corresponding decline in Soviet power. As a result, Britain emerged as the chief guarantor of Persia's territorial integrity. Relations constantly improved between 1935 and 1938. British finance again assumed the leading role in Persia's economic life, and the British navy's oil supply from Abaddan was assured. The new influence of Britain became visible in 1937, when Persia (now Iran), Afghanistan, Iraq, and

Turkey signed at Saad Abbad a treaty of friendship and non-aggression. The treaty was no doubt an expression of the growing feeling of unity among the Near Eastern states and served their common interests well; it is probable, however, that it would never have been consummated without the promptings of British diplomatic representatives, who had begun to solidify again the pre-1920 wall around the Indian Empire. Early in 1939 it became obvious that were a crisis to develop in the interior of Asia, Persia would no longer allow herself to be turned into the spearhead of anti-British activities. On the contrary, Persian leaders admitted that under certain conditions the Shah might even find it advisable to co-operate with Britain against a third power.

To bring about reconciliation with Afghanistan was more difficult. Soviet penetration had gone farther there than in Persia, while the disorganized state of the country made concentrated political work difficult. The assassination of Amanullah brought no improvement. The British were delighted that the spearhead of the Soviet penetration had been removed; on the other hand the anarchy under the bandit-ruler Bacho Sakao, which might have served as an excuse for Soviet intervention, was an even greater menace. In 1929, consequently, Britain financed Nasir Shah to stage a revolution which resulted in his assumption of the Afghan throne. About a million dollars was placed at his disposal, and, what was more valuable, around ten thousand rifles. Nasir Shah was successful; careful work among the most important feudal grandees persuaded them to flock to his colors. After that Afghanistan resumed its place in the British orbit. There was even an increase in British activity as compared with the pre-war years.

Relations between Turkey and Britain became idyllic after 1933. The new policy at work in other parts was implemented in an even more radical manner in Turkey. Although at first suspicious of British professions of benevolence, the Ghazi became convinced of their sincerity during the last years of his life. "Ankara," wrote the semiofficial organ of the Colonial Office, has made "too much of a bogey of 'capitalist imperialism' that under present day conditions is a figment of Turkish imagination."

Britain's first object was to bring Turkey into the League of Nations, thus to start her looking westward instead of eastward where her natural ally was Russia. Success came in the summer of 1932, when Turkey became a member of the League. Britain then began to supplant Russia in developing Turkey's modern industries; trade relations improved; and at the Montreux Convention in July, 1936, it was British support that enabled Turkey to win consent of the powers to abolish the clauses of the Lausanne convention demilitarizing the Dardanelles. On that occasion one British publication commented, "Of late... the interests common to both states have been more sharply perceived, and Anglo-Turkish relations are today on a plane of such happy cordiality as is gratifying not only for its own sake but also for the sake of the whole Near East.... A nation's policy must confirm its strategy; there is every reason, therefore, that these good relations should endure."

Efforts by the Axis powers during the few years preceding outbreak of the war to oust Britain from her position of supremacy failed completely. A vast amount of propaganda went into Turkey from both Germany and Italy; Berlin spent millions of dollars to tie Ankara to its economic chariot; cultural missions were sent to Ankara, and Turkish delegations were taken to the Reich, at the latter's expense of course. Germany's most polished diplomat, Herr Franz von Papen, was sent to convince the Turks of the value of an alliance with Berlin. All in vain. An Anglo-Turkish accord was signed on May 12, 1939, binding the two governments to co-operate in case of aggression that might lead to war in the Mediterranean, and Turkish authorities made it clear that they would do nothing that might alienate British support. Never, not even during the last years of the last century, were relations between the two countries so intimate.

Different tactics were necessary to bring back Greece to the imperial fold. Dictator John Metaxas having followed a pro-Axis policy to strengthen his regime and against the wishes of the overwhelming majority of the people, who prayed that their traditional ally should resume her interest in Greece, no choice was left to the British government but to issue, without regard to the wishes of the dictator, a unilateral guarantee of Greek territory. London knew that such a step would meet with the full approval of at least 90 per cent of the Greek nation. On April 13 Prime Minister Chamberlain told Parliament that His Majesty's Government "have come to the conclusion that, in the event of any action being taken which clearly threatens the independence of Greece and Rumania.... His Majesty's Government will feel themselves bound to lend at once to the Greek or Rumanian government ... all the support in their power."

The declaration had its effect. Metaxas did not protest; indeed, he found it advisable ... but after a significant delay of more than forty-eight hours, as contrasted with his speedy response to Mussolini's guarantee of Greek integrity ... to "express the Government's thanks" for the declaration. Important, however, was that Mussolini refrained from completing his invasion of Albania with an attack on Corfu, as he seemed to have planned; and Greece assumed her traditional place in the British sphere of influence. A section of the British Mediterranean Fleet paid a "friendly call" at Phaleron Bay during the summer of 1939, and—for the first time in years—high Greek naval officers were permitted to accept the hospitality of British ships. To dislodge Germany from her privileged position in Greek trade, the British Treasury approved a loan of about $15,000,000. The significance of these developments were not underestimated in Berlin and Rome. The Axis powers had to recognize that Britain had again at her disposal the innumerable and excellent Greek naval bases.

The reconstruction of this part of the imperial structure gave to the British Empire a new aspect by the spring of 1939. That the arrangement partook of the nature of a *mariage de convenance* was obvious; but to interpret that as an element of weakness, as did fascist statesmen, would be a grave error. On the contrary, the fact that Britain had succeeded in harmonizing her own interests with those of almost a dozen fully independent states could not but be a source of strength. Since they had rejoined the British system of their own accord, Britain would no longer have to waste material and human resources to hold them in the imperial orbit; having gained in strength since 1920, the members of the Outer Empire would be better able to protect their own interests and therefore those of the Empire. In a very real manner, at least as far as the members of the Outer Empire were concerned, the British imperial system had become a miniature League of Nations, and the only effective form of collective security.

XI

THE EMPIRE AT WAR

THAT GREAT BRITAIN was eager to avert outbreak of another
world war goes without saying; and, in conformity with the
policy pursued during the previous years, London appealed
for a peaceful solution of the Danzig question as late as
August 30, 1939. During subsequent days, after Hitler's
armies were in Poland, the door to a negotiated compromise
was carefully kept open. Indeed, so obvious was London's
search for an honorable peace that liberals throughout the
world feared and suspected appeasement until the end of
October, 1939.

British statesmen knew that war—even a victorious war—
is bound to shake the foundations of the political and economic system evolved by their ancestors. The truth is that
Britain can no longer win a war. Under the very best circumstances she must lose the war—or rather the peace after
the war—even if she wins on the battlefield.

In this respect Britain is in a far worse position than
Germany or any of her potential rivals except Russia. She
loses more in defeat than any other state can conceivably
lose; from victory she cannot possibly profit as much as her
rivals. What can, say, Germany give her which she does not
have already? Victory will not enable Britain to turn Germany into a colony for the exploitation of British capitalists;
no one is so naïve as to believe that British officials could
rule the Reich. Nor can more than an insignificant fraction
of Germany's wealth be transferred. Experience since the last
war has demonstrated that reparations over a long period of
years, in the form of industrial and agricultural goods, cannot be transferred without creating grave disturbances in
the economy of the victor. As to onetime levies, which can

be transferred with safety, does anyone imagine that the Krupp works, Germany's chemical and dies factories, her railways which are in a sad state, and metaled roads could somehow be removed to England? Germany has no gold or foreign investments; her shipping does not amount to much. Italy could of course lose her colonies—if they were worth anything.

On the other hand, the fascist states need only to help themselves to the crown colonies to solve most, if not all, of their economic problems and to multiply manifold their wealth. A few of the African colonies could, if developed, satisfy all their food requirements, much of their needs for industrial raw materials, and provide room for tens of millions of immigrants. Egypt, Tanganyika, and a few other African territories could supply all their cotton needs; the empty spaces of Iraq, Trans-Jordan, and Syria are rich in petroleum and various other mineral resources, and offer almost unlimited possibilities for agricultural development. The list is almost endless. Britain's great merchant marine and navy, her gold and foreign investments would add greatly to the wealth and power of the "have-not" states.

The German rulers understood this—apparently all too clearly. Besides, they did not believe that sufficient energy was left in British veins or that the will to live was still sufficiently strong to enable the British to stand up against the new "master race." Haushofer, one of the chief Nazi theoreticians, had assured the German public with oracular omniscience that the pacifism was a "symptom of the flagging English will to Empire." Berchtesgaden and Munich had been the destination of Mr. Chamberlain's flight in 1938; a German Canossa would be the end of the inevitable flight in 1939.

There was, however, to be no Canossa nor even a second Munich. As usual, the Germans did their political arithmetic too crudely. They overlooked not only a number of concrete facts, but, what is at least as important, the intangibles in the British character. They failed to recognize the significance of the change that had come about in England after the invasion of Czechoslovakia. They forgot that if the British aversion to shaping long-range policy had made possible the first Munich, the same trait might prevent them from looking too far into the future in dealing with the menace at hand. Having at last grasped the full implications of Hitler's sinister plans, the British, whose resolution is never "sicklied o'er with the pale cast of thought," preferred to face the ills of the moment rather than worry about the others that they "know not of."

The issue of course was neither Danzig nor even Poland. At stake were the future of the Empire and the independence of France. It was obvious that Hitler did not want Poland for its own sake. Poor and overpopulated, Poland could not solve any of the Reich's alleged economic problems; like Austria and Czechoslovakia it would indeed aggravate them. Even its military and strategic value was not great. What was important to Hitler was only the symbolic significance which Poland had assumed. Hitler saw correctly that if he could bring Britain to her knees in the struggle over this symbolic imperial rampart—one of the three states in Europe the territorial integrity of which Britain had guaranteed since the invasion of Czechoslovakia—the future could hold for the Empire nothing but disintegration. Britain, too, realized the significance of the challenge; and war became inevitable.

A UNITED EMPIRE

Outbreak of the war presented Britain and the Empire with a host of new problems. Here was the supreme test of the success of the efforts at imperial reconstruction during the past few years. First, what would be the attitude of the Empire, and especially of the Dominions, now free to determine their policies? What of the spheres of influence now that membership in the British system might mean national suicide? The answer to these questions is now a matter of history. We must, however, analyze also certain problems the solution of which remains hidden in the future. Where will the war spread? How much can the various parts of the Empire contribute to the struggle? And over all there hangs the question: Whither the Empire when it emerges from the war effort?

Britain had not yet declared war before it became obvious

that the forces of unity would generally win. Pro-Empire efforts during the past few years had not been in vain; and Hitler had been even more useful in welding the parts together. His wanton aggressions—in contrast to the "long-suffering" attitude of Great Britain—gave the war an ethical and humanitarian aspect which appealed strongly to Dominion idealism; and all parts now justly felt that their security was at stake. Yet, the situation everywhere was very different from that of 1914. No longer did all the Dominions become automatically involved the moment Britain declared war; the struggle between the elements favoring neutrality and those demanding participation was very severe in at least two, and a third—Eire—decided to remain neutral. All the forces of disintegration analyzed in preceding chapters came to the surface, as well as the centripetal ones, which proved the stronger. And the events of September, 1939, are of more than historical interest: they are pregnant with implications for the future.

As was to be expected, the commonwealths in the Antipodes were first to declare their loyalty. "New Zealand pledges unanimous aid in any eventuality," Acting Prime Minister Fraser said in a broadcast announcing that the government had already assured Britain that it "strongly endorses the steps taken by Prime Minister Chamberlain to honor the pledged word" to Poland. "We stand or fall together, in war or peace, in defeat or victory," Prime Minister M. J. Savage said when offering to send a division to any imperial battlefield. Hardly less determined was the attitude of Australia. "Britain and France," said Prime Minister R. G. Menzies in a radio speech announcing the declaration of war, "struggled to avoid this tragedy. They have patiently kept the door to negotiations open and have given no cause for aggression, but their efforts failed. We, therefore, as a great family of nations involved in this struggle must at all costs win, and we believe in our hearts that we will win." Newspaper editorials were unanimous in pleading for Australian support, and the voluntary rush for enlistment was the best sign of public opinion.

More problematic was the attitude of Canada, where, we have seen, the forces toward separation had operated powerfully since 1920. As late as the end of March, 1939, Prime Minister Mackenzie King, Liberal, and Dr. Robert Manion, head of the more pro-imperial Conservative party, had united to issue a joint statement that "Canadian youth should not be conscripted to fight outside the borders of Canada." In his most sanguine moments Dr. Manion did not envisage greater co-operation than "through volunteer units, through supplying ammunition [at a price], food, and other necessities." French-Catholics were solid against all commitments, and nearly a dozen important organizations in Quebec went on record against participation in any European war. In a speech devoted to an enumeration of what Canada would not do, the Prime Minister assured the Dominion House of Commons on March 30 that his government would never conscript Canadians for service overseas. "A strong and dominant national feeling is not a luxury in Canada; it is a necessity," he concluded.

Much propaganda was necessary to change the general coolness into something like enthusiasm; but as the summer months drew on it became evident that Canada would not remain neutral. During the parliamentary debate on foreign affairs the Minister of Justice, acting as the Prime Minister's chief lieutenant, pointed out that it would be impossible for Canada to remain neutral if Britain were at war. The Veterans' Association issued a ringing manifesto demanding conscription of Canada's "wealth, its man power and its industries." "We, the returned soldiers of Canada, feel," they asserted, "that the preservation of this Dominion is wholly dependent upon the continued security of the British Empire." During the critical August days all the important English newspapers announced in chorus that Canada was "ready, aye ready" to fight.

Significantly, in a broadcast address on September 3 announcing outbreak of war, the Prime Minister emphasized that "Canada, as a free nation of the British Commonwealth, is bringing her co-operation voluntarily. Our effort will be voluntary." He did not declare war in that speech; nor did Canada become "automatically" involved through the action of Great Britain, as was the case in 1914. Formal declaration of war came on September 10—full seven days after that of the United Kingdom—when, setting a precedent, the Canadian Government issued its own declaration. Yet more so than the action of any other Dominion, Canada's entry into the war demonstrated that the Empire was a reality, not a myth; for, unlike all other parts, Canada was in no way menaced by the fascist states. Quebec's ratification of the government's action during an election in November constituted an important victory for the Empire.

The greatest surprise, however, to those who were convinced that the empire is on the verge of collapse was the action of South Africa. The Boers had been and still are in the "militant phase" of their nationalism; at one Imperial Conference after another Union spokesmen had formed the vanguard in breaking down imperial girders. The leader of the Nationalist Opposition, Dr. Malan, declared as late as the fourth week of August that, "The war threatening Europe is not worth one drop of Afrikaander blood. The Nationalists of South Africa desire that South Africa should live up to its freedom and remain neutral." Of all Afrikaander statesmen only General Smuts dared to take a different attitude. "We are greatly indebted to Britain for this system of democracy, and for not having to be dictated by a dictatorship," he said. "I therefore implore you, stand together and keep our overseas friends. If we lose our friends and get into trouble you can be sure that South Africa will be the cockpit of the world's troubles."

Britain's declaration of war confronted South Africa with a critical situation. The English population mobilized all its power to secure co-operation with the rest of the Empire; Afrikaander nationalists became more vociferous than ever. The cabinet itself split over this supreme problem. But when Prime Minister Hertzog recommended to parliament that relations with Germany should "persist unchanged and continue as if no war was being waged," the forces of imperial co-operation won the day, though with a small majority of fourteen. General Hertzog resigned and General Smuts assumed office with the intention of co-operation with "friends and associates in the British Empire." The battle had not been an easy one in South Africa, but the imperial connection managed to survive the supreme test.

Ireland's decision to remain aloof was no doubt a severe blow to the Empire; yet who can say that it came unexpectedly? The bitter anti-British tradition, the "wrong" of Ulster, the exaggerated nationalism of the Republican Army—all these came to the surface. On September 2, Premier de Valera recommended a policy of neutrality to the Senate: "I know that there are strong sympathies in this country with regard to the present issue," he said, "but I do not think that anyone would suggest that the official policy of this state should be other than neutrality." A few Senators opposed this policy; "If Britain, France and Poland are defeated," said one, "everything the Irish race has stood for spiritually will go down and this country will be reduced to a state of rags and beggary that it has not known for centuries." Public opinion, however, favored the Premier's policy, and Eire has so far remained outside the Imperial family.

No different essentially was the reaction of the colonial empire. Britain's strong moral position and her recent progressive activities had everywhere profound effects; non-support, which would aid Germany and facilitate a fascist victory, offered an alarming prospect. The colonies therefore took a strongly loyal stand. In Palestine more than one hundred thousand Jews offered their services; and the whole Arab world united during the first few days of September to make common cause with the democracies. In Jamaica the National party immediately ceased agitation, and the labor unions, which had previously provoked extensive unrest, placed themselves at the disposal of the government. In Bermuda, more than a fifth of the total male population—negro and white—between 18 and 38 offered to join the volunteer forces. All African colonies placed their resources at the disposal of the British government.

India, however, failed to present a united front. All princes declared their loyalty and came out with offers of help. The Moslems, too, placed their services at the government's disposal. M. C. Rajah, leader of the depressed classes, issued an appeal to all "on the side of democracy" to come to the aid of the Empire. But the National Congress decided to remain aloof. For this, however, Britain had nobody but herself to thank.

THE EMPIRE CAN HELP

Oratorical declarations of loyalty are not enough. The important question is: Can the Dominions and colonies of the British Empire make a significant contribution to the struggle which they have made their own? Before outbreak of the war not one of the colonies had a military organization approaching that developed by Mussolini in his African possessions. The Dominions had come closer to complete disarmament than had any other modern state except Luxemburg, which is hardly a state; and the total miltary strength of the sixty-odd colonies was less than 30,000 men, most of whom were in semipolice organizations. Of what value, then, can the far-flung empire be to the mother country in this war?

The Imperial General Staff knew that for a year or so after outbreak of war England would receive little aid of value from the Empire. Indeed, during this period the Empire would be a liability. British military leaders foresaw that English troops would have to be kept in the Near East and in other places; the British navy would be unable to throw its whole strength into blockading Germany because it would have to guard the back doors of the Empire; officers badly needed for the enlarged army at home and in France would have to be sent to the imperial backwoods.

These weaknesses were inevitable; but military officers in Britain and the Empire knew also that time would radically change the situation. Basically the Empire was in a far stronger position than the Reich. In a war of attrition, not the number of guns on hand at the outset, not even the amount of stored materials, would determine the issue, but the amount of accessible raw materials in the ground and the capacity to exploit them. From these points of view, it was obvious, the advantage would be overwhelmingly on the side of the British Empire. Increasingly important also would be the human reserves, no less for expanding production than for replacements in the battle line. And the longer the war lasted, the more important would inevitably be the Empire's contribution.

Germany began the war with a population of almost 91,-000,000, which is somewhat larger than the combined population of France and Britain. The Reich acquired, moreover, some 20,000,000 Poles, hundreds of thousands of whom were soon compelled to do useful work. However, the entrance of the Dominions swept into the conflict 25,000,000 whites on the side of the Allies. And while Germany experienced a shortage of labor even before the hostilities began, the Dominions had a surplus population—the unemployed—able to enter production. In addition, the empire has 450,000,000 colored inhabitants. Tens of millions of these have been engaged in the production of necessary raw materials, but the pages on social conditions in the colonies and India have shown that tens of millions more can easily be found for expanding present industries. The colored empire is an inexhaustible source of manpower.

For imperial reasons, the British were not eager at the outbreak of the war to use this immense human reservoir for military purposes, and they refused to raise colonial armies. Before 1939 had come to an end, however, millions of colored men in the colonies and India offered to bear arms for the king. Their names were placed on special registers, to be called for service when necessary. Long after the exhaustion of Germany's human resources, the British Empire will be in a position to have millions of men at its call.

Allied military leaders realized that a year or perhaps more would have to elapse after outbreak of hostilities for the Empire's direct military contribution—in terms of soldiers, guns, airplanes, shells—to make itself felt. For one thing, as has been pointed out above, even the Dominions were almost completely disarmed as late as the end of 1938; for another thing, which is the more important, the Empire had no general staff to organize the military efforts of the various parts and to co-ordinate their war machines. "The Empire is without a brain," Major General Fuller of the Imperial General Staff wrote a few years ago. "There is no common brain; in fact, the Empire has become a hydra—a monster of political discord." For twenty years or more each Dominion had been full master in its own house; even for the colonies no co-ordinating organization had been set up, and every effort to remedy this deficiency had met with uncompromising opposition from the Dominions. The seriousness of this handicap should not be underestimated. The first World War showed the dangers of multiple control, although all Dominion forces were then under the authority of the British commander-in-chief. It was expected that absence of unified control would prove exceedingly costly.

But there are indications that the self-governing Dominions are slowly overcoming previous prejudices. The idea of calling Dominion ministers to London for purposes of consultation was a master stroke. Although Dominion governments opposed during the last months of 1939 suggestions to form an imperial war cabinet, many admitted that the logic of realities might bring about a change even in this. Besides many counted on the pre-war personal contacts which had been established between ranking military officers of the Empire to aid in facilitating the removal of some of the worst features of the old system. The highest officers not only know each other well; they all tend to have the same point of view.

The importance of the Dominions as arsenals for the production of finished arms, munitions, and planes cannot be overestimated. Far removed from the scene of conflict, and with an almost inexhaustible supply of labor and available raw materials, they have tremendous possibilities for production. Even in 1917 Canada produced munitions costing £333,000,000—compared with £28,000 in 1914. Three years after the outbreak of the first World War, the Ministry of Munitions spent in Canada no less than 15 per cent of its total expenditures.

The outlook in 1939 was far better than in 1914. It is of decisive importance that the Dominions and India have become great industrial nations, the production capacity of the former having increased by about 60 per cent over the 1914 level. Canada is now the fifth or sixth industrial nation in the world, and India ranks eighth; in 1914 industry had not gone far in either. Every Dominion is now equipped to turn out finished war materials; and the speed of production can be increased in a comparatively short time; unlike 1914, when no one thought of the Dominions as potential arsenals, plans had been laid long in advance of outbreak of hostilities.

Help from the Empire is of special importance in a war involving other parts of the world. Canada sent a highly mechanized expeditionary force to Europe in the early days of the war; it began a scheme to train tens of thousands of aviators; but the main importance of the Dominions' military effort is the strengthening of British garrisons in Asia and the Pacific. These should act as sedatives on excited militarist nerves in Italy and Japan. Britain and the Dominions realize that the best way to prevent the various other hungry fascist states from undertaking military adventures, individually or in unholy union, is to show them that the Empire is prepared.

Accordingly, both New Zealand and Australia planned their military efforts with an eye on Asia and the Pacific, where, due to their geographic position, they can exert the greatest influence and where lies their own interest. They coordinated their work with the Royal Navy and the Royal Air Force in the Far East; and infantry from these Dominions can play a decisive role in Singapore, the Near East, and perhaps India. Even their efforts for territorial defense constitute a distinct imperial contribution; and the other parts of the Empire are also making desperate efforts to become as self-sufficient as possible for withstanding attack. India with her immense human reservoir can play an especially important part in this scheme. However, ugly political problems must be solved before India's military resources can be exploited fully.

It is in the form of material resources that the overseas Empire can make its greatest contribution. In this respect it has an overwhelming advantage over the enemy. Long after the exhaustion of Germany's industrial raw materials, food, and other necessities, the Empire need no more than have scratched the surface of its immense resources and potentialities. The excellent studies of the Imperial Economic Committee on the Empire's resources and production capacity, which have been discussed in a previous chapter, were no doubt dug out from library shelves as soon as war broke out and utilized for shaping concrete policy. And the longer the war, it must be emphasized, the more valuable is bound to be this contribution of the overseas parts of the Empire.

Food resources of the Dominions and the colonies, first of all, are nearly inexhaustible. In 1937 the Dominions alone produced some 12,000,000 tons of beef and veal, more than 600,000 tons of mutton and lamb, and almost as much pork. The Empire produced more than 255,000,000 quintals of wheat against Germany's 78,000,000, more than 320,000,000 bushels of barley, and millions of bushels of rye, maize, oats, rice, and other products. Again, the important point to bear in mind is that while Germany cannot possibly expand its acres under cultivation, a different situation prevails in the British Empire. Production of most foodstuffs can be rapidly expanded.

The British Empire has been the world's largest producer of the agricultural raw materials necessary for industry. Even before the outbreak of war Germany suffered from a shortage of cotton, wool, flax, hemp, jute, rubber, and vegetable oils. The British Empire, on the other hand, had a superabundance of all these. The whole clip of the world's two greatest producers of wool, Australia and New Zealand, was taken over by Britain as early as the autumn of 1939; in 1936 their combined production totaled close to 1,300,000,000 pounds. Not only need Britain fear no deficiency in wool; it can resell to neutrals on a profitable basis. No different is the situation with regard to rubber, in which the British and Dutch empires share a monopoly. Germany, of course, manufactures synthetic rubber, but this requires raw materials it can ill afford for this purpose and a tremendous amount of human labor, and the durability of the finished product is much less than that of natural rubber.

The Empire lacks only one important raw material—oil. Although it has produced about six times as much crude petroleum as the Reich, it has had to meet almost its whole need with imports from the outside. But even in this respect Britain is in a far better position than the Reich. For not only can production be increased under the stimulus of necessity and higher prices, but much of the Empire's crude petroleum comes from countries which, while not marked red on British maps, fall within Britain's sphere of influence, and their resources are exploited by British-controlled companies. Both Iraq and Iran are outside the boundaries of the Empire; yet Britain has the final word as to the destination of their petroleum. The British government is the largest shareholder in the Anglo-Iranian Petroleum Company; Mosul oil is produced by an Anglo-French consortium and flows through territory controlled by the British and French.

The Empire has also become a large producer of vital minerals. While not more than a hundred thousand tons of asbestos were produced in 1914, close to half a million were extracted in 1937. Against Germany's production of 71,000 tons of copper can be pitted the 560,000 produced in the Empire. Canada alone mines about eleven per cent of the world's supply of this most necessary metal. Very little nickel was produced in 1914; Canada furnished 87 per cent of the world's total supply in 1938 and production in Burma and Rhodesia has been on the increase. Against Germany's 190,000 tons of lead, one must put the Empire's production of more than half a million tons; against the former's 4,000,000 tons of iron, there is the 10,000,000 tons extracted in Britain and the Empire. During the last twenty years the Empire has become an important producer of aluminum, bauxite, barium, chrome, manganese, tungsten, zinc, tin, and many other minerals of supreme importance in war. Practically no tungsten ores, which are so important in munitions, were produced in the British Empire in 1914; in 1937 about 8,000 tons were mined. The empire also accounted for about 35 per cent of the world's supply of zinc in 1937.

The truth is that the British Empire is so rich that no one knows what and how much it really has. Every year proves that it is far richer than anyone had suspected. The Empire's mineral resources are almost inexhaustible and can be produced in quantities to meet any demand. Engineers prophesied twenty-five or thirty years ago, to cite one example, that, the gold supply of South Africa would give out in twenty years; yet today more gold than ever is being taken out and the end is as far as ever from sight. Hardly a year passes that new resources are not discovered and new companies started to exploit them. Hundreds of mines have been closed since 1920 because of a glutted market; hundreds of concessions have been granted which have not been used; self-denying agreements have been made to cut production. Even the low production of petroleum is due far more to

politics than to scarcity. Britain followed until 1939 a consistent policy of keeping Empire oil production as low as
possible; it preferred to see the Western Hemisphere exhaust
its resources. So rigidly was this policy followed that both
Iran and Iraq, which needed the royalties, protested more
than once against the restrictions.

War budgets passed by the various Dominions show best
the seriousness with which they early began devoting themselves to the war. Having made the struggle their own, they
threw into limbo all previous separatist policies, and abundantly made clear their determination to see the war through.
Australia spent £19,600,000 (Australian) during the first year
of the last war; during the last few months of 1939 appropriations were boosted from £19,600,000 to £40,000,000 and
again to £59,500,000 for the 1940 financial year. The Canadian government borrowed some $200,000,000 for war pur-
poses in 1939, and the Minister of Finance estimated that
the cost of the first year of war would be at least $315,000,000
(Canadian). In addition, a scheme to train 10,000 pilots from
Canada, Australia, and New Zealand would cost Canada
about $350,000,000 in three years, while the other Domin-
ions would spend more than $100,000,000.

The spirit animating the Dominions can be expressed no
better than in the words of the Canadian Minister of Defense, Norman Rogers. "Canadians are not a warlike people,"
he said in a broadcast announcing the selection of the first
squadron of the new Canadian Air Force. "But when peace
is threatened, when our free institutions themselves are
challenged, Canada can gird for war. She did so twenty-five
years ago with the proud achievements of which we are all
aware. She does so again today. We are pledged to the defense of freedom whatever the sacrifice may be."

IS WAR INDIVISIBLE?

These calculations figured prominently in Allied councils
during September, 1939, and the subsequent months. But it
was obvious that the situation would change profoundly were
the Reich to be joined by Russia, Italy, Japan, or by all
of them. Such an alliance, by extending the war from Europe
to Asia, Africa, and perhaps even to the Antipodes, would

create new problems for the British Empire. Aided indirectly
by Britain's foreign policy in past years, those states, as we
have seen, have become first-rate powers; and an alliance
among them would demand of the Empire far greater military efforts than would be needed to cope with the Reich
alone.

That inherent antagonisms deeply rooted in history would
operate against such a world-wide combination was fully
understood. British statesmen consoled themselves with the
hope that Mussolini, for example, would be satisfied to gain
less from an Allied victory than to gain more territory by
co-operating with the Reich. To what avail the new imperial
expansion with the Axis if Italy itself become a German
colony?

However, an empire possessing as many interests as the
British could not possibly rely for its safety exclusively on
antagonisms between potential enemies. The possibility had
to be kept in view that, each one eager to grab a share of
the immense booty which would become available in case
of Britain's defeat, the so-called "have-not" powers might sink
their fundamental antagonisms if the war were to go badly
for the Allies on the western front. Once before the prospect
of great booty from the disintegration of a vast empire had
repercussions as far away as Central Asia. Peoples from Mongolia and China had set out in their tens of thousands to
western Europe when word went round that Rome was on
the verge of collapse.

It was also obvious that the Reich would spare no effort
to consolidate a world-wide military combination directed
against the Allies. The Triangle—and to a large extent the
Axis as well—having disintegrated with the signature of the
Berlin-Moscow convention, the Nazi diplomats set themselves the task of constructing a new combination to include
not only Italy and Japan but Russia, too. Unable to play
any longer on the anti-Comintern note, they began to con-
coct new slogans to suit the new reality. Before 1939 had come
to an end an important Berlin newspaper published a call for
the formation of a "Eurasian Bloc of Young Nations" which
should be composed of those powers eager to "free themselves
of the control exercised by the British group" for the sake

of the full development of their respective "living spaces." Berlin began to speak of a war of the "proletarian" nations against the "plutocratic" British Empire and France. The Reich Labor Leader, Dr. Robert Ley, went so far as to issue the call, "Workers of all lands, unite to smash the rule of English capitalism!"

What resources could Britain bring into play were such a military combination to materialize? Clearly, alone and unaided the Allies would be totally unable to cope with it. The Dominions, and India and the colonies, although able to render valuable service after their military machines are put in order, could certainly not withstand protracted attacks from Italy, Russia, and Japan.

It is in this connection that the other parts of the Empire assume vital importance. Victory or defeat would be decided, in a real manner, by the states of the outer and financial empires. Their geographic position, their human and material resources, would play a leading role in dealing with the other three aggressive powers. Indeed, the mere knowledge that those states are prepared to co-operate with Great Britain if the necessity were to arise might prevent the consummation of the combination.

Outbreak of the war strengthened Turkey's determination to abide by its connection with the British. Mussolini learned that if he were to undertake adventures in the Near East he would have to confront not only British, Egyptian and Arab troops but Turkish soldiers as well. Greece, Iran, Egypt, Iraq, and other Near Eastern territories also placed themselves within the British orbit more decisively than ever before. Anti-British propaganda was abruptly terminated in this region; Germans were expelled; commercial relations with the Reich were greatly reduced or ended. Greece's trade with Germany, for example, declined during the second month of war to about a quarter of what it had been the year before, and it declined further in the following months. The Turkish Foreign Minister, Sükrü Saracoglu, expressed the attitude of all these states when he told the Balkan Conference early in February, 1940, that his country was "not neutral but merely out of the war." Although not one of these states has a military machine comparable to that of Italy or Russia, their mountainous terrain would enable them to hold an enemy at bay for months or perhaps even years.

Unlike the situation up to 1935, the road to India and other Far Eastern territories is no longer open—a fact that should make Japan and Russia think more than once before courting trouble. Britain has been hard at work to win the Islamic world, including Moslem Afghanistan. Nor would nationalist India remain neutral were the menace of aggression to come close to the gate. It is easy to foresee that nationalist India, reluctant to co-operate with British imperialism in the war against Germany until granted suitable political concessions, would not hesitate to change tactics if the far greater evil of Japanese or any other imperialism were to appear on the horizon. The Congress is no friend of either Germany or Italy—or imperialist Japan. As to those who had looked longingly to Soviet Russia for salvation, they had been accenting the word Soviet in the name and have probably changed their views since Moscow began to emphasize the more traditional appellation.

Britain's longstanding emphasis on salt-water boundaries makes the Empire much more defensible against foreign attack than is commonly realized. No other political structure has so long a belt of salt water; nowhere does the coastline form so large a proportion of the total area. Not one of the potential aggressors can do very much damage as long as Britain rules the waves. This concentration on salt-water borders has not only made imperial communications a series of excellently integrated lines, with convenient stations from London to Hong Kong or Melbourne; it has given the Empire power far greater than is justifiable by the number of guns and airplanes it possesses. British officials do not have to threaten Rome and Moscow with military invasion; sufficient for Mussolini and Stalin is the knowledge that men-of-war are ready to cut their sea-communications with the outside world. As to smaller states, they have no choice but to submit to London's orders.

Britain's financial power would be of supreme importance in combating an attack from the four "proletarian" nations. It is not only that her great financial holdings turn the world into a workshop for producing the sinews of war, thus increasing vastly the number of people actually engaged in combating the enemy; financial power places Britain in a very strong position to obtain more direct co-operation. Already Germany has felt this aspect of Britain's might. The Scandinavian countries, although menaced directly by Reich guns, have not given the aid Berlin expected; the Balkan countries have also remained tied to London's financial kite; and Uruguay, where British capital has played a preponderant role, would most likely have adopted a different attitude had a British, instead of a German, cruiser run in for shelter. By forcing the *Admiral Graf Spee* to put out to sea, Uruguay removed a serious menace to British shipping and delivered a blow to Nazi naval morale. Constantly one confronts the fact that it is an extremely well-integrated system that the British have constructed, enabling them when the need arises to call on the support of many more peoples and states than is generally realized.

ENTER ENGLAND

It is obvious, however, that, whatever skirmishes or even campaigns take place in the outlying parts of the Empire, Germany is the chief enemy and victory or defeat will be decided in Europe. Britain will have to fight on three distinct fronts. First, much military effort will have to be devoted to the metropolitan or home front, progress in aviation having made the densely populated, highly industrialized British Isles possible objectives for Germany's high-powered bombing squadrons based 350-600 miles away. Second, British troops and airplanes will have to participate in operations in Europe. Finally, there is the naval front on the high seas. It is very likely that the outcome of the war will be decided on this, Britain's traditional front.

Were one to narrate now the full extent of the decline in Britain's military and naval might between 1920 and 1935, the story would only with difficulty be believed. Every branch of the service was starved; the number of actives declined; equipment became antiquated; no attempt was made to keep up with developments in armament construction. It seems incredible that a power as great and as rich as England should

have so neglected her defenses; yet we have the word of
competent observers that only a few months before the spring
of 1939 "the shortage of equipment was so great that many
Territorial units were drilling with the equivalent of broom-
sticks and thousands of militiamen had never handled a modern machine-gun or antiaircraft weapon." Although the
total expenditure of the British government increased from
£197,000,000 in 1913-14 to about £800,000,000 in 1934-35,
the amount devoted to all armed services increased only from
£77,000,000 to about £112,000,000. The personnel of the
regular army fell from 250,000 to 195,000; that of the territorial army from 250,000 to about 130,000: the personnel
of the Royal Navy—the main defense of the Empire—actually
declined by more than half, falling from 200,000 to 90,000.
In 1913 close to 200,000 tons of naval construction was
launched; in 1935, a grand total of 23,000 tons, and even
less was launched in some previous years (10,665 tons in
1933). Having officially relinquished the two-power standard
with regard to the United States, it seemed that it would not
be long before other powers as well would obtain parity with
Britain.

More serious even was Britain's backwardness in the air.
In this field, not one but three or four powers had far sur-
passed her in number of machines, in type of construction,
in speed and everything else. How far Britain had fallen can
be seen from the following list of official pronouncements:
In 1934 the government announced an aircraft expansion
program which provided for 1,304 first-line planes by July,
1939! (Italy, Russia, and probably Germany already had
more than that.) One year later Mr. Baldwin expanded the
program to 1,500 planes by March, 1937. Only a few months
had to pass, however, before the government practically admitted that even this program was not being implemented
and a new schedule—only 1,750 completely new planes by
March, 1939—was announced. The schedule was amended
for the fourth time in May, 1938, when it was decided to
build 2,370 first-line machines by March, 1940! Unfortunately, in May, 1938, "Germany *already* had some 1,000 more
front-line machines" than Britain expected to have in 1940.
More alarming still, Germany's productive capacity was es-

timated to exceed Britain's by as much as three or four hundred per cent.

It was not till the spring of 1938 that Britain began to devote serious attention to her military defenses; but having recognized the seriousness of the situation, the government spared neither efforts nor money to remedy it in as short a period as possible. To detail here the various measures that were taken would serve no useful purpose. Army and navy budgets swooped upwards; production was greatly expanded; personnel was increased; a big broom was carried into the dust-laden war office. Much attention was devoted to the home front. Hundreds of new airplanes were assigned to guard this front and antiaircraft guns appeared everywhere. Prime Minister Chamberlain's bill of April 26, 1939, introducing conscription of all youths between twenty and twenty-one years of age constituted nothing short of a revolution. As late as the end of March the Premier had refused to have anything to do with conscription, and in angry debate in the Commons rejected all promptings from members of his own party. The inexorable march of events, however, forced a complete change in less than a month.

Figures of aircraft construction (although all such figures have to be taken with more than a grain of salt) show how much progress had been made until outbreak of the war. "In April, 1939," a competent authority reported, "Britain is believed to have produced perhaps 500 planes, about 600 in May, and 650 to 750 in June," when her total air strength was reported to be in the neighborhood of 4,000 planes. The quality of British machines had greatly improved, comparing favorably in this respect with those produced by the enemy. Above all, British manufacturers had greatly expanded their productive capacities and they had no need to worry about raw materials.

The effect of these efforts became evident soon after the war began. Germany did not unleash the oft-promised *blitzkrieg* on England by sending over fleets of, say, one hundred planes ten times a day to rain death and destruction. While no amount of antiaircraft defenses or even fighting planes could make England completely immune to aerial attacks, Reich military leaders had to recognize that the losses in mass attacks would have to be immense. Whether the prospect of inflicting great industrial damage on England could compensate the Nazis for their immediate losses in airplanes appeared doubtful.

Also, the one justification for risking hundreds of planes in mass attacks—the prospect of delivering a knockout blow to the enemy—was largely removed before the end of 1939. The British did much to decentralize their key industries, especially those connected with war production, and to spread the population over the countryside. Going further afield, they made extensive preparations for starting production of the most essential war requirements in the Dominions. And all experience of aerial bombardment in China, Spain, and even Poland tends to show that squadrons of bombers, while able to inflict tremendous damage, cannot wipe out large cities or put out of commission vast industrial centers, especially if opposed by antiaircraft guns and an adequate number of fighting planes.

Even if a series of gigantic air attacks could inflict all the damage foreseen by some romantic writers, it seemed questionable whether that would eliminate Britain—and far less the British Empire—from the war. No doubt, the sporadic flights over the British Isles during the first few months of the war could not be accepted as indicative of Germany's capacity or intentions. However, it was obvious that the murder of tens of thousands of British civilians would not seriously affect the military aspect of the war. There would not be even a serious reversal in morale. Savage air raids would indeed bolster up the morale of the Empire and strengthen the will to resist.

The crucial front now, as in 1914-18, is the naval. The shifting fronts on the high seas constitute the very heart of the Empire and Britain's own future. Naval action provides also the cheapest and perhaps most effective way for putting the Nazis out of commission—whether as a result of slow military defeat, or, which seems the more probable, of internal revolution. On this point, Britain's success during the first six months of war was even greater.

Although inferior in number of ships and in tonnage to 1914, it was not long after outbreak of war that the British navy made good its mastery of the seas in a manner more convincing than in 1914. German shipping was swept off the seas—about 1,200,000 tons of it. A number of enemy vessels were captured; the majority ran for shelter into neutral ports. Germany's overseas imports declined rapidly; as early as September 9 the British Ministry of Information was able to announce: "The cutting off of Germany from overseas sources of war supply is now virtually complete except for the Baltic.... Already there are practically no German merchant ships on the high seas." The strangulation was completed in November by a British Order declaring German exports contraband of war.

Britain's financial power played a very important role in enforcing the blockade. No longer did a blockade consist of throwing men-of-war on the enemy's sea lanes; now war vessels were only the finishing touches to a very long and complicated process which started in commercial offices and in which Britain's finance, insurance connections, and commercial agents throughout the world played a supremely important role. Sources of supply to the enemy were carefully watched, and the work of impeding shipment started long before the cargo put to sea. Purchases were blocked at the source by threatening the financial standing of the selling firm; insurance connections were used to deny insurance to offending firms; financial operations were impeded; finally, a great network of intelligence was set to work to inform the Admiralty authorities of the presence of contraband on certain ships.

On the other hand, it was not long before events demonstrated that Britain could not be cut off from the world. German submarines, magnetic mines and aerial attacks took a heavy toll of Allied and neutral shipping; however, the balance of forces indicated that unless the Nazis produced totally unforeseeable instruments of naval destruction, Britain would retain mastery of the seas.

During the first week of the war, according to a review given to the House of Commons by Winston Churchill, First Lord of the Admiralty, British losses amounted to 65,000 tons. Even this huge loss compared very favorably for the British with their losses during the first week of unrestricted warfare in 1917. In the second week, however, losses declined to 46,000 tons; in the third week they were 21,000 tons; during the fourth week of war only slightly more than 10,000 tons was lost. Afterward the situation improved steadily and greatly; and during the first five months of warfare British losses totaled less than six hundred thousand tons—an average of less than 3,800 tons daily. Total Allied and neutral shipping losses during this period amounted to 360 vessels of 1,213,500 tons—a daily average of 6,750 tons. This must be compared with an average of 22,060 tons sunk daily during the first five months of unrestricted submarine warfare in 1917.

To appreciate the full meaning of these figures—for they are the best available indication of future developments—one must bear in mind, first, that the British Empire owns about twenty-one million tons of shipping and that on an average, about two thousand ships flying the Union Jack are strewn each day over all seven seas. As to the world merchant marine, it numbered in 1938 a total of 31,186 vessels of about seventy million tons. Second, sinkings during the first five months of unrestricted sea war were considerably below building capacity. In 1938, although Britain's docks were not working to capacity, 1,030,400 tons of new shipping was launched—almost double the amount sunk in five months. It is reasonable to assume that the amount under construction has increased to two million tons since outbreak of war. In the same year the world's total of new building was about three million tons. This means that somewhat more new shipping was built each month in 1938 than Germany sank during the first few months of war.

At this rate, as the First Lord of the Admiralty told Parliament, "We should have to go back to a hundred years of war to provide sufficient time and scope for such inroads upon our mercantile marine to become seriously effective.... In the month of November nearly a quarter million tons of shipping entered or cleared from our harbors for every 1,000 tons lost, a proportion of 250 to 1."

Certainly the above figures of Britain's shipping losses cannot be taken as indicative of the future. On the contrary, there are reasons for believing that attacks will become greater and will entail more serious losses. The Royal Navy and Air Force have an extremely hard task before them, which is likely to strain Britain's resources to the limit. Mr. Churchill never ends his optimistic reports without sounding an alarm that dangerous days lie ahead. Moreover, the blockade of the Reich cannot become sufficiently effective to assure rapid victory. German trade with the Balkan and Scandinavian countries—whence come food supplies and important raw materials—was expanded greatly during the first five months of war and will no doubt be expanded even more; development of *ersatz* (substitutes) has made the Reich less dependent on outside supplies than it was during 1914-18.

All these forces will operate during the war. In the aggregate they mean that Nazi Germany is in many ways stronger than the Imperial Germany of 1914, and that Britain was in some respects weaker in 1939 than it had been at the outbreak of the first World War. Then the home front, to mention only one difference, was comparatively immune. But against these disadvantages one must balance the greater strength of the British Empire as a whole, and especially the aid which the Outer Empire will render should such aid become necessary for victory.

FROM NAPOLEON TO HITLER

That the war will be long drawn out is only too likely; probably it will demand greater sacrifices than the last one. It may ruin England financially; it is pregnant with menaces to the whole imperial construction greater probably than any confronted thus far; it raises problems many of which, as will be shown in the following pages, appear at present to defy satisfactory solution. But the doubting Thomases who think that the British will lay down the sword—or, scuttle the boat, to use a more appropriate metaphor—can do no better than reread the history of the Napoleonic wars. The challenge then was no less than that of Germany and the other powers of aggression today.

The Napoleonic wars occupied England almost continuously for twenty-three years and taxed British resources to the breaking point. The government budget, which had stood at £18,000,000 in 1792, reached the alarming sum of

£113,000,000 in 1814; the public debt jumped from an insignificant total to the, in those days, gigantic sum of £861,000,000 in 1815. To realize what this figure meant it must be borne in mind that the population of England was only 8.5 millions, and the national income has been estimated at £140,000,000. No wonder that the public debt— more than the total national income in six years and comparable to a public debt for the United States of $540,000,-000,000—caused general "consternation," and evoked the most pessimistic prophecies. Defeat and annihilation seemed imminent more than once during that quarter of a century; in Parliament and outside people could foresee nothing but darkness ahead.

Pitt the younger and his successors were very much disturbed by the apparently unfavorable fortunes of war and the prospect of ignominious financial bankruptcy. But they knew that there could be no turning back. Whatever the losses of victory, those of defeat would be incomparably greater. Bankruptcy, defeat, loss of Empire notwithstanding, England carried on—and carried on the war till the end desired by London became a reality. The sword was not sheathed until Napoleon was safe at St. Helena, an allied army in Paris, and Canning was laying down the law to the nations of Europe.

The situation today is very similar to that existing at the beginning of the last century. The British people realize that however great the cost of war, while it lasts and afterwards, the price of a Canossa—or even of another Munich—would inevitably be far greater. The peoples of the Empire, too, realize fully the kind of future that would await them were the war to be ended by a peace without honor.

XII
WHITHER THE BRITISH EMPIRE?

THE IMMENSE RESOURCES of the Empire will enable it to continue the struggle for years—or decades if necessary—until a satisfactory settlement is secured. But wars invariably create more problems than they solve; and this war can certainly be no exception. More dangerous even than the war itself is the crisis which lies in wait for the British Empire as soon as the war ends, and which is bound to be far more severe than any confronted hitherto. For it seems inevitable that Britain should lose the peace even if the Empire wins the war.

If the first World War released forces which brought the Empire perilously close to disintegration, it is inevitable that this war should strengthen those centrifugal forces and, in addition, create new ones working in the same direction. The internal forces bent on dissolution of the Empire will remain under control as long as the foreign threats to the security of the various parts remain on the horizon—only to break loose the moment victory is assured. And what will make the aftermath so dangerous is that the explosions will occur simultaneously over the far-flung Empire, ruling out the possibility of concentrated action necessary for coping with each explosion separately.

The last point deserves closer analysis. We have seen that the engineering principles of the British Empire are different from those which underlay every other imperial structure. The reason for this has been that Great Britain, the foundation of the edifice, has been in the final analysis a very poor base. Britain's population has been small; territorially Britain is almost insignificant; her heavy industry has ranked third or fourth in the world. Indeed, that Great Britain was able to construct the greatest imperial structure known to history has been due to a series of accidents and to the resourcefulness and energy of the British people, not to objective material reality.

The system was able to survive as long as it was not seriously threatened from within. When centrifugal forces became powerful in any one territory, Britain was invariably compelled to make concessions; for well did London know that it did not have the military power for holding down the whole Empire. Moreover, the British did not have to worry about separatist movements as long as those were sporadic and confined to a few territories. For two reasons: First, England was always strong enough to deal with one or two completely disarmed territories; second—and this factor is of far greater significance than is usually recognized— the strength drawn from the various passive parts made it possible to control the discontented ones. In a very real manner, the colonies and India were their own subjectors.

But an unprecedented situation is bound to develop as soon as the war ends. No longer will revolts be sporadic and confined to one or two territories. War creates all sorts of social, economic, and political forces which must everywhere stimulate demands for separation and independence. And no longer will Britain be able to draw power from one territory for keeping down the other. A country like the United States with 130,000,000 inhabitants and its potentially immense military resources might be able to cope at one and the same time with a dozen or more revolutions in different parts of the world. The United States, in other words, has a base potentially adequate for an immense imperial superstructure. Britain is obviously in a different position.

DOMINIONS TRIUMPHANT

All the Dominions with the exception of Eire answered loyally the King's appeal for a united front. Having entered the arena, and realizing that they are fighting for their own safety against aggression, not for Britain, they will undoubtedly harness all their human and material resources to assure victory—"to the last man and last shilling," as Premier Menzies of Australia said. As long as the war lasts the Commonwealth will remain more united than at any time since 1918.

What will happen the moment after the whistle blows? Thrice during the past forty years the Dominions were called to fight imperial battles, and each time their response was less enthusiastic. A profound reaction against the Empire, their own statesmen, and the whole culture which produced the gigantic slaughter swept over them at the end of the last war, and received revolutionary expression in Canada during the Chanak incident in 1922. At that time, instead of rushing to the defense of the Empire in response to an S.O.S. signal from the British Premier calling upon the "United Empire" to rise as one man, Canada replied coolly that no war measures could be taken without the approval of Parliament, then not in session. Twenty years were necessary to live down the anti-Empire sentiment engendered in 1914-18.

There was less enthusiasm for King and Empire in September, 1939, than in August, 1914. The cultural reaction at the end of this war will undoubtedly be far greater. Now that very little remains of the old legal and political ties, and the right to secession—undreamed of in 1914—has had to be acknowledged, public sentiment has become one of the most important bonds tying the Dominions to the mother country; and if public sentiment goes, very little remains. Faith in the *mystique* surrounding the concepts of "King," the "Empire," "Briton," and other ideals—so fundamental in the maintenance of imperial unity—was shaken by the last war; this one may see their disappearance as important cultural factors.

With the disastrous results of past foreign policies only too apparent, the Dominion governments pledged themselves shortly after the outbreak of hostilities to insist, at the next peace conference, on the establishment of a functioning system of collective security under a League of Nations with resources to enforce international law and order. They knew that only a powerful League could prevent another world war in the future. More idealistic and less conscious of the intricacies of the European political pattern, they are determined to remove the ground from beneath those conflicts from which, once they break out, they cannot isolate themselves. "The idea that every twenty years this continent which has done all it can to run itself should feel called upon to save periodically a continent that cannot run itself, seems to many a nightmare and sheer madness," the Canadian Prime Minister, W. L. Mackenzie King, told the House of Commons in 1939.

However, a League able to enforce international law and order will certainly not strengthen the Empire. Until now fear of aggression and the inability to protect their vital interests without the aid of the British navy has been the strongest imperial tie; what, then, will happen to the Empire once fear of foreign aggression ceases to play a role in Dominion politics? Will they be so ready to follow British leads on vital questions? Will they be so eager to abide by the imperial connection? Able to dispense with the potential aid of the British navy, the Dominions will be in a position to translate into daily practice their sovereign rights to independent foreign policies, which until now have remained to a large extent on the theoretical plane.

British statesmen have not been blind to the menace which a strong League would constitute to the Empire. Their foreign policy was torn between the conflicting aims of international security which would lead to imperial disintegration, or chaos in the former sphere to maintain a measure of unity in the latter. The British government could assert with truth, as it did in the White Paper on Disarmament of March, 1935, that "the establishment of peace on a permanent footing is the principal aim of British foreign policy." On the other side, there was the theory that, to use the words of the Air Minister in a speech at Newcastle (October 27, 1933), "a convention to eliminate war...was an idealistic conception." Instead, to avoid the dangers of war and the no less real menaces of peace, it tried to chart a different course. "We must do our best to influence people in every part of the world that war shall be postponed as long as possible." This obviously was a totally different policy from the one outlined in the White Paper; but it was the more realistic and better adapted to Britain's peculiar problem.

Now Britain's difficult predicament is reaching a solution; and this time the solution will not be left to Downing Street. The Dominions will make the choice for Britain, and force her hand—as they are already doing. A manifesto issued shortly after outbreak of the war by two important Canadian leaders, to cite one example, demanded an Imperial Conference to "lay down the principle and the plan by which the federated resources of the Empire will guarantee a new order of security." The peoples of all the Dominions are willing—indeed eager—to sacrifice the limited security afforded by the Empire for the more complete security that only a League of Nations can give.

And the Dominions will be able to enforce their views should the mother country prove recalcitrant. As important contributors to the Allied victory, they will be able to speak at the peace conference with a voice of authority. The war will have strengthened their economies, which will be relatively more stable than that of Britain; and the experience gained during the past score of years in the international arena, limited as it has been, will stand them in good stead. The inevitable economic consequences of the war will also not make for greater imperial unity. The trend toward industrialization, begun by the war of 1914-18, will have received a powerful stimulus. Their chief producer of industrial goods busy manufacturing armaments, the Dominions will have been compelled to develop industrial plants of their own to replace imports from Great Britain. Many special industries connected with military needs will have sprung up. And industrialists in the Antipodes Dominions, India, and the colonies are better prepared to take advantage of Britain's predicament than they were in 1914. Obviously, Britain, too, will profit from the experience of the last war and will do her utmost to purchase as little ammunition from the Dominions as possible while making every effort to keep up industrial exports. Ugly necessity, however, may make short shrift with long-range calculations, and dependence on Dominions for munitions will grow the longer the war continues.

It is inevitable that such developments should contribute greatly to the atomization of the Commonwealth. Unable to

administrators presents colonial governments with the alternative of leaving undone necessary tasks or admitting natives to positions hitherto closed to them. In 1914-18 the former alternative was followed everywhere—if only because the colonies did not yet have trained professional men of their own. Now, especially with the demand for greater social services, natives will have to be used in positions hitherto beyond their reach; and the process thus begun will not be easily stopped. "Why should we pay British officials ten times the salary paid to a native for the same kind of work?" they ask; and having learned the taste of power, the natives are not likely to forego it. Much of the trouble in India after 1920 was the result of just this factor.

And to prevent complications during hostilities, Britain will be compelled to make promises about independence, self-government, and liberty, which are not easily forgotten. Experience in the Near East showed that they were discussed widely and constantly cited; native intellectuals saw to it that peasants in the remotest villages should hear about them. Nor will Britain be free to exercise discretion about the quantity and quality of the propaganda; the enemy began to force the pace even before outbreak of war. The radio, a powerful instrument in the hands of Germany, is used to capacity to make trouble in India and the colonies. And it is inconceivable that the speeches of British leaders about fighting to "destroy Hitlerism, fascism, the rule of force and tyranny," which have been disseminated by all British news agencies, should not make an impression on the colonies. "Why is fascism bad in Europe and good here among us?" a hundred colonial newspapers have already asked. Censorship and police tyranny can no longer put an end to such questions.

These forces will inevitably produce an upswing of nationalism in the colonies. Experience shows that there can be no turning back. Nationalist uprisings, hitherto sporadic, may become universal as soon as the war ends; and Britain will not be able to crush them with force. For one thing, this war will produce as great a reaction at home against brute violence as did the last one, only more so; for another, Britain will not have the necessary soldiers for coping with all the revolts. Besides, nationalism is not a force that can be crushed with guns, except for very short periods of time. To sit on bayonets is not only highly unpleasant, but exceedingly costly. For bayonets have a way of requiring more bayonets as time goes on. If ten bayonets suffice to crush one rebellion, twenty-five or a hundred will be required for crushing the next one.

In addition, the war will set in motion economic forces which must reinforce the cultural and political ones. The Near East would not have exploded in 1919 had it not been enriched by the war. As war demands force up production of agricultural and industrial raw materials, prices soar, and, although the lion's share of the benefit goes to the European owners, labor obtains higher wages, and there is more money in circulation. A demand for all kinds of industrial goods is created, which British industry, busy manufacturing implements of death, cannot supply; and the same process as we have observed in the Dominions, though of course on a much smaller scale, repeats itself in the colonies.

The effects of this process go far beyond economic limits. It is important that industrialization—contact with modern machinery—revolutionizes native habits of life and thought. The new industrial laborers constitute a great political force, for they can be disciplined, taught, and directed as peasants cannot. More important even is it that the war prosperity creates a middle class—a social group which had been absent in most eastern and colonial societies. This class, which came into existence in Egypt during the first World War and was immensely strengthened in India, is conscious of its wealth, of its interests, and of its power. Political liberty is to it not a slogan but a question of life and death. It is ambitious as no Asiatic class has ever been before; and it counts too many members to be able to come to terms with imperialism, as did the old feudal classes, on the basis of division of spoils.

There is no escaping the fact that an extremely critical situation is developing in the colonies. Possibly Britain will be far-sighted enough to take effective measures to lessen the force of the explosion; indications are that she realizes the dangers ahead. It is extremely unlikely, however, that

London—and to an ever larger extent the "men on the spot" —will voluntarily renounce sufficient authority to satisfy native nationalism. Never before has vested interest acted thus; and the tendency will be to underestimate the strength of the new movements. On the other hand, shrewd realists that most colonial politicians are, they will seize on the moment of Britain's greatest weakness—right after the war— to start trouble, just as Egypt, Palestine, Syria, Iraq, Persia, Turkey, India, Afghanistan, and other territories did immediately following the last war. And to crush the coming insurrections will be more difficult even than it was in 1919-21. The dark races are now better armed, better trained, and politically more conscious. The flames will burn also in many more places than they did in 1919 and in areas widely separated one from another, which will prevent Britain from concentrating her forces to cope with each.

INDIA ON THE EVE

More radical than the colonial leaders, left-wingers in the Indian Congress were not willing to wait for peace before launching a new attack on the Empire. They decided to take advantage of England's preoccupation in Europe to place her in a terrible predicament.

Hardly had the present war broken out than the Viceroy, Lord Linlithgow, was confronted with an ultimatum demanding immediate realization of Britain's oft-repeated promise that Dominion status is the ultimate goal of India's constitutional development. The National Congress was in deadly earnest. Having worked out its tactics carefully in advance, it was determined to force Britain's hand since the latter was occupied with a first-rate war and was in need of India's aid to resist actual foreign aggressors and even more to prepare against potential ones, which might spring into action at any moment. Of course, the British refused to act according to the dictates of the Congress.

More than that: with exemplary bad manners, as if determined to insult the Indians, they categorically and abruptly refused to discuss constitutional reform during the war. They forgot Macaulay's words of wisdom uttered during the Reform Debate in 1832: "Reformers are compelled to legislate in times of excitement because bigots will not legislate in time of tranquillity." All their moves seemed to be studiously calculated to enrage the nationalists. India was declared at war without anyone being consulted; the federation scheme passed into abeyance merely because London so ordered. Lord Linlithgow's statement on future British policy was annoyingly vague. To the resolution of the all-India Congress Committee affirming "that Indian freedom must be based on democracy and unity," the Viceroy replied requesting a "consultative group representing all the major political parties in British India and of the Indian princes"—a policy certain to offend all nationalists. All he had to offer was the possibility of revision of the India Act after the war "in the light of Indian views."

Matters consequently moved from bad to worse. All the Congress ministries which since 1937 governed eight of the eleven provinces of British India resigned in November, 1939, forcing Britain to resort to autocratic administration. Civil disobedience again raised its head. Although Gandhi appealed for "restraint in word and deed," radical groups were clamoring for a more militant policy. They were determined to gain their goal as rapidly as possible and had no scruples against exploiting Britain's preoccupation in Europe and her needs in Asia.

Yet there is no denying that there was a great deal of reason for Britain's refusal to grant immediate Dominion status. Neither the internal nor the foreign situation made the moment propitious for constitutional experiments. Clouds blacker and more impenetrable than ever before hung over India's northern frontier, making necessary an alert vigilance. Even from the point of view of India's interests, as distinct from those of the Empire, internal experiments could not be risked till Stalin's intentions became clearer. Nor was it the best time for disturbing the eighty million Moslems, who have constantly rejected unqualified and immediate home rule. Europe has shown those Moslems how tragic can be the fate of minorities; they have no reason to believe that the Hindu majority would act in a more civilized manner. The princes, too, opposed the Congress conception of India, and constituted a serious stumbling block.

All these considerations, important though they are, are superficial compared with the real problem involved. What really faces Britain is a choice between two allies—whether she will work with the nationalists (mainly Hindus) or with the minorities and the princes. Never before was the issue so squarely placed; never before was choice so difficult. Statements like that made by Sir Samuel Hoare in the House of Commons, that the British Government now believes that its mission is "not to govern other people but to help other people to govern themselves," only befog the issue. Britain has confronted a similar issue in Palestine, where she had to choose between Zionists and Arabs. But at least since 1933 the choice in Palestine has been infinitely simpler than in India, because there could be no doubt as to which of the two was the more valuable ally. Not so in India, where the scales are more balanced.

On the one side, Britain cannot afford to antagonize the minorities—especially the Moslems—and the princes. She needs them all badly to help pull the war chariot. The Moslems are the martial people of India, and Britain may need them on the battlefields; she may need even more the Moslems of the Near East, Iran, and Afghanistan, who take a profound interest in the fate of their Indian co-religionists. Moslem support would become a question of life or death were Italy or Russia or Japan to throw in their lot with the Reich; and hardly had the war broken out than Britain began carefully building an all-Islamic bloc. Nor could she afford to antagonize the princes. They all offered their services to the Empire and some contributed material aid as early as September, 1939. London knew that they could and would give more as the war dragged on; and it would be inglorious indeed to let down the "faithful allies of the Crown."

On the other side, there stands Congress India, daily becoming politically more mature, more restless, and stronger. Influence of the Congress has grown rapidly during the past few years, which is bound to make the revolt, when it comes, more widespread than any in the past. The tens of millions of peasants who have economically benefited somewhat from Congress rule have perceived for the first time the direct connection between political freedom and their economic interests and are now more than ever at the call of the nationalist leaders. Were the Congress to let loose a full-fledged rebellion during the war, Britain's position would become unenviable, especially as she would be unable to afford the necessary military force to crush the outbreak. Even before the end of 1939, the war in Europe made necessary a serious reduction in the Indian military establishment. Nor could Britain overlook the fact that, driven by desperation, Congress leaders might decide on co-operation with her foreign enemies. Either Japan or Russia would be only too delighted to be of assistance to the Indian revolutionaries.

Nevertheless, the chances of India embracing such an alliance are not very great. Most of the nationalist leaders are hard-headed realists and they know that, whatever the momentary advantages, in the long run India would have to pay a frightful price for making common cause with either Russia or Japan. It is possible even that, his eyes glued on the distant future, Gandhi will succeed in restraining his overzealous followers from making trouble during the war. These factors are likely to enable Gandhi to carry through his policy; and India may not flare up in a great revolution until the Allies win. Perhaps, although this is more unlikely, the Congress might even decide on active co-operation with Britain if the outlook in Europe changes seriously for the worse. After all, victory of the fascist imperialists cannot possibly be to India's advantage. India could no more defend herself without Britain's aid than could the colonies— and she is the far more desirable prize.

It is perfectly obvious, however, that a frightful explosion will take place the moment fear of foreign aggresssion is removed. India will then be in a position to launch a revolution compared with which all the previous ones will have been child's play. The hardship and suffering of the war years will have added to the bitterness of the national cause, and the power of the Congress will have increased. And, her hands tied in a dozen places throughout the world, Britain will be unable to throw her whole weight into crushing such a revolution. The only way to avoid such an aftermath is to grant all the demands of the nationalists before the end of the war. Unfortunately, the Moslems and princes are not likely to stand idly by while being sold down the Ganges to the nationalists; nor can Britain be certain that a liberated India, not tied to her by blood, religion, or language, will not make use of the right to complete secession from the Empire—a right which is implied in Dominion status.

A time there was when Britain could have united the various groups in India and thus spared herself the present terrible dilemma. She did not do that—whether because of laziness or imperialistic selfishness does not concern us here. A choice of only two alternatives confronts her in India, the sweetest of which is bitter indeed.

ECONOMIC PROBLEMS

Extremely serious will be the financial and economic problems which will arise immediately following cessation of hostilities. Britain's industrial collapse bids fair to be far greater at the end of this war than was the collapse in 1920. Necessity to produce vast quantities of military products will have worn out Britain's industry, and there will be the difficult and costly problem of converting machinery for the production of swords into machinery for the production of plowshares. A large part of the merchant marine will be at the bottom of the seas; foreign trade will be ruined, the markets captured by neutral rivals; foreign investments will have been consumed for financing imports at a time when exports were a fraction of their normal average. Yet investments and credits have in the past been the lifeblood of the Empire, feeding the heart while keeping alive the far-flung parts.

If Britain's foreign investments declined by less than a quarter during the last war, the decline is likely to be far more serious now. In 1914 the Dominions had to borrow in London to finance the large expeditionary forces they sent to all the theaters of war, which enabled Britain to make new investments while old ones were being repatriated in payment for war purchases. But it was the United States that then saved Britain from bankruptcy. Immediately after out-

break of the war Britain had to sell heavily on American
financial markets to obtain dollars to pay for war materials.
Something like $3,000,000,000 of American railroad, indus-
trial, and government securities held in England were repatriated. It was obvious that continuance of this process
would force Britain into bankruptcy; and America rushed
to grant credits amounting to about five billion dollars.
Thanks to these manipulations only a quarter of Britain's
foreign holdings had to be sold to finance the last world war.

Entirely different conditions prevail now. All the Dominions are following a clear autarchical policy, aiming to
spend as little as possible outside their frontiers. Instead of
sending to Europe large expeditionary forces which would
create even larger debts in London, they decided to limit
their war efforts largely to militarization at home and to
send small highly mechanized units which could be pro-
visioned from home. Nor is the United States likely to rush
credits to provide American exchange. Experience with foreign investments generally and with the last war debts specifically have made American investors shy of foreign loans.
Britain as well as her allies will have to pay cash for their
purchases. The financial alliance with France, far from being a help, makes Britain's problem greater than ever. France
is a liability, notwithstanding her large gold hoards.

The first effect of the war was to divert British industry
from normal production of consumption goods for the home
and foreign markets to the production of necessities of war.
Hundreds of cotton factories were converted to armament
production; machine and metal establishments catered primarily to the army. Raw materials once used for manufacture
of goods for export were devoted to uneconomic production. At the same time, imports had to be increased.

War is a great consumer, and the imports to keep the war
fires burning will more than compensate for the decline in
ordinary consumption. Nor will Britain be able to restrict
imports to raw materials which British labor will finish into
implements of war. To keep up with Germany in armaments
production, Britain will be driven more and more to resort
to the labor markets of the United States, Italy, and other
industrialized countries by importing the finished products

of laborers in those countries. Obviously this will compel her to export vastly more gold or foreign currency than if purchases could be restricted to raw materials.

At the same time, however, exports of domestic produce—the most healthy form of payment—will decline to new lows. The longer the war is protracted and the more intense it becomes, the less will Britain be able to afford the machinery and manpower necessary for the production of goods for export; nor will she be able to afford either the shipping or the raw materials for producing and transporting commercial goods. A shipping shortage has appeared already. A large percentage of British ships have had to be diverted from the normal carrying trade to transporting men and materials of war; submarines scared away neutral shipping. Shortage of shipping has already diminished considerably the amount of raw materials available to industry; and this factor will become increasingly important the longer the war goes on.

Twenty years of peace were insufficient for recovering from the effects of the first World War on Britain's foreign trade; the second may prove ruinous. Markets lost during the war cannot be picked up like lilies of the field after the armistice is signed; competitors will have established themselves and new trade connections will have been formed. The large Latin American market will be largely lost: American businessmen are already rushing in whence the British have been compelled to withdraw. Edward J. Noble, Under-Secretary of Commerce of the United States, has been at work since the outbreak of the war to increase trade between the United States and Latin America. British trade will suffer losses which may prove irretrievable in the Scandinavian countries, in the Balkans—even within the Empire.

The war, it was pointed out above, is forcing the Empire to industrialize itself at breakneck speed. Not only are new industries springing up, which will permanently reduce imports from England; the Dominions and colonies are placing orders in the United States for goods they can no longer obtain in the mother country. Orders valued at tens of millions of dollars have already been placed by Australia, India, and Canada for machine tools and machines to manufacture goods of consumption, which will inevitably lead to new or-

ders in the future as parts break down and improvements
develop.

The first months of war revealed these tendencies in full
operation. In the month of September imports to Great
Britain declined by one-third as compared with the same
month in 1938; exports, however, fell by no less than 42 per
cent. Perhaps, as the *Economist* says, "that exports should
have fallen heavily in the first month of war was only to be
expected.... But by the second month there should have
been an improvement." Unfortunately, actual trade retu: ns
show that matters became worse. While imports declined 22
per cent as compared with October, 1938, exports fell by
44.5 per cent—or almost half. Exports increased considerably
during November, although still lower than in the same
month in 1938; on the other hand, the gain was more than
offset by larger imports, and the balance of trade was actually twice as unfavorable as during September. These figures
are indeed disconcerting, as a London financial publication
puts it.

It is probable that slight improvements will take place
before the end of the war. British industrial and financial
leaders are making every effort to keep up exports. "It cannot
be too often reiterated that Great Britain must export or die,
that the present state of the export trade is disastrous and
that not nearly enough is being done about it. It is our worst
failure of the war, and will bring down all the rest unless
drastic action is taken at once," shrieked the normally calm
Economist at the end of November. British newspapers and
financial publications became filled as soon as the war regime
was set up with complaints against the governmental bureaucracy which was alleged slowly but surely to be strangling
the export trade; British industrialists complained of inability to obtain raw materials to fill foreign orders. Probably,
these administrative handicaps will be reduced as the system
of governmental control gets into full swing; bureaus of
control will be established to control the present "controls"
with a view to diminishing bureaucratic "controlitis"; and
every effort will be made to capture some of the markets
previously supplied by the Reich.

Unfortunately, the improvement cannot be more than

slight under the very best circumstances. It is not "controlitis" that will produce unfavorable trade balances, although it may aggravate them; the real difficulties are those analyzed before, and those cannot be dealt with so easily. To pay with exports for the imported materials consumed by war, Britain would have to send out at least twice the amount of manufactured goods she exported before September. However, (a) shortage of labor, and (b) lack of shipping—even if the markets could be found—rule out such a solution.

How then will Britain pay for her large imports? Unable to pay with merchandise, she will have to pay in cash. Her gold reserve of about three billion dollars would suffice to pay for a good deal of ammunition. Unfortunately, Britain cannot afford to use the whole, or even the major part of this fund. Depletion of the gold reserve would rapidly send the pound sterling toppling down, and create a host of serious difficulties. First, the price of necessary imports would skyrocket in terms of her currency, thus reducing further her ability to compete in world markets. Second, the moment British currency became unreliable the Sterling Bloc would disappear, as the various countries would unhesitatingly switch their allegiance to the dollar. It will therefore be necessary to keep a large part of the gold in reserve for emergencies.

The only other way by which Britain can pay for imports is to use her holdings of foreign securities, which amount to about sixteen billion dollars—a sum large enough to pay for Britain's total imports during five years. Careful investigations made by the *Economist* of London disclosed that investors in the United States would be interested in at least a quarter of these securities, which would give Britain large amounts of dollars for buying American products. British investments in the United States alone amounted in 1934 to $1,297,000,000, $619,000,000 of which represented marketable stocks.

In the event of war [wrote the London *Economist* in the summer of 1939] we should lack the formidable financial protection of our pre-war holdings of American railway securities. But there are three additional items which might combine as substitutes. Direct British investments in the United States, though

originally made for reasons of industrial strategy, could presumably be mobilised in case of extreme need. Second, there are
holdings in certain neutral countries which might be of interest
to American financial houses or investors as they were in the
last war. Finally, holdings in mining and transport undertakings
in the Dominions might appeal to the United States public or
Treasury.

In the Dominions, too, Britain will have to sell securities.
Since the outbreak of the war she has contracted to purchase
the whole exportable surpluses of Australia's wool, Canada's
copper, wheat, and other products, of New Zealand's wheat,
butter, and wool. Egypt's cotton crop will be taken over by
London, and negotiations are proceeding for purchase of
other strategic products. To pay for all these, securities
issued by the Dominions and other countries which are at
present held by British nationals will have to be repatriated.
Britain will send back the 2.2. billion dollars' worth of Canadian securities, the £950,000,000 of Australian and New
Zealand, and £250,000,000 of African negotiable papers. The
same method will be adopted to pay for imports from Argentina, Egypt, and other countries.

Without doubt, this policy will enable Britain to pay for a
great deal of war imports; the after-effects, however, may be
very grave, politically no less than economically. Unless her
whole economy is reformed radically, first, the standard of
living will have to decline, in the postwar years even more
than in the immediate future. Income from investments
abroad and from banking services connected with them, which
have netted her about £300,000,000 annually, will disappear
and will be missed the more as foreign trade will also have
declined. How then will Britain feed her enormous population? Second, London, for more than a century the banker
of the world, may lose its position of financial supremacy.
The present situation can bring to a decisive conclusion the
struggle with New York, by which, the latter, not the political
capital of the Empire, would come to hold the Empire's
financial strings.

The political consequences of such a revolution can be
glimpsed rather than foreseen. Credit and debt has formed
one of the most lasting ties connecting the Dominions to

the mother country; what will happen when the loose ends of these strings will be held in New York? How long under such conditions will the Empire continue? Will the Finance Minister of New Zealand be as obliging in trade terms to the mother country when he will have to go to New York instead of to London to beg for a new bond issue? The answers to these questions are disturbing in the extreme.

But when the peace is made the financial debacle will not come alone. While Britain will confront financial and industrial problems more perplexing than any she has confronted until now, all the other forces aiming to break up the Empire will be at work. There will be India, either in the thick of a life-and-death struggle or at its commencement; the colonies will be ready to launch revolutions, and if they synchronize their plans, all the King's horses and all the King's men and all his ships and airplanes thrown into the bargain will be powerless to check them. The Dominions, too, may not abide by the status quo. They will be tired of the system which had forced them to make tremendous sacrifices in three distinct wars in a third of a century; financially and industrially they will now be independent of London.

Are we, then, witnessing the heroic last gasp of the once-mighty British Empire? No doubt it was a realistic appreciation of the forces which war must inevitably release that made British statesmen, irrespective of political creed and party affiliation, so reluctant to embark on any policy which might lead to war. The vision of a disintegrating Empire, not fear of military defeat, made them all devotees of peace until peace could no longer be purchased except at a price which meant immediate dissolution of the Empire. But are they combating one external menace only to create numerous internal ones, which will be even more difficult to fight? Arms and soldiers will avail very little against the latter menaces.

Whither the British Empire...? Not since the days of Napoleon has this question been as pregnant with ominous meaning as at the present time.

XIII
THE EMPIRE WILL NOT DIE

A CRISIS MORE SEVERE than any Britain has hitherto confronted is certainly inevitable as soon as the war ends; and
the prophets of the immediate "Decline and Fall of the
British Empire"—an increasing tribe—no longer appear as
unjustified as in the past. Logic and history seem to point
to the conclusion that the days of the Empire are numbered.
"Babylon, Egypt, Rome, Spain, all traversed the same track,"
exclaims a great English scientist; "Our peculiar quality of
superior mentality seems but a suicidal acquisition hastening
and intensifying the imminent doom," he concludes somewhat illogically. Mr. Briffault wrote not long ago of "the
meteoric Empire" whose career—note the tense—has "been
singularly brief."

What is usually overlooked is that the contemporary
Jeremiahs are a good deal less original than they appear to
be; the most astounding thing about the British Empire has
been its inexplicable ability to outlive its oratorical mourners.
The inevitable death and disintegration of the Empire has
been foretold more often and for many more years than the
contemporary prophets of doom probably realize. As early as
1807, Lord Byron declared in a Memorandum that "another
century will sweep our Empire, our literature, and our
name, from all but a place in the annals of mankind." The
noble lord at least gave himself a century for the realization
of the gloomy prophecy; most others of the prophetic tribe
were not as prudent. Yet today the British Empire is still
very much with us.

Writers indulged in the refreshing sport during periods
which, as we look back over the past, seem to us to mark the
height of British power and glory. A hundred and eleven

years ago the conservative *Quarterly Review* could see no other future than disintegration of the Empire: "It is pretty much with colonies as with children; we protect and nourish them in infancy; we direct them in youth, and leave them to their own guidance in manhood; and the best conduct to be observed is to part with them on friendly terms." "There is not a man in the Empire who does not look forward to the dissolution, at no distant period, of the connection between Canada and England," the other great British journal, the *Edinburgh Review,* wrote a few years later. And in 1830 it demanded "the instant emancipation" of Canada, because it would only mean "anticipating by a few, a very few years, the inevitable separation." Viscount Bury wrote a book in 1865 to prove that the imperial connection is against the best interests of Canada; and he pleaded for "an amicable, not unfriendly separation."

One can go on citing quotations like these *ad infinitum.* "We are two peoples to all intents and purposes," wrote Cobden in 1865 about relations with Canada, "and it is a perilous delusion to both parties to attempt to keep up a sham connection and dependence which will snap asunder if it should ever be put to the strain of stern reality." Nobody expects "Canadian regiments to storm the Redan side by side with the English soldiers," wrote Lord Thring in the same year. "Nobody hopes to see Australians or New Zealanders volunteer for service out of their own country." Goldwin Smith, Sir Charles Dilke, Cornwall Lewis, Lord Morley—practical statesmen and profound observers all—delivered themselves in an identical vein. "Nobody believes," wrote the last, that Australia would contribute "money for a war, say, for the defense of Afghanistan against Russia or for the defense of Belgian neutrality." Yet not only have Australia and New Zealand and the other Dominions voted funds to pay for just such a war, but they have sent their men to every part of the globe; and have done so not once but three times since the beginning of this century.

So convinced had British statesmen during the first part of Victoria's reign become of the inevitable dissolution of the Empire that they persuaded themselves, with typical British stolidity, to contemplate the prospect with no little relish. "I have an idea," Trollope wrote in 1862, "that it would become the Canadas to rebel and assert their independence . . . unless it be conceded to them without rebellion." Visiting colonials were annoyed and pained at the defeatist attitude that had become all but universal in the mother country. "I am more than ever disappointed at the tone of feeling here as to the colonies," the Canadian statesman Alexander Galt wrote to his wife during a visit in England in 1867. "I cannot shut my eyes to the fact that they want to get rid of us." Another Canadian statesman, Sir Richard Cartwright, became convinced that "the leaders on both sides, Gladstone and Disraeli included, would have been still more pleased if we had asked for our independence at once." Lord Clarendon replied to a letter from Lord Lyons, Gladstone's Minister for Foreign Affairs, with the following words: "I agree in every word you say about our possessions in North America, and wish they would propose to be independent. . . . We cannot throw them off, and it is very desirable that we should part friends."

No less gloomy have been prophecies of Britain's economic prospect since, say, 1500 A.D. Not a decade—I suppose that sufficient research would show that not a year—passed without one-eyed prophets foreseeing uninterrupted decline in England's prosperity. The economic adviser to the Bank of England was in the best British tradition when he moaningly admitted in 1931: "There can be nothing in the future for this country but slow decline." Long before England reached the summit of Victorian glory, very competent authorities shed tears because the prospect of England becoming the workshop of the world "is already a dream of the past" since "the singularity of our position has gone." Even the normally optimistic Froude saw in 1870 "symptoms which suggest, if not fear, at least misgiving as to the permanency of English industrial supremacy." Yet today, three score and ten years later, England's industrial exports almost equal those of its nearest rival, the United States, which has a population three times as large.

As to similar prophecies and wishes in later years, and especially since the beginning of this century, their number is legion. Where is the shrewd politician who has not prophesied the "distintegration of the British Empire in the not distant future"—whatever that may mean. German statesmen before 1914, including the Kaiser, were convinced that the imperial bonds would not stand the strain of war; but we know what happened in 1914. The interval between the first and second world wars witnessed a spontaneous growth in such prophecies; and American journals have been filled with expert analysis proving conclusively that the day when New Zealand and Australia—not to speak of Canada—would flock to our standard cannot be far removed. Yet far from showing any inclination to become partners in the American commonwealth, they have not only retained their independence but even their membership in the British Empire. Nor has Britain lost a single colony since 1776. She has relinquished sovereignty over the Ionian islands of her own free will, and has returned Java to the Dutch; and that has been all.

Prophets of doom would do worse than bear in mind the past experiences of the British Empire. Obviously the fact that it has not collapsed until now does not mean that divine Providence has ordained an eternal life and that disaster is therefore ruled out. But history should make us chary of easy jeremiads and set us looking into the causes which prevented their realization. No doubt today the Empire confronts more serious problems than ever before; the forces of destruction are greater and the compensations for cohesion smaller. But there never has been a time when all was perfect in the Empire and no cloud marred the glorious horizon. Inevitably so. In an empire the size of Britain's where so many interests are at stake, there must always be dangers and menaces; it is too great to lead the quiet existence of a Tibet. One Empire, it is well to remember, Britain has lost; yet 1776 did not sound Britain's death knell, as contemporary statesmen feared. A new and greater Empire came into being; and that Empire too has stood on the brink of disaster more than once during the past hundred years.

THE LAW OF CHANGE

What has enabled the Empire to outlive its pessimistic mourners is that, in bold contrast to all other imperial nations, who hoped to prevent decay by reducing everything to a dead status quo, the British have incorporated the natural laws of change and growth into the basis of their political system. Having learned during centuries of experience that in the political, no less than in the physical, world only solids break under the impact of opposing forces, they have intentionally refused to hoist a hard political and ideological framework on the Empire. Lack of rigidity has saved the Empire in the past, for the British knew how to adapt themselves to changing conditions; I am convinced that the same factors will enable it to weather the coming storms.

A completely transformed British Empire will occupy the center of the political stage when the dust and smoke of battle clears; not a dead one. The Empire which will emerge after the war will have little in common with the one we know now, just as the present Empire has very little in common with that of a century ago—or even with the Empire of 1914. Indeed, the very name has changed; and it is a truism that names remain after all real meaning has undergone a revolutionary transmutation. So profound, however, have been the changes in the constitution and economic nature of the British Empire that statesmen felt impelled to evolve a new terminology, which brought into existence the British Commonwealth of Nations. In analyzing the history of the British Empire one must ask not what has changed during the past hundred or twenty years; the question should be, what has remained unchanged? Yet, as in the world of nature, the more everything changed, the less fundamental the changes became; and beneath all the outward changes there remained a solid substratum.

One needs only to look at the Dominion empire, where the transformations have been of revolutionary magnitude, to see how these principles have worked themselves out. Obviously the Canada of 1830 had nothing at all in common with that of 1859, which enacted the first tariff in the Empire directed against British manufactures; with the Canada at the beginning of this century, which was taking the first steps towards diplomatic independence; with the Canada of 1919, which was accorded a separate seat in the League of Nations; and, finally, with the Canada of 1931, which had become independent of Britain in every possible way—much more independent of British power and influence than, say, Rumania, which has never been a member of the Empire. Nevertheless Canada has continued to attend Imperial Conferences; she entered of her own volition into special economic relations with the mother country in 1932; and today she is meeting the supreme test of allegiance by participating in an imperial war.

The changes have not been nearly as great in the territories inhabited by dark races; yet neither has this part of the Empire remained stationary. There are real and fundamental differences between the position of India or Ceylon in 1900 and their status in 1939. Very little has remained of the absolute power Britain enjoyed in these parts as late as a quarter of a century ago; British officials are no longer free to act according to their discretions or according to orders from Downing Street. Natives have taken over a large measure of effective power; and if the changes have not been as great as in Canada or in Australia, that is due to a larger extent than native nationalists would admit to the weaknesses and backwardness of the peoples concerned. Even in those colonies where British officials still have a theoretical free hand, their power is now limited—and very effectively—by public opinion, which played no role at all a score of years ago.

Change has been the first law of the British Empire. That—nothing else—has enabled it to survive innumerable crises in the past; and there is no reason for believing that it will be less adroit in the future. There is, indeed, every reason for believing that, to avert disaster, the British will try to march in the future in closer accord with reality. Unlike 1914, when they plunged into the war with the blissful ignorance of children, the British started thinking about the aftermath the moment war was declared. Today they recognize the perils of war, and are preparing beforehand to cushion the blows. The press is filled with highly intelligent discussions on all phases of the imperial problem as it will emerge after the war; some of the finest brains in the world are devoting all their thoughts to the problems enumerated in the previous chapter.

No one can foretell the forms which the Empire will assume when the war is over, just as no observer a century or a generation ago predicted the lines it has followed. The outline which has emerged so far is extremely vague. Indications are that the most fundamental changes, as was to be expected, will affect India and the colonial empire. The idea that colored peoples could be admitted to full membership in the Commonwealth—that Britain could treat with India, Malaya, or Jamaica as an equal—has until now, notwithstanding the declaration that Dominion status is the "ultimate goal" of India's constitutional development, placed a very severe tax on the British imagination. Indications are that this prejudice is now rapidly disappearing.

A new conception of Empire is gradually emerging. It is now recalled that a few years ago Wickham Steed, who has been so often ahead of his time, threw out an idea which might well serve as the cornerstone of the new structure. Foreseeing that an Empire based on British "race superiority" —the fundamental principle of the Empire until this day— was no longer sufficient to hold the immense structure together, he advocated a new test for membership in the British Commonwealth which would not automatically exclude the overwhelming majority of the population now living in the shadow of the Union Jack. He saw this test in community of civilization. Not the degree of pigmentation should henceforward constitute the acid test to political maturity, but the extent to which "British civilization" and its ideals of justice, personal liberty, freedom of minorities, have spread and taken root; and the bond uniting the Empire shall consist of community civilization, not absence of pigmentation. To realize how great a metamorphosis this view represents one needs only to recall that only a few years ago Lord Milner, although one of the most advanced of the liberals of the old school, said: "I am a Britisher—indeed, primarily an English-Nationalist. . . . My patriotism knows no geographical, but only racial limits. . . . Hence, we probably took the wrong road in trying to convert India into a Dominion." But Wickham Steed told the Royal Empire Society Summer School at Oxford in 1936 that he has "definitely come to the conclusion that British Race Patriotism is not enough." India, where British ideals have struck deeper roots during the past two centuries than in any other territory inhabited by dark races, will of course be first to be admitted to full equality in the Commonwealth. She will not for long be the only one. Other colonies will follow in rapid succession. There will be Burma, Ceylon, Jamaica, Bermuda, Malaya, and so forth.

Interestingly enough, the British have already taken far-reaching steps toward removing the color bar in personal status, where it normally remains long after political independence is achieved. That they have been driven to take this step by the exigencies of war does not matter. Just as the present Tory Government found it necessary to introduce egalitarian reforms in England to win the support of the masses for the war, so it has found it necessary to put down the color bar in the colonies. Natives are now being admitted to offices in the colonial services hitherto closed to them; Lord Zetland, Secretary of State for India, has announced in the house of Lords: "The British Government had decided ... that ... Indians, Anglo-Indians or Burmans resident in the United Kingdom are on the same footing as British subjects of pure European descent in regard to voluntary enlistment in the armed forces. Similarly, their eligibility to be considered for the grant of emergency commissions will be on the same basis."

In the meanwhile changes no less revolutionary in their ultimate effects are being projected for the more backward parts of the colonial empire. Lord Hailey recently indicated the future trends in these parts when he told the Royal Institute of "the necessity of educating the Africans not merely to take the routine of administration off the shoulders of the European officers, but to take part, in a real sense, in the actual work of administration." There is even some talk already of admitting colonials to the newly formed Colonial Civil Service organizations which were intended exclusively for Englishmen, just as the Indian Civil Service was originally an all-British show. Before the war a storm of opposition would have met any suggestion that natives be admitted to these organizations; now the matter is being discussed quite dispassionately, and it is almost certain that sooner or later the step will have to be taken.

The Empire which will come into existence as a result of these and other reforms which cannot even be outlined at this stage, will of course be totally different from the one which the world knew in September, 1939. But will these reforms suffice? They obviously do not affect the Dominions and do not touch on any of their problems. As far as the Dominions are concerned the only possible reform is extinction of the Empire. But even with regard to the colonies and India it is more than doubtful whether these reforms can do so much as to forestall rebellions. They might have been sufficient if implemented before the war; their therapeutic value for the diseases which the war will create is less obvious. Other factors entering upon the situation have to be considered.

FUNCTIONS AS JUSTIFICATION

Fundamentally the fate of the Empire will be decided not by its constituent parts but will depend on and be determined by the shape of the world as a whole. It cannot be too often emphasized that, in contrast with all other imperial structures, brutal military force ceased to play a significant role in holding the British Empire together long before outbreak of the war; *mutatis mutandis,* it will not be Britain's lack of force that will bring about the collapse after the war. The Empire survived the innumerable menaces in the past because there was a real need for its services. It performed functions vitally necessary for the outlying parts; and its ability to perform those services was in the last analysis its justification and mainstay. The Empire will exist as long as there is a need for it, as long as it fulfills a necessary service, as long, in other words, as no social organization is created which performs its functions better, more cheaply, more altruistically, more reliably.

The Empire's function was, first of all, in the field of defense. More than any other political organization it has been able to give security to its members. Australia and New Zealand have been able to devote all their energies to socially constructive work because the Empire was there to give them protection. This is even truer of the small colonies which, in contrast to even tenth-rate European states, have devoted to defense nothing at all or totally insignificant parts of their budgets. The net profit from this service remains immensely large even if the debit occasioned by the necessity to participate in all-Empire wars is deducted. Direct and indirect contributions of the Dominions, India, and the colonies to all the wars of the Empire amount to a fraction of the expenditures they would have had to incur, in money and resources, had they been completely independent.

Defense, extremely important though it has been, has not been the only service. Membership in the Empire has brought invaluable financial services, as the undeveloped parts have been able to borrow money at much lower rates of interest than prevailed on world financial markets, and on terms a good deal less onerous. Sir Theodore Morison pointed out correctly in 1911 that the imperial connection has enabled India "to borrow money at an average rate of $3\frac{1}{2}$ per cent, whereas, judging from the example of Japan, she would otherwise have to pay at least $5\frac{1}{2}$ per cent. The saving of 2 per cent interest" amounted even then to £5,340,000 a year. No less important, members of the Empire could always rely, in contrast to independent countries which have had to go begging from one financial market to another, on the London money market to supply them with funds whenever needed for development schemes, and without having to submit to London's normally extremely careful questioning. This service has been especially great since 1930, when, financial resources on all world markets having dried up, priority in London for imperial countries was semiofficially decreed. Thanks to their political connection, also, various countries have been able to carry through extremely advantageous refunding operations which save them tens of millions of dollars annually.

Nor should the value of the administrative services be underestimated. At a comparatively small cost to themselves the backward parts of the Empire have obtained the services of administrators, scientists, physicians, teachers, and the like, among the finest in the world. An independent Nigeria would certainly not have obtained men of the caliber Britain has sent her for $5,000 a year or less. Of course, Britain has not performed these services for the colonies for the love of humanity. She expected to profit, and did profit. Construction of Egypt's irrigation system meant jobs for hundreds of

Englishmen; British firms received no mean orders; even British shipping profited. It is true also that the British colonial officials have not been as progressive as they should have been; selfish interests have too often determined their policies. There is no denying, however, that they have given the colonies a great deal and have been progressive agents.

One needs only to compare Tanganyika or Fiji with Abyssinia, or Tibet, or Afghanistan to realize what the British have accomplished. While Abyssinia or Tibet remained completely stationary, although tens of millions of dollars accumulated in the treasuries of the Negus or the temples; while no schools were built and no hospitals were constructed; while government remained synonymous with tyranny, justice with corruption, and not the slightest effort was made to introduce modern industrial and agricultural improvements, Tanganyika and Fiji under the British have made notable progress in all these directions. Or one needs only to compare the present state of Afghanistan with India. Certainly the British have no reason for being proud of their Indian record; yet who can doubt as to which is now more prepared to play a role in the modern world, and that notwithstanding the fact that the potential per capita wealth of Afghanistan is much greater and its people have always been more vigorous than that of India. The British have built a system of irrigation for Egypt which would have cost probably ten times as much and would not have been nearly as efficient had the Egyptians built it themselves. And the Egyptians know it. They know that the dams built before 1882 with foreign aid cost many times their value and were operated inefficiently; they know that a new spirit has reigned in the Irrigation Department since the British first assumed charge.

The colonies have their grievances of course; in many cases, probably in most, all-too justifiable grievances. The disturbances which have taken place in the past are the best evidence of that. But the most enlightened elements in the colonies realize perfectly well that they cannot yet stand alone under the strenuous conditions of modern life. They need and want foreign assistance; many need even foreign direction and control. Iraq and Egypt, completely independent states now and able to hire and fire officials as they please, have not dispensed with British assistance. Realizing that the British know about their own countries more than they do themselves and are better equipped for the task of ruling, the new native authorities have not dismissed the British officials, and have not been too arrogant to ask, and usually act upon, their advice.

Gloomy prophets of the immediate disintegration of the British Empire could do worse than consider these factors. Proof that these services have been of real value is provided by the Dominions, which have not severed their connection with the Empire although they have been free to do so. Indeed, their participation in the present war shows the value they place on membership and the enormous price they are willing to pay. Even India has been less bent on asserting her complete independence than a few noisy intellectuals would have the world believe; otherwise the tarbushes, topees, lungis, and even Congress caps of the three hundred fifty million Indians would have sufficed for suffocating the six or seven thousand British officials and sixty thousand British soldiers (now less) spread over the whole continent.

However, two crucial questions remain to be answered. Granted that Britain has performed vital services in the past, will she be able to play the same role after this war? Will she not be too weak, too poor, too exhausted? Second, even if Britain could fulfill all the functions as in the past, is there not likely to emerge after the war an international organization which will perform for the Dominions, colonies, India, and the spheres of influence all the services performed by the Empire, and do so at less cost, more altruistically and more progressively? British statesmen, it will be recalled, had been uneasy since 1920 lest the extremely limited, basically powerless League of Nations should undermine imperial unity; will not the new League, which will probably be far stronger and with wider interests simply push the Empire out of existence?

IMPERIAL FUNCTIONS IN A NEW AGE

Not much need be said about the security problem. There is no reason for believing that the united power of the Empire will not be able to give as much security to the individual members after the war is ended as before. On the contrary, the security it will be able to give will be far greater than at any time since 1930. The greatest military power in the world having been defeated by the might of the British Empire, which enemy will dare to measure strength with it? Certainly not Italy or Japan; nor even Russia, unless I am greatly in error.

From a purely military point of view the Empire will be far stronger at the end of the war than it was at the beginning. To say that war exhausts is as much nonsense as that exercise weakens. Exercise can kill one suffering from heart disease, and a state lacking manpower or raw materials or industrial capacity can be ruined. But the British Empire certainly does not lack the first two; its industrial capacity to produce, already tremendous, will be vastly expanded during the war.

In this connection it is important not to overlook that the mere winning of the war will add greatly to the prestige of the Empire; and empires as great as the British live on prestige. The present war became inevitable in 1936, when Mussolini contemptuously dismissed Britain's veto of his Abyssinian adventure. "The most important aspect of Il Duce's recent *coup de théâtre* in Ethiopia," I began an article for *The Nation*, written in the Near East during the summer of that year, "is that without firing a single round of ammunition, he defeated the greatest imperial and naval power in the world. . . . If only to recapture lost prestige . . . England must win a war." [1] It was perfectly obvious that once the halo was removed there could be nothing but slow or rapid decline. But the Empire's prestige will be far greater at the end of this war than at any time since the last century. Not only will it have demonstrated again its military might; more important, it will have shown its effective unity in times of stress.

Less certain is Britain's ability to perform the financial services it rendered in the past. There is of course an immense difference between her behavior now and in 1914, when not the slightest understanding of the inevitable economic consequences of the war was shown. Britain is no longer squandering her resources. A Ministry of Supply was created the moment war was declared, instead of waiting three years; all foreign investments have been mobilized by the government,

[1] *The Nation*, August 15, 1936.

which is holding on to them very tightly; every effort is being made to encourage exports. An attempt will no doubt be made to fill the vacuum created by the embargo on German exports. However, how far these measures, albeit very useful, will succeed in overcoming inherent weaknesses cannot be foreseen.

Yet even the economic weaknesses, although the most serious chinks in the imperial armor, may not prove as destructive as they would have under more normal circumstances. First, a reorganization in the imperial banking, monetary, and industrial systems, as the war may well make necessary if it lasts long enough, would create a new unity, which would go far to help solve all future financial problems. Those problems would then assume to a larger measure than at present an intranational nature; and a flexible banking system can solve all intranational financial problems, as Germany and Italy have demonstrated. Britain would then assume the role of imperial banker to an extent even greater than at present; for its functions would be made vitally important.

Second, Britain may well attempt to establish a new financial relationship with the Dominions by which the latter will become vitally interested in her economic well-being and in the maintenance of imperial integrity. Instead of repatriating Dominion bonds to pay for the large war purchases, Britain is likely to decide to float loans in the various Dominions and hold on to the pre-war securities. For the first time in their histories, the Dominions would thus become Britain's creditors on an extensive scale instead of, as until now, her somewhat jealous debtors. And such an arrangement is likely to be welcomed by the Dominion governments. Ottawa does not welcome the prospect of becoming the creditor of the various provinces, as it would have to become if the provincial securities now held in Britain were repatriated. The provinces would be much less careful to meet their obligations if their bonds were held locally, in which case the federal governments would eventually have to assume the burden.

Reforms executed under duress of war and threat of rebellion immediately afterwards, will greatly enhance the beneficial results of British colonial administration. Compelled now to co-operate with native nationalists and reformers, the British officials will have to render more progressive service, while the chances for carrying through selfish policies will be less. In some colonies they will be even under the control of native governments; and experience has shown that under such conditions British officials can perform invaluable work. The fact is that countries like Iraq, Turkey, Iran, and various Baltic states have discovered after experimenting with officials and experts from all over the world that the British give far more devoted and disinterested and useful service. A British expert in, say, the new Turkish government would not think of informing his ambassador of what is taking place inside government offices; the same cannot be said about other European nationals. There is every reason for believing that under the new political conditions in the postwar world Britain will execute her traditional function in the backward parts of the Empire far better than hitherto—because the only alternative will be loss of the colonies.

THE LEAGUE AND THE FUTURE

That a League of Nations could perform all the services hitherto rendered by the British Empire and do so infinitely more effectively, more cheaply, and with greater benefit to the world as a whole, I do not doubt for a moment. Only an international organization could remove the last tinges of selfish interest in the performance of all these services; only world co-operation can realize the dream of permanent peace. Moreover, bitter necessity will probably force the world to create eventually such an organization, as the only alternative to chaos and the disintegration of Western culture.

Unfortunately the problems connected with the creation of such an organization are far more complex than is generally realized. Take the first and simplest task which such an organization would have to perform—provision of security on a world scale. However, it is surely not sufficient to lay down the rule, as was done in the League Covenant and the Kellogg-Briand Pact, that no nation may resort to force to obtain satisfaction of its demands. Such a law would be a strangling rope around a nation which had developed new needs from the time of its enactment, even if it were possible to obtain the co-operation of the world for its enforcement. To obtain real international security provisions going far beyond establishment of an international police force to penalize aggressors will have to be made. In international as in national life violence can be outlawed only after real justice has been made accessible to all.

An extremely complex economic machinery will have to be created before there can be permanent world peace; a totally new conception of trade will have to gain acceptance; above all, there will have to be a cultural revolution and new loyalties will have to be developed. Such diverse fields as immigration, foreign exchange, nationality, civil legislation, labor and trade regulations, shipping, air transportation, and a thousand other matters today regulated on national lines would have to be placed under international control. The revolution which such an arrangement would necessitate in all our cultural ideas is too obvious to need elaboration. Yet— as the last League has demonstrated—no organization which does not take into consideration all these factors can give more than a limited and highly precarious security.

Security, far-reaching though its ramifications be, is, however, not the only matter with which the new international society will have to deal if it is to become of universal importance. It will have to evolve the necessary machinery for dealing with a host of financial demands; with problems of raw materials; with emigration and immigration, and so forth. An organization not very unlike the present British Colonial Civil Service will have to be created for administering the backward peoples of the world.

Machinery for dealing with all these problems could certainly be created. Experiences of the last League indicate that, given proper guidance and stimulus, an efficient international civil service with international loyalties is possible. The colonial and other services could be staffed from the successful competitors in an examination to which men and women from all over the world would be eligible. Policy could be laid down by, and the civil service would be responsible to, a Board of Control sitting in Geneva and appointed by the executive or legislature of the League. But one needs only to draw the simplest lines of such an organization to realize how unprepared the world is as yet for it.

An international society will undoubtedly come into existence at the end of the war; but it is more than doubtful whether its ramifications will be so wide as to be able to displace entirely the present British Empire by performing all the services of the latter more efficiently and at less cost. Far more likely is it that the new League will be, as a British publication recently put it, "a loose rather than a close federation, at least until experience tightened its bonds. It would be, in effect, a union for certain purposes only—all important purposes, but few in number compared with the whole range of public affairs." And unlike Minerva, it will not spring up full grown from the head of Zeus nor will it spring from the depths of world chaos. At the very best, it will develop during a protracted period of time, gradually assuming greater and wider burdens as age and experience strengthen its limbs.

Reality is, therefore, very likely to give the lie to the prophets of the immediate dissolution of the British Empire as a result of the emergence of a more embracing world organization. The new League would be unable, under the best circumstances, to deliver all the services rendered in the past by the Empire; and until experience proved the value and reliability of the new organization, the British Empire would have to continue. In the immediate future it will have to remain as a secondary insurance organization; and though smaller and in the long run less useful than the larger association, it would certainly be the more effective and reliable at the outset.

What is likely to happen is that for many years—probably decades—the two organizations will exist side by side and co-operating with each other. It should be borne in mind that such co-operation will be easier in the future, if only because the British Empire as well will have assumed more truly the form of a co-operative commonwealth, each member—not only Britain—playing a role in the formation of policy and each contributing a more proportionate share in the executive work than at present.

Addressing the Imperial Conference of 1902, Joseph Chamberlain, one of the greatest of England's imperialists, told the Dominions, "The weary titan staggers under the too vast orb of its fate." That was in 1902—and the "weary titan" has staggered on somehow until now; he will stagger on in the future. There will be no decline and fall of the British Empire. Like all other political structures, it, too, will come to an end—but as a result of slow evolution and fruition into a higher social organization.

And toward the development of the new League of Nations the British Empire can contribute more than any other existing political organization. Co-operation has been developed here to a fine point; the Empire's experience in dealing with the delicate problems of sovereignty should prove invaluable. The British theory of nationality, rather than that of all other states, would have to be the League's ultimate goal; the British Colonial Civil Service would have to be the model on which to base, albeit not without major modifications, the larger organization of the future; and British methods and theories in all-Empire legislation, operation of international finance, and in similar matters would have to be the League's safest guide.

ENGLAND AND THE ENGLISH

England will have to change to meet the problems which will develop after the war. She will have to overhaul her economic system; delicate social and political adjustments will be necessary. But change is not synonymous with decline. If old avenues of enterprise close, new ones will be created which may yet give this amazing little island a greater influence on world affairs than previously. The years which are bound to elapse between the emergence of the new League and the final disappearance of the Empire will facilitate an orderly transition to, possibly, something ethically better and socially more useful. And the first steps in such a transition have been taken already.

Fundamental in a nation's history is the virility of its people. A nation does not decline until its citizens become physically and morally corrupt, their energy is gone, and their will to live is sapped. The "glory that was Rome" was not ended by the barbarian invaders; as St. Augustine knew, they only delivered the final blow to a people that had become rotten and had degenerated. On the other hand, the greatest military defeat in history was not sufficient for crushing the German people. Less than half a dozen years afterwards, Germany was again occupying a leading position in the family of nations.

Who can say that the British people are less energetic, less virile, less courageous, less able than a century ago? Who can say that the British hand has lost its cunning, the British brain its extraordinary powers to understand everything human? Have they less determination to win a race they enter, less will to live? Are the men of Britain less cultured than their forebears of a century ago, less successful in commercial and intellectual enterprises? One needs only to pose these questions to perceive that there can be only one reply.

Few countries can boast as high a type of manhood as that produced by the public schools of England. The courage, tact, coolness of judgment, political insight, intellectual attainments, and administrative ability of an Englishman of this class is not the less amazing for his studied moderation and his practiced efforts to belittle personal accomplishments. I have seen Englishmen go out to rule provinces from which their predecessors had not returned—and do so with no more outward concern than if they were taking a joy ride. I recall a newly wed Scotch couple that went out to the Sudan-Abyssinia frontier a day or two after the news arrived that the party of engineers the husband was supposed to join had been murdered. I have seen Englishmen walk into the jaws of death among bitterly hostile crowds, and with patience, tact, coolness gradually gain control.

I do not want to write an essay upon the virtues of the British, but the prophets of doom could do worse than pay attention to the human material, which in the long run is a more decisive factor than industrial raw materials. No doubt the British can be exasperating to foreigners; often one wants to shriek to high heaven against what appears to be brazen-faced hyprocrisy; the middle classes especially are guilty of a mental smugness that is annoying in the extreme. These qualities, however, have nothing to do with their ability to survive and to win, which is only enhanced by their overwhelming sense of selfishness. The masses of England are among the most ingenious, the most skilled and hardworking in the world; the upper classes produce more men of the highest intellectual and administrative attainments per thousand of the population than their counterparts anywhere else in the world. The septuagenarian Neville Chamberlain is symbolic of the virility of the English people.

Such a nation is neither lost nor declining. Britain will make contributions to whatever social organizations arise in the future; and the world will be ready to pay for those. Her prosperity is not dependent on any one factor; and her flexibility makes change easy. Obviously in a day when Egypt, Ceylon, or Tanganyika produces cotton goods, England cannot base her economic structure on the export of Manchester prints; but it will be many long years indeed before any of these countries will have the technical knowledge and skill to build their own machines to produce cotton goods, their own electrical equipment, or high-grade internal combustion engines. And having at last grasped that world economy has changed, Britain has been diverting her industrial machine to the production of articles requiring the highest technical skill, for which possession of the finest body of skilled workmen in the world has eminently equipped her.

Nor are England's exports limited to industrial goods. She exports brain power, and there is every indication that this type of export will be greatly expanded during future years. British writers and poets; British journalists, scholars, and lecturers; British explorers, scientists and mathematicians have held the front rank of their professions since the last half of the last century, and their intellectual products find a ready market the world over. This type of export is as profitable to the exporting country and as useful to the world as exports of coal and cotton prints. Against every American writer working for a British publication I can cite a score or more British writers who draw salaries from America; to every foreign professor in England there are—even if the colonies and India be excluded—probably a hundred who lecture in universities all over the world, and who send part of their earnings back to England. This type of export England

will undoubtedly develop, if one may judge by present indication, in the future.

It was an Indian nationalist who a year or two ago pointed
out to me that the decline of Manchester may spell a glorious
fruition of Oxford, Cambridge, Edinburgh, London, and
other intellectual centers. Although by no means kindly disposed to British rule in India, he saw that centuries of careful
training had prepared England to become the finishing school
of the world. Himself an Oxford graduate, he had every
intention of sending his sons to the same university; "I fight
for political independence," he said, "but once that battle is
won, I will certainly favor co-operation with England and
with the other Dominions in financing research institutions
for the benefit of all, which can flourish in England probably
better than in any other place in the world." Of course those
institutions will not be staffed exclusively by Englishmen, as
the few already set up show; but they will have their seat in
that island and contribute to its total wealth.

And the backward areas of the world will continue to give
employment to thousands of Englishmen, whatever the system of administration evolved in the future. If the old type
of colonial rule is thrown overboard as incompatible with
the our greater sense of justice and scientific progress, and a
system of administration by an international civil service
under the jurisdiction of the League of Nations is evolved,
Britain will still contribute the overwhelming number of administrators. There is no escaping the fact that the British
have been more successful in dealing with backward peoples
and in helping young nations than any other of the so-called
Great Powers. The number of Englishmen in all the other
international civil services which may be created will also be
out of all proportion to what their total population would
justify. The various British civil services are not only among
the most honest in the world, but, what is far more important,
among the most creative, most capable, and least enslaved to
deadening routine.

The war will certainly result in profound changes in England's economic and social system. Large-scale emigration will
probably become necessary; she may even become agricultur-
ally slightly more self-sufficient than at present. The major

changes, however, will be in different directions. Increasingly England will become the world's industrial specialist, producing goods which call for the highest labor skill and the least raw materials; her shipping, insurance, and banking services will become more important. Especially the last, for she is better equipped to become the financial nerve center of the world than any other nation. Above all, there will be a large expansion in the cultural and scientific and administrative services, which will continue to give Britain a far greater influence on world history than mere numbers of population justify.

Is it dangerous to base a nation's existence on such intangibles? Of course it is. But England has always lived dangerously, and it is difficult to see that she has been the worse for it. Rapid industrialization at the expense of agriculture was dangerous; very much so, and there was no dearth in prophets of doom who foresaw all kinds of catastrophic results. Yet instead of becoming poor, England has become the second richest country in the world—and on a per capita basis possibly the richest—although her natural resources, or the absence of them, would entitle her to a rank not much above Italy and lower than that of Germany. One should not forget that England's natural resources, either industrial or agricultural, simply cannot be compared with those of the United States. She ran tremendous risks when free trade was embraced, and again when it was abandoned, though in both cases the decisions proved eminently wise; Lord Durham's recommendations, although inevitable, were dangerous, and the recent reforms in India and the colonies even more so. A nation of forty-seven millions which aspires to world leadership must live dangerously. Whether new policies are hazardous is not important. The crucial question always is: Are they wise? History is the best answer to that question.

APPENDIX

THE BRITISH EMPIRE

THE COLONIAL EMPIRE

EUROPE
Gibraltar
Malta
Cyprus

ASIA
The State of North
   Borneo
Brunei
Sarawak
Ceylon
Aden
Perim
Socotra
Hadramaut
Kuria Maria Islands
Palestine
Transjordania
Laccadive Islands
Maldive Islands
Straits Settlements
Federated Malay States
Unfederated Malay States
   Johore
   Kedah
   Kelantan
   Perlis
   Trengganu

Hong Kong

AFRICA
Gambia
Sierra Leone
Gold Coast
Nigeria
Togoland
Cameroons
Anglo-Egyptian Sudan
Kenya
Uganda
Tanganyika
Nyasaland
Southern Rhodesia
Northern Rhodesia
Bechuanaland
Swaziland
Basutoland
Zanzibar
British Somaliland
Ascension
St. Helena
Tristan de Cunha
Gough Island
Seychelles
Mauritius
Rodriguez

335

Amirantes
Penguin Island
Prince Edward Island
Marion Island

INDIAN OCEAN
Chagos Archipelago
Penang
Andaman Islands
Nicobar Islands
Cocos Islands
Christmas Island (No. 1)

AUSTRALIA AND OCEANIA
Papua
Bounty
New Guinea
Bismarck Archipelago
Antipodes Island
Stewart Island
Campbell Island
Auckland Island
Macquarie Island
Gilbert Islands
Ellice Islands
Emerald Island
Ocean Island
Santa Cruz Islands
New Hebrides (British)
Norfolk Island
Lord Howe Island
Palmyra Island
Washington Island
Fanning Island
Christmas Island (No. 2)
Jarvis Island
Malden Island
Starbuck Island
Tongareva

Chatham Islands
Manihiki
Cook Islands
Pitcairn
Ducie
Rarotonga
Kermadec Islands
Tonga Islands
Samoan Islands (British)
Tokelau Islands
Phoenix Islands
Johnston
Howland Island
Baker Island
Solomon Islands
Fiji Islands

CENTRAL AMERICA
British Honduras

WEST INDIES
Bermuda
Bahamas
Jamaica
Trinidad
Barbados
Tobago
Grenada
Windward Islands
Leeward Islands

SOUTH AMERICA
British Guiana
Falkland Islands
South Georgia
South Sandwich Islands
South Shetlands
South Orkneys
Graham Land

BRITISH POSSESSIONS IN THE ANTARCTIC

THE INDIAN EMPIRE

India
Burma

Kashmir
Baluchistan

THE DOMINION EMPIRE

Australia
Canada
Eire

Newfoundland
New Zealand
Union of South Africa

THE OUTER EMPIRE

Greece
Turkey
Egypt
Iraq
Bahrein Islands
Kuweit
Iran
Saudi Arabia
Afghanistan
Tibet
Portugal

Portuguese colonies:
Goa
Damao
Diu
Macao
Timor
Cape Verde Islands
Guinea
São Thome
Princip
Angola
Mozambique

THE FINANCIAL EMPIRE

Sweden
Denmark
Norway
Argentina
Bolivia

Brazil
Colombia
Paraguay
Finland
Esthonia

SELECTED BIBLIOGRAPHY

NO ONE SERIOUSLY interested in the British Empire, especially in the colonial part, can dispense with the numerous and excellent volumes published by His Majesty's Stationery Office. About fifty *Annual Reports on the Social and Economic Progress of the Peoples of the Colonies, Protectorates and Mandated Territories* are issued each year by the Colonial Office; since 1938 the Colonial Secretary has published an annual Statement on *The Colonial Empire,* Cmd. 5760 (1938) and Cmd. 6023 (1939); in addition, there are the invaluable reports of commissions and other special publications. The following are of special importance: *Report of the Commission Appointed to Enquire into the Financial and Economic Position of Northern Rhodesia* (A. W. Pim), Colonial No. 145 (1938); *Rhodesia-Nyasaland Royal Commission Report,* Cmd. 5949 (1939); Report of the Commission on the *Trinidad and Tobago Disturbances, 1937,* Cmd. 5641 (1938); *A Survey of Agricultural Education in the Colonial Empire,* Colonial No. 124 (1937); *Labor Conditions in Northern Rhodesia,* report by Major G. St. J. Orde-Browne, Col. No. 150 (1938); *Palestine Royal Commission Report,* Cmd. 5479 (1937) and two volumes of *Evidence,* Col. Nos. 133-4; *Report of the Royal Commission on Labour in India,* Cmd. 3883 (1930); *Report of the Commission Appointed to Enquire into the Disturbances of the Copperbelts Northern Rhodesia,* October, 1935, Cmd. 5009 (1935); *Commission of Inquiry into the Administration of Justice in Kenya, Uganda and the Tanganyika Territory in Criminal Matters,* May, 1933, Col. No. 96 (1934); *Correspondence Relating to the Constitution of Ceylon,* Cmd. 5910 (1938); *Memorandum on the Education of African Communities* by Advisory Committee on Education in the Colonies, Col. No. 103 (1935); *Higher Education in East Africa,* Report of the Commission appointed by the Secretary of State for the Colonies, Col. No. 142 (1937); *West Indies: Report of the Closer Union Commission,* Cmd. 4383 (1933); *Correspondence Relating to the Welfare of Women in Tropical Africa, 1935-37,* Cmd. 5184 (1938); *Nutrition Policy in the Colonial Em-*

pire, Col. No. 121 (1936); *Colonial Development Advisory Committee,* Eighth Annual Report, Cmd. 5537 (1937); *Report of the Commission on Closer Union of the Dependencies in Eastern and Central Africa,* Cmd. 3232 (1929); *Report of the Kenya Land Commission,* September, 1933, Cmd. 4556 (1934); *Nutrition in the Colonial Empire,* Cmd. 6050 and Cmd. 6051 (1939); Imperial Economic Committee, *Annual Reports;* Air Ministry and General Post Office, *Empire Air Mail Scheme,* Cmd. 5414 (1937); Cable and Wireless Limited, *Statement of Proposed Changes in the Arrangements between His Majesty's Government and Cable and Wireless Limited, and of a Reduction in Empire Cable and Wireless Rates,* Cmd. 5716 (1938); *Imperial Economic Conference at Ottawa, 1932,* Cmd. 4174 and 4175 (1932); *Imperial Committee on Economic Consultation and Co-operation, 1933, Report,* Cmd. 4335 (1933); Imperial Conference, 1937, *Summary of Proceedings,* Cmd. 5482 (1937); *Report on Indian Constitutional Reform* (Montagu-Chelmsford Report), Cd. 9109 (1918); *Report of the Indian Statutory Commission* (Simon Commission) Cmd. 3568 and Cmd. 3569 (1930); *Indian Round Table Conference 12th Nov. 1930—19th Jan. 1931, Proceedings,* Cmd. 3778 (1931); *Government of India Act, 1935,* or *XXV & XXVI, Geo. V, ch. 42.*

Needless to add, the volumes of *Parliamentary Debates* constitute an inexhaustible mine of information on all developments in the Empire. The annual debate in connection with the Colonial Office Estimates (e.g., June 14, 1938, vol. 337, No. 126) is of special interest.

ABBOTT, J. F. *Turkey, Greece and the Great Powers.* R. N. McBride & Co. New York. 1917.

ALLIN, C. D. *Australasian Preferential Tariffs and Imperial Free Trade.* The University of Minnesota. Minneapolis. 1929.

ANDREWS, C. F. *India and the Simon Report.* Macmillan. New York. 1930.

ANGELL, NORMAN. *The Defence of the Empire.* Hamish Hamilton. London. 1937.

ANSTEY, VERA. *The Economic Development of India.* Longmans, Green & Co. London. 1929.

ARCHER, WILLIAM. *India and the Future.* Alfred A. Knopf. New York. 1918.

BOSE, SUBHAS C. *The Indian Struggle—1920-34.* Wishart & Co., Ltd. London. 1935.

BUELL, R. L. *The Native Problem in Africa.* Macmillan. New York. 1928.

BIBLIOGRAPHY

CANADA, Bureau of Statistics. *Trade of Canada with the British Empire Countries and the United States.* Ottawa. 1932.

CHIROL, SIR VALENTINE. *India.* Ernest Benn, Ltd. London. 1926.

CLEARY, VINCENT F. *British Imperial Preference in Relation to Australia.* The Catholic University of America. Washington. 1934.

COPLAND, DOUGLAS B. *Australia in the World Crisis, 1929-33.* Macmillan. New York. 1934.

CROMER, EARL OF. *Modern Egypt.* Macmillan. New York. 1908.

DARLING, M. L. *The Punjab Peasant in Prosperity and Debt.* Humphrey Milford. London. 1925.

DAUTREMER, JOSEPH. *Burma Under British Rule.* (Translated by Sir G. Scott). T. F. Unwin. London. 1913.

DRUCKER, PETER. *The End of Economic Man.* The John Day Co. New York. 1939.

DUTT, R. PALME. *World Politics 1918-1936.* Random House. New York. 1936.

GWYNN, S. L. *Ireland.* Charles Scribner's Sons. New York. 1925.

HANCOCK, W. K. *Australia.* Charles Scribner's Sons. New York. 1930.

———. *Survey of the British Commonwealth Affairs.* Oxford University Press. London and New York. 1937.

HARRIS, H. L. *Australia's National Interests and National Policy.* Melbourne University Press. 1935.

HOFMEYR, JAN H. *South Africa.* Charles Scribner's Sons. New York. 1931.

IRELAND, P. W. *Iraq: A Study in Political Development.* Macmillan. New York. 1938.

JOHNSTON, SIR H. H. *A History of the Colonization of Africa by Alien Races.* University Press. Cambridge. 1913.

KEITH, ARTHUR B. *A Constitutional History of India.* 1600-1935. Methuen & Co. London. 1936.

———. *The Constitutional Law of the British Dominions.* Macmillan. London. 1933.

———. *The Constitution, Administration and Laws of the Empire.* Macmillan. London. 1924.

———. *The Dominions as Sovereign States.* Macmillan. London. 1938.

———. *The Governments of the British Empire.* Macmillan. London. 1933.

———. *The King, the Constitution, the Empire and Foreign Affairs.* Oxford University Press. London and New York. 1938.

KIEWIET, C. W. DE. *The Imperial Factor in South Africa—A Study in Politics and Economics.* University Press. Cambridge. 1937.

KENNEDY, W. P. M. *The Constitution of Canada.* Oxford University Press. London and New York. 1938.

KOHN, HANS. *A History of Nationalism in the East.* Harcourt, Brace & Co., New York. 1929.

LENIN, NICOLAI. *New Data for Lenin's "Imperialism."* Edited by E. Varga and L. Mendelsohn. International Publishers. New York. 1939.

LOVELL, REGINALD. *The Struggle for South Africa.* 1875-99. Macmillan. New York. 1934.

LUGARD, SIR F. D. *The Dual Mandate in British Tropical Africa.* Wm. Blackwell & Sons. Edinburgh and London. 1922.

MANSHARDT, CLIFFORD *The Hindu-Muslim Problem in India.* Allen & Unwin, Ltd. London. 1936.

MARTIN, CHESTER B. *Empire and Commonwealth: Studies in Governance and Self-government in Canada.* Clarendon Press. Oxford. 1929.

MAYHEW, ARTHUR. *Education in the Colonial Empire.* Longmans, Green & Co. London. 1938.

MOREL, D. *The Black Man's Burden.* B. W. Huebsch, Inc. New York. 1920.

NEHRU, JAWAHARLAL. *India and the World.* Allen & Unwin, Ltd. London. 1936.

NORTHCUTT, CLARENCE H. *Australian Social Development.* Columbia University. New York. 1918.

PALMER, GERALD E. H. *Consultation and Co-operation in the British Commonwealth.* Oxford University Press. Humphrey Milford. London. 1934.

QUICK, SIR J. *The Legislative Powers of the Commonwealth and the States of Australia.* C. F. Maxwell. Melbourne. 1919.

READ, MARGARET. *The Indian Peasant Uprooted.* Longmans, Green & Co. London. 1931.

ROYAL INSTITUTE OF INTERNATIONAL AFFAIRS. *The Colonial Problem.* Oxford University Press. London and New York. 1938.

———. *The British Empire.* Oxford University Press. London and New York. 1938.

SMITH, WM. R. *Nationalism and Reform in India.* Yale University Press. New Haven. Oxford University Press. Humphrey Milford. London. 1938.

STOYE, JOHANNES. *The British Empire: Its Structure and Problems.* Bodley Head. London. 1938.

SUTCH, W. B. *Recent Economic Changes in New Zealand.* Institute of Pacific Relations, New Zealand Council. 1936.

TONSILL, C. C. *The Canadian Reciprocity Treaty of 1854.* Johns Hopkins University. Baltimore. 1922.

TOYNBEE, ARNOLD J. and K. R. KIRKWOOD. *Turkey.* Ernest Benn, Ltd. London. 1926.

——. *Survey of International Affairs.* Royal Institute of International Affairs. Oxford University Press. London and New York. 1925—to date.

TROTTER, R. G. *Canadian Federation, Its Origin and Achievement: A Study in Nation Building.* J. M. Dent & Sons. Toronto and London. 1924.

WOOD, ERNEST. *An Englishman Defends Mother India.* Ganesh & Co. Madras. 1929.

The Cambridge History of the British Empire. Macmillan. London and New York. 1929—to date.

The Cambridge History of India. Macmillan. London and New York. 1922-1937.

INDEX